MARY THE MOTHER OF JESUS

MARY

THE MOTHER OF JESUS

FRANZ MICHEL WILLAM

Translated by Rev. Frederic Eckhoff

 Scepter

Originally published in 1939 under the title
Das Leben Marias, der Mutter Jesu

English edition first published in 1949 by B. Herder Book Co.
St. Louis, Missouri

Nihil obstat
F. J. Holweck, Censor librorum
February 2, 1938

Imprimatur
Archbishop Johannes J. Glennon
February 3, 1938

ISBN 1-59417-003-7

Scepter Publishers, Inc.
P.O. Box 211, New York, NY 20018
www.scepterpublishers.org

Text composed in ITC Garamond, Letraset Dolmen

First printing
Printed in the United States of America

CONTENTS

I.

Before the Annunciation

In the land of Israel, a father and a mother were rejoicing at the birth of a daughter. Because they were devout Israelites who confidently awaited the coming of the Redeemer in their generation, a boy would have been more welcome. At least, in the opinion of their neighbors, the birth of a boy would have been an event of greater honor. The infant was washed and bound tightly in swaddling clothes. The parents called her Miriam, or Mary. The meaning of the name is not known to us with certainty; perhaps even then those who conferred the name on the child were equally ignorant of its meaning. The name was used frequently, and people did not inquire into its meaning. In the Gospels we find a Mary Magdalene, a Mary of Bethany, and a Mary wife of Clopas; nor was the name confined to the ordinary people. In fact we find a series of Marys in the family of King Herod. No one surmised that this child was destined for anything unusual, that she was to be the Mother of the Redeemer.

We should be happy today to know something more definite about this child and her parents, but the Scriptures reveal nothing to the inquirer. Not even the names of the parents are recorded, and we can easily understand how people later on supplied the missing details with imaginary stories and legends describing the wonderful things that surrounded the father and mother and the growing child.

The first incident recorded in the life of Mary is found in the following passage of St. Luke's Gospel:

In the sixth month the angel Gabriel was sent from God to a city of Galilee named Nazareth, to a virgin betrothed to a man whose name was Joseph, of the house of David; and the virgin's name was Mary. And he came to her and said, "Hail, full of grace, the Lord is with you!" But she was greatly troubled at the saying, and considered in her mind what sort of greeting this might be. And the angel said to her, "Do not be afraid, Mary, for you have found favor with God. And behold, you will conceive in your womb and bear a son, and you shall call his name Jesus.

9

> He will be great, and will be called the Son of the Most
> High;
> and the Lord God will give to him the throne of his father
> David,
> and he will reign over the house of Jacob for ever;
> and of his kingdom there will be no end."
> And Mary said to the angel, "How can this be, since I have no husband? "
> And the angel said to her,
> "The Holy Spirit will come upon you, and the power of the
> Most High will overshadow you;
> therefore the child to be born will be called holy, the Son
> of God.
> And behold, your kinswoman Elizabeth in her old age has also conceived a son; and this is the sixth month with her who was called barren. For with God nothing will be impossible." And Mary said, "Behold, I am the handmaid of the Lord; let it be to me according to your word." And the angel departed from her (Lk 1: 26-38).

This record discloses three things in the life of Mary prior to the Annunciation. The angel designates Mary as being "full of grace"; this expression reveals to us her inner life with God. By means of various expressions he intimates to Mary that the Son whose birth he has come to announce is the promised Redeemer, and these expressions, which the angel presupposed were familiar to her as a child of her people, reveal to us the ideas by which she referred to the coming Redeemer. Certainly it was the angel's mission to convey the message, which God had charged him to deliver, with unmistakable clearness, and he used terms designed to make his message clear rather than to obscure it. Therefore, when the angel said, "And behold, you will conceive in your womb and bear a son, and you shall call his name Jesus. He will be great, and will be called the Son of the Most High; and the Lord God will give to him the throne of his father David, and he will reign over the house of Jacob for ever"; the name "Jesus," the expressions "Son of the Most High," "the throne of his father David," and "reign over the house of Jacob" must have been already known to Mary. Finally, this narrative tells us that Mary had separated from her family and was espoused to a man named Joseph, even though she had resolved to continue a life of virginity. Thus in the story of the Annunciation we are afforded three vantage points from which we may look back on the years that preceded this hour of her great decision.

Mary as a child

Hail, full of grace . . . you have found favor with God (Lk 1: 28, 30).

In Nazareth the angel Gabriel greets Mary with the words "Hail, full of grace," and he uses these words instead of the proper name. According to the words of the angel, Mary is, therefore, in the sight of God and, according to the divine dispensation, full of grace in such a singular manner and to such an incomparable degree that, in comparison with her, no other woman can be called full of grace. She is called full of grace, not as if she had acquired this attribute, but as having been endowed with it from the very first moment of her existence, and the angel addresses her as though she had always been full of grace. In the same manner, the angel of the Lord addressed Gideon and said to him: "The Lord is with you, you mighty man of valor" (Judg 6: 12). This designation of Gideon is intended to express a personal characteristic, just as when the angel addresses Mary as being full of grace. From the first moment of her life, therefore, Mary was full of grace, fully endowed with holiness.

A holy child. How rare a creature in this sinful world, how unusual will be his life surrounded by sinful humanity! Like other children he is born of a mother and begins life as a helpless infant; he grows as do other children, until that time when the soul within expresses itself in words and actions. Soon parents and relatives will realize that the child differs greatly from other children they know. While the parents express their wonderment, the child's playmates will sense his unusual qualities. They will love him; something draws them to him, yet there is also something holding them aloof. Now there is something attracting them to him, now something filling them with awe in his presence. At all times they feel a mysterious reverence that prevents them from treating him as one of themselves.

The child grows, and his parents, observing him closely, are at a loss whether they should rejoice or be concerned at the unusual character of their child, for such is the fate of the unusual that its nature is not readily appreciated. Time and distance must intervene, often the lapse of many years and great distance, sometimes even death, before a man is judged in his true light. In all respects a holy child is usually a normal child, not wise or grave beyond his years. While other children readily adopt the evil they see in their elders rather than the good, and gradually show a faculty for concealing the evil that they do, a saintly child does not follow in the footsteps of others but remains constant in doing good, even against the wishes of his companions. His faults are so trivial that they serve merely to call attention to his perfections, even as the rustling of the leaves in a secluded mountain valley seems to make the silence audible. Other children are fickle and unstable in prayer, but this child seems to have the experience of a lifetime of prayer and the contemplation of the things of God so that the exercise of prayer seems to have become a part of his being.

All these things, which persons in more intimate relationship with saintly children can observe, were seen exemplified in Mary in a more perfect degree, for Mary was more intelligent, saintly, and unblemished than other children endowed with the grace of sanctity. As the neighbors of Zechariah and Elizabeth remarked at the birth of John the Baptist, so now those who observed the child Mary might frequently have asked one another: "What an one, think ye, shall this child be?" For the hand of the Lord was with her.

To record what was meanwhile taking place within Mary's soul, to follow the course of the inner life of her who was full of grace, is impossible for us because we lack the knowledge of corresponding religious experiences upon which to base our comparisons. We must be content to draw what comparisons we may from our superficial knowledge of the inner religious life of the soul. All who lead the inner spiritual life have experiences that must forever remain exclusively their own; to divulge these experiences will only cause other persons to misunderstand them or even to deny their reality altogether. Silence, therefore, is the only refuge of these souls. This is true of the inner development of a child; the great experiences of a child especially chosen by God remain, as a rule, beneath the ordinary external behavior, hidden from the observation of parents and companions.

Mary's development in her youthful years was in accordance with the laws that govern the development of human lives. But in the soul of her who was full of grace, in that soul free from the least taint of sin or any inclination to sin, occurred events that could not be revealed to others, so that the question never arose whether she should tell them to others or not. Mary spent these years in a profound loneliness, which had a determining influence on her soul and made her the silent contemplative who "kept all these things, pondering them in her heart" (Lk 2: 19, 51).

Mary's solitude

Because of a sensitiveness natural to them, children live in a world of their own, into which adults gain admittance only with great difficulty. Among themselves children associate with ease and a sense of security, compared to the manner in which adults approach each other, sometimes awkwardly hesitant and uneasy. On certain occasions this difference between adults and children is particularly evident. When two groups, for instance, each comprising adults and children, meet during an outing in the country, before the adults have been formally introduced, it will be noticed that the children have already become acquainted and have formed a little world of their own. They cannot, of course, give a personal description of one another, but for all immediate purposes they accept one another as though they were lifelong friends.

The loneliness of a child living only with adults is an inadequate but serviceable illustration of Mary's solitude. Mary, full of grace, in the highest and most perfect sense a child of God, lived among people who had, all of them, lost their status as children of God and who, to a greater or less degree, had fallen into sin and had yielded to their evil inclinations. Usually man comes to know the difference between good and evil by doing evil and then becoming aware of the reproaches of his conscience, indeed, by hearing the voice of conscience and setting it aside or perhaps by doing the evil thing and refusing to heed the warning of conscience. Such knowledge of evil does not come from God, but from man's separation from God.

In her youth Mary had no such experimental knowledge of evil; at no time was she made aware of the warning voice of conscience as though she were inclining to some evil. When her conscience spoke, it suggested the good, and even then it needed not the urgency of appeal with which conscience speaks of conversion to the ordinary sinful man; because Mary conformed to the least movement of divine inspiration with complete surrender.

Endowed with this spiritual characteristic, Mary would not have known unusual suffering had she been placed in some retiring place where the outward solitude would have been like

13

the solitude of her soul. But her life was set in a small Eastern village, where she was obliged to live in close proximity to men and women who knew evil through curiosity and temptation and often by actual commission. These people lived in a world with which Mary had no contact, for she never took even the least part in any sin: when others spoke an unkind word, she did not listen with pleasure or approval; when disputes arose between those about her, she took no part in the angry exchange of words. The numerous social ties and connections in this world of ours often arise, not from good deeds, but from unchecked ambitions and inordinate desires; in all these things Mary was excluded from the lives of her fellow villagers. Yet never for a moment in her life was she able to escape the grief of her soul for the sin of a single human being; she never put it out of her mind with the reflection that, after all, it was the sinner who had committed the evil, not she, and that it was no concern of hers. Mary, who was without sin, saw in every sin something monstrous, an insult offered to the Most High, a disruption of that order which God's love had planned for mankind. She beheld the desolation sin caused in men's souls, and sin-laden mankind round about her knew less of the state of their souls than she did.

At the same time, she could not understand why she was so different from all others; her great humility did not permit her to believe that God had endowed her with most extraordinary graces. However, countless instances made it clear that she stood alone, that no other human being was like her; yet she could not understand the reason for all this. This impression was deepened by these repeated experiences, and Mary felt like a child in the company of adults, lonely and misunderstood.

Her habit of silence, which later became more and more noticeable and is expressly mentioned by the Evangelist, was a natural consequence of her position among the people with whom she lived. Her special relationship to God immured her in silence with regard to her religious experiences; her special relationship to sin placed another seal of silence upon her lips. No one has ever been obliged to such complete silence; no one has ever been obliged to conceal so much; nor has anyone ever kept these secrets so perfectly in his heart.

In all these incidents, increasing day by day and reminding her that she stood alone, she had but one refuge, to fly to God. Her living with God and in Him was an indispensable necessity, even as breathing is for the physical life of man. Without an appreciation of Mary's loneliness in this world, we cannot understand her life and the extraordinary progress she made toward God.

What impression did Mary's silence make on others, and what was their reaction to it? Recalling the narrow circumstances of a small village in the Middle East and the vivacity of its inhabitants, we immediately have presentiments of sad and tragic consequences. The greater number of her women companions, for Mary had contact only with women, sensed this peculiarity. But they lacked that magnanimity and generosity toward others with which Mary was so richly endowed. In circumstances like these, people always leap to the same conclusion; if someone among their acquaintances is different from themselves or superior to themselves, such a one is harshly judged and condemned as proud and arrogant, as having illusions of grandeur, as considering himself "too good" to associate with ordinary people. Doubtless Mary, from the time of her youth, had to suffer much from such unkind and rash judgments by the inhabitants of the little town of Nazareth, who were known to be a contentious people.

Perhaps frequently, Mary, who was the humblest of all, was called proud and a disgrace to the house of David and was treated accordingly. When in the *Magnificat* she rejoices that God has put down the mighty from their seats and has sent the rich away empty, while exalting the humble and filling the hungry with good things, she is giving expression from the fullness of her heart to things she herself has experienced. Her own exaltation followed a period of deep humiliation.

Vows among the Jews

The Holy Scriptures describe Mary at the time of the Annunciation as possessing two relationships, each of which is unusual. We are told explicitly that she was espoused to a man named Joseph of the house of David; at the same time she clearly indicates to the angel that she knows no man, that therefore she had no relationship as would naturally be thought necessary for the announcement of the birth of a son. These unusual circumstances can be explained only if we suppose that Mary had made a vow of virginity.

Among every truly religious people, vows have always played

15

an important role. We need simply recall the history of such times as, for instance, the Middle Ages, to realize that vows, promises made to God, were a part of their religious life. So it was among the Jewish people. Ever since the time of Moses and the kings, vows were an important element in the religious life of Israel. We read in the Law: "When you make a vow to the Lord your God, you shall not be slack to pay it. . . . But if you refrain from vowing, it shall be no sin in you. You shall be careful to perform what has passed your lips" (Deut 23:21-23). "Let not your mouth lead you into sin [by vowing rashly], and do not say before the messenger [afterward] that it was a mistake; why should God be angry at your voice, and destroy the work of your hands? " (Eccles 5:6).

In Mary's day, too, the making of vows was an accepted and cherished aspect of the people's worship of God. In connection with vows, certain customs and abuses also made their appearance. The abuses are perhaps the best evidence that the making of vows had become an established practice; because such abuses arising from human weakness generally appear when a custom has been widely accepted. Our Lord Himself pointed to abuses that had crept in during His time. When the Pharisees remonstrated with Him because His disciples did not observe the ceremonies of purification, He countered by saying: "And why do you transgress the commandment of God for the sake of your tradition [the customs introduced by the Pharisees]? For God commanded, 'Honor your father and your mother,' and, 'He who speaks evil of father or mother, let him surely die.' But you say, 'If anyone tells his father or his mother, What you would have gained from me is given to God [i.e., shall be Corban, an offering vowed to the Temple], he need not honor his father' [i.e., shall not be obliged to support his father or mother]" (Mt 15:3-6). According to this reproach by our Lord, vows were made in order to free the person making the vow from the obligation of supporting his parents. A son would say to his parents: "I have made a vow to give such of my possessions as you might expect for your support as a sacrificial offering to the Temple." Since such an offering was sacred, no one, not even the parents, could take it for themselves.

In profane writings also we learn that the custom of making vows continued without interruption. Vows were made to renounce certain things; and for these vows forms were adopted similar to those in use for oaths. How widespread the abuse had become to make rash and inconsiderate vows may be judged by the practice of making a counter-vow to secure oneself against the obligations of such rash promises. A solemn declaration like this would be made: "All vows that I make shall be invalid." Every possible case would be enumerated that could make a vow invalid, and every possible reason would be adduced to exempt from the obligation of a vow. Express mention is made of the instance of a father or a son disinheriting each other by a vow; the form cited by our Lord—"That which you would have gained from me is given to God [Corban—a sacrificial gift]"—is identical to that advocated by the doctors of the Law.

Vows concerning marital relationships and recorded in secular writings are of special importance in the life of Mary. We know several instances of vows by which a husband interfered with the life of his wife by forcing her to accept added obligations. For instance, it is recorded that a man required his wife to vow that she would never again lend anything, never wear any ornaments or jewelry, and never again visit the home of her parents. Such vows, of course, were binding upon the woman only when she had given her consent; but if the husband insisted upon the vow, she was permitted to separate from him.

Since the husband was not allowed to force upon his wife the observance of vows that interfered with the conduct of her life, the woman was all the more prohibited from making vows that affected her husband's manner of life without his consent. By their very nature, such vows were rare. One instance, however, is recorded in the Bible. Hannah, the mother of Samuel, made a vow, saying: "O Lord of hosts, if thou wilt indeed look on the affliction of thy maidservant, and remember me, and not forget thy maidservant, but wilt give to thy maidservant a son, then I will give him to the Lord all the days of his life, and no razor shall touch his head" (1 Sam 1:11). It was Hannah, the wife, who made the vow; but her husband, Elkanah, must have given his consent to the promise.

We have also instances of vows that touch upon the marital relationship itself. A certain man made a vow to lead a life of continence in marriage; and the commentator remarks: "He shall not violate his word but according to the word spoken by his mouth he shall do." This vow, therefore, was accepted as legal and binding. In another place, explicit directions are given how to proceed in deciding a case in which confusion has arisen out of a vow at the time of a betrothal: if a man espouses himself to a woman with the condition that there "are no vows resting on her," the betrothal is invalid if she does not reveal her vows before the betrothal. If, after the betrothal, the couple have already entered the new home and it is discovered that there "are vows which she has concealed," she is to be given a bill of divorce and dismissed without repayment of the dowry. If, therefore, because of such concealed vows, a woman can be divorced without repayment of her dowry, evidently an essential for a valid betrothal is that the woman reveal to her husband any vows that may bind her for the future. This much light from non-biblical sources is cast upon the question of Mary's vow of virginity within marriage. We would, of course, be gratified if we could cite an instance of a woman vowing herself to God with the consent of her betrothed or of her husband. But no instance of this sort has been found. We have simply come to the end of that period during which the ordinary religious customs of the people prepared the way for Mary's vow.

Although historical testimony is not sufficient to show that Mary's resolve was something that can be explained as a natural consequence of the circumstances of her time, still ample evidence is available to show that the practice of making vows was firmly established among the people, and that the connection between the promises of vows and the promise of marriage was generally understood. Therefore, if Mary had resolved to vow herself to a life of virginity, she must have known that under these circumstances she was obliged to reveal her resolve to her spouse before the betrothal. Furthermore, for her to be certain that after the marriage no difficulties would arise from this vow, she could not have been satisfied with an oral agreement but must have required some surety that her spouse would not change his attitude afterward. From these historical data we may say finally that in Mary's time women were not accustomed to renounce marriage for the love of God and to consecrate their virginity to God by vows. But could not Mary in some other way have come to this resolve, influenced by views commonly accepted in her day? What was the accepted view of marriage and continence in her time? The answer to this question will furnish additional light as to Mary's attitude.

Marriage, widowhood, and virginity among the Jews

To marry and grow old, surrounded by numerous children who like olive branches had sprung from the parent trunk, and to live to see their children's children was the ideal of the average men and women of Israel. Marriage was considered an obligation for young men, and the lives of most of the people conformed to this viewpoint. Children and posterity were the important consideration for those who married, in order that the line might be extended until the days of the Messiah. That pious people looked upon marriage and entered into it with this thought is exemplified in the prayer of Tobias.

Alongside this ideal, the state of virginity was much esteemed among the people. Virgins were permitted to accompany the ark of the covenant with kettledrums, and in the lamentations they were mentioned after the priests. Widows who refrained from entering into a second marriage and lived in chastity and piety as if in a second virginity were honored and respected. Judith was taken as the model for such women, and on the threshold of the New Testament another widow appeared, the prophetess Anna, who consecrated her widowhood to the service of God and who with the aged Simeon was privileged to greet the Savior in the Temple.

Esteem for the celibate life grew apace with the religious development of the people, but only for those who had dedicated their lives to some definite religious mission. Several of the prophets (for example, Elijah; Elishah, his disciple, who was greatly revered by the people; and Jeremiah, the prophet of the captivity) led lives of celibacy. The last of the great prophets, John the Baptist, marking the transition from the Old to the New Testament, who had placed the entire people under his strictures, was likewise a celibate; nor do we read that the people reproached him for his celibacy. They must, therefore, have had some understanding of the ideal of celibacy and regard for it. Several generations before the birth of Christ, a new religious sect arose among the Jews. Its members were bound to celibacy and, since, according to Flavius Josephus, their number was about four thousand in his time, they must have attained considerable importance. The origin of this sect, which declined to serve at the sacrifices in the Temple, has not yet been fully explained. But the appearance of a religious group adopting the practice of celibacy is a sign that the ideal of celibacy had at that time obtained a certain degree of favor with the people. We may surmise that some religious sect, appropriating an idea that until then had lain obscure and vague in the consciousness of the people, made it the basis of a religious system.

What we have said thus far concerns the men. The women had naturally a different attitude toward marriage, since they did not marry but, according to our Lord's expression, were given in marriage. Hence, strictly speaking, there could be no commandment for them to marry; but insofar as such a commandment existed or was thought to exist, its obligation rested upon the father or the guardian. Public opinion was not focused upon this question as it was upon the marriage of young men, and so the Scriptural sources have very little to say on this question as it concerns women. In general, we may conclude that at a time when the celibacy of men was accorded reverence and esteem, at least in certain circumstances, the possibility of a woman's refraining from marriage for religious reasons was not entirely excluded.

Keeping these circumstances in mind, we may adopt the view that current opinion had to some extent prepared the way for Mary's resolve to preserve her virginity. However, particular obstacles stood in the way of such a resolve for a young woman like Mary. She was one of the daughters of the house of David, out of which, according to the prophecies, the Messiah was to come forth. These prophecies had at this time been so deeply impressed upon the consciousness of the people that the Messiah was referred to as the "Son of David," as also later during the life of Christ. Every daughter of the house of David knew these prophecies and knew that she was one of that small group who might be the mother of the Messiah or, at least, His ancestress. In that instant, however, when a daughter of David consecrated herself to God, every hope of the motherhood of the Messiah had to yield to this life of virginity, and for this profoundly religious reason, Mary may have hesitated before making her vow of virginity.

How she passed over such considerations is indeed difficult to say. The problem would be simple if we were able to offer proof that at that time a commonly accepted belief existed that the Messiah was already born. Although such opinions were abroad among the people, they do not help to solve our problem, for they were not commonly accepted. We may further surmise that

Mary considered herself unworthy to be the mother of the Messiah and that she thought His cradle would be found in some Davidical family that had preserved more of its ancient brilliance and nobility. This would imply that Mary had expressly pondered the question whether she was chosen to be the mother of the Messiah. More probably, in her great humility and because of her outwardly lowly circumstances, Mary had never thought of herself in connection with the Messianic prophecies. In any event, we must not lose sight of the fact that, by her vow of virginity, she had separated herself from the other daughters of the house of David, at least insofar as they were the bearers of the Messianic prophecy. However, we may do well not to limit ourselves to any one explanation. The question of how Mary came to make her vow of virginity we may let remain a mystery that, under the guidance of Providence, was the beginning of her personal preparation for the coming of the Messiah.

Mary's vow of virginity

As we have remarked, the custom of making vows was generally well known and favorably received by the people during the years of Mary's adolescence, although we are unable to find recorded any instance of a vow that might have served as a model for Mary's consecration of herself to God. What reasons or considerations, we may ask, moved her to vow her virginity to God? The possibility of a special divine revelation, which could have been perceived by the senses, such as the appearance of an angel, must be excluded, for in that case she would have referred to it in some way in her reply to the angel at the Annunciation. Insofar as it is humanly possible to discover any factors that may have influenced Mary in making her vow of virginity, the peculiar circumstances—that she was under the special direction of Providence, that she was full of grace—must be accepted as the only reason for her consecration of herself to God.

Her living completely in God not only isolated her in an inexpressible loneliness, it also awakened within her a longing that absorbed her whole being, a yearning to belong completely to God. This longing grew as she advanced in years. Even as the spring is constant in the murmur of its waters, as the wind ever sings the same melody, as the flames of fire ever reach upward, so Mary's thoughts and longings were ever directed to God alone. The constancy of this longing gave to her life something unchangeable and invariable, which makes it difficult for us, with our ceaseless desire for change, to understand her life, because we strive against unchangeableness, even against remaining unchanged in God. In this constancy Mary resembled the angels. The resolves she had once made out of her love for God were so firm that she never afterward had the least desire to recall them. In a very special sense Mary is the "Virgin most faithful" of the Litany of Loreto. Noteworthy also is the fact that this perseverance in God was especially effective in those years when growing girls are outwardly and sometimes inwardly most changeable and fickle, the years when the child matures into young womanhood.

Mary's life would not have been truly human if these years had not been of special importance also for her; for now she too became conscious of her relationship as a young woman to the other sex and to the community in which she lived. At an age when many young people separate from God, she united herself still more intimately to Him and consecrated her whole life to Him. On this point St. Augustine expresses his mind by saying that Mary made a vow of virginity. His words may lead us to believe that Mary promised to do something that others had already promised and that the expression "vow of virginity" was already in common use. This, however, is not true. Her action is rather to be compared to the flower that opens its petals to the rays of the sun; it was a movement from within, not from without. Mary did not follow the example of others, she brought to realization what was inwardly possible to her who was "full of grace."

At what time did Mary make this vow? At what age? A vow is an action that must be made at a certain time and in a certain place; it is not something that takes place without the person's being conscious of it, like a change of attitude. According to tradition, a girl had to be over twelve years of age to make a vow validly. Mary was therefore certainly over twelve years old when she vowed herself to God. Where did she make this vow? There is, of course, no record to guide us. But, in view of the religious life of the people and past manifestations of divine grace, it seems most probable that Mary made her vow on the occasion of one of the feasts in Jerusalem. In later life, also, these feasts were of great importance. We cannot suppose this moment in Mary's life was unaccompanied and unassisted by the mysterious power of divine grace. It is not improbable that this step was preceded by inward struggles, by doubts and uncertainties, such as Joseph, her spouse, suffered before his espousal; because Mary had determined upon something unprecedented, but something for which, without knowing it, she herself was to become the model. She knew the mental attitude of her relatives; she knew also the customs and opinions of the people well enough to know that her vow would bring persecution and much tribulation in its train.

Mary's genealogy

The book of the genealogy of Jesus Christ, the son of David, the son of Abraham.

Abraham was the father of Isaac, and Isaac the father of Jacob, and Jacob the father of Judah and his brothers, and Judah the father of Perez and Zerah by Tamar, and Perez the father of Hezron, and Hezron the father of Ram, and Ram the father of Amminadab, and Amminadab the father of Nahshon, and Nahshon the father of Salmon, and Salmon the father of Boaz by Rahab, and Boaz the father of Obed by Ruth, and Obed the father of Jesse, and Jesse the father of David the king.

And David was the father of Solomon by the wife of Uriah, and Solomon the father of Rehoboam, and Rehoboam the father of Abijah, and Abijah the father of Asa, and Asa the father of Jehoshaphat, and Jehoshaphat the father of Joram, and Joram the father of Uzziah, and Uzziah the father of Jotham, and Jotham the father of Ahaz, and Ahaz the father of Hezekiah, and Hezekiah the father of Manasseh, and Manasseh the father of Amos, and Amos the father of Josiah, and Josiah the father of Jechoniah and his brothers, at the time of the deportation to Babylon.

And after the deportation to Babylon: Jechoniah was the father of She-alti-el, and She-alti-el the father of Zerubbabel, and Zerubbabel the father of Abiud, and Abiud the father of Eliakim, and Eliakim the father of Azor, and Azor the father of Zadok, and Zadok the father of Achim, and Achim the father of Eliud, and Eliud the father of Eleazar, and Eleazar the father of Matthan, and Matthan the father of Jacob, and Jacob the father of Joseph the husband of Mary, of whom Jesus was born, who is called Christ (Mt 1: 1-16).

Throughout the religious writings of the Jews and in the conversations that have been recorded, we find expressions such as these: "So it is written"; "the Scripture saith"; "thus it is written"; "so it is written in the book of the prophet." In the New Testament similarly we find: "So it is written"; "How readest you?" "What is written?" Thus the conviction that the Scriptures were the expression of the will of God was deeply impressed upon the minds of the people. Knowingly or unknowingly, each one was persuaded by these repeated expressions that the future of his people, no less than its past, was no haphazard jumble of incidents or accidental occurrences. Accordingly, each individual had a special vocation and a destiny within the race; each one was a unit in the great whole of his people, not an isolated individual. So completely had this viewpoint won the mind of the people that the most insignificant individual became important in the great design God had given the people. This belief in the divine ordering of events included even things that are generally regarded as being under the simple control of nature. Marital life and the establishment of a family were also thought to come within the provisions of God's plan for his people. For the Israelite, marriage was not a personal concern affecting only himself and his immediate relatives, because in marriage he entered into the great religious undertaking of his people, to continue the succession of generations until the appearance of the Messiah who was promised by the Scriptures. To be childless was a religious disgrace, a sign that God had excluded the childless man or woman from His plans. The childless person remained, as it were, stationary; he did not go forward through his children to the days of the Redeemer.

While we are accustomed to follow only the direct line in genealogical lists, the people of the Middle East were perhaps more realistic in reckoning also the relatives in the collateral lines. This inclusion of all the branches permitted a certain latitude in establishing a family tree. As one may return to the trunk by any of the branches of a tree, so, in tracing the descent of an individual, not all the branches of the family were indicated, not even those directly returning to the main stem; often the line was traced through collateral branches back to the main stem. This fact should be kept in mind when we consider the two family trees recorded by the Evangelists, who manifestly do not trace the same line of descent. The Evangelists themselves and their earliest readers were not disturbed by this apparent discrepancy, for they were cognizant of the methods in use in tracing descent. Particularly accurate family trees were kept for the families of priests and Levites and for all who occupied positions of honor in the Temple. Before marriage, the woman's family tree was thoroughly investigated. When a priest married a woman of priestly descent, the rule was that her genealogy must be traced back through eight generations of maternal ancestors. Flavius Josephus, a contemporary of the Apostles, speaking of the Jewish practice of investigating the genealogy of the priests, writes as follows: "This is our practice not only in Judea, but wheresoever any body of men of our nation do live; and even there an exact catalogue of our priests' marriages is kept; I mean at Egypt and at Babylon, or in any other place of the rest of the habitable earth, whithersoever our priests are scattered; for they send to Jerusalem the ancient names of their parents in writing, as well as those of their remoter ancestors, and signify who are the witnesses also." A permanent commission, which held its sessions in the Temple, investigated and certified the genealogy of priests and Levites. Certain documents indicate that the ancestry on the maternal side was also considered. In order that the record of a relationship might be complete, consideration had to be given also to the various ramifications by which the priestly class was related to the ordinary people. The Middle East was always concerned with such details and, according to records that have come down to us, these border lines of relationship were not lost sight of.

The knowledge of these general practices will throw some light on Mary's genealogy. Although nothing is recorded of Mary's father, we are expressly told that she was related to Elizabeth, the wife of the priest Zechariah. Being a priest, Zechariah had to keep the lists of descent for his family; in these lists would be found the record of Mary's ancestry. This question of descent was accorded more than ordinary attention by the members of noble families, among which the house of David was reckoned as one of the first families of the people. Explicit mention is made of those who, like Mary and Joseph, traced their descent back to David; for example, Hillel, the famous doctor of the law, who was descended on his mother's side from David.

Mary's descent from David, however, is not conclusively established from the genealogical list in St. Luke's Gospel. More conclusive evidence is to be obtained from the narrative of the Annunciation, in which the descent from the house of David is expressly mentioned. We read: "The angel Gabriel was sent from God . . . to a virgin betrothed to a man whose name was Joseph, of the house of David; and the virgin's name was Mary." Does the expression "house of David" refer to Mary or to Joseph? Since the whole account concerns chiefly not Joseph but Mary, we may

25

with considerable probability take the phrase as referring to Mary. We find frequent mention of women's ancestry, especially in the case of the more prominent members of a family. Thus it is recorded that Elizabeth, the mother of John the Baptist, was a daughter of Aaron, and that the prophetess Anna was the daughter of Phanuel, of the tribe of Asher. Joseph's descent from David, moreover, is given separate mention later (Lk 2: 4). Therefore we may reasonably conclude that the words "house of David" refer to Mary and that she is here introduced as a daughter of David.

The words of the angel Gabriel addressed to Mary are reliable evidence that she was descended from the house of David, and they also reveal that she was aware of her descent. The angel announced to her: "And behold, you will conceive in your womb and bear a son, and you shall call his name Jesus. He will be great, and will be called the Son of the Most High; and the Lord God will give to him the throne of his father David." By the words "you will bear a son," the angel designates Jesus as the son of Mary; and in the words, "the Lord God will give to him the throne of his father David," he designates Him the descendant of David. This would be true only if Mary belonged to the house of David, for only then could Jesus be both the descendant of David and Mary's Son. Upon hearing the angel's words, Mary mentioned her resolve not to use the rights of marriage; but further than this, she did not ask or say anything. Therefore she must have known of her descent from the house of David when the angel referred to it in his message to her.

The daughter of the house of David

The Lord God will give to him the throne of his father David (Lk 1: 32).

A traditional story, current among the Jews, shows that they considered descendants not only as heirs of the promises and merits of their ancestors, but also as heirs of their guilt and punishment, and that they felt obliged to pray and atone for their ancestors. This is the story. While Chijja, a doctor of the law, stood in the Temple and prayed, Rabbi Kahana, another doctor of the law, also came to pray and stood behind him. When Chijja had finished his prayers, he sat down to wait, because he did not wish to pass in front of Kahana and disturb him. But Kahana prayed a very long time, and Chijja waited. When Kahana finally ended his prayers, Chijja said to him: "Perhaps it is your custom in Babylon thus to torture your teachers with endless prayers." Kahana then begged Chijja's pardon and said: "I belong to the tribe of Eli, of whom it is written: 'The iniquity of his house shall not be expiated by sacrifice or offering for ever' (1 Sam 3: 14). The punishment that God decreed for my ancestors who violated the sacrifices and offerings for the altar is that now they can be helped only by prayers and that sacrifices and offerings avail them nothing. Forgive me, therefore, if I have prayed for them so long." Chijja was moved by these pious sentiments of Kahana and promised henceforth to join him in these prayers of atonement, and, the story concludes, God was pleased with Chijja's resolve. The important point is not whether the event ever actually occurred, but that the story was told and retold and universally accepted and that it reflects the thoughts and sentiments of the people.

According to the story, Kahana was descended from the tribe of Eli; this fact he learned from his family lists. Accordingly, he paid special attention to those parts of the Scriptures in which his family was mentioned, and he was deeply affected by the misconduct of his ancestors. To atone for them, he devoted his life to prayer. This pious resolve won the approval of the devout Chijja, who is even moved to support Kahana's prayers with his own. The story presupposes the existence of detailed family lists, which, unlike our public registers, were something vital, the history of the tribe, an epitome of the good and the evil of its inheritance. They were the record of the inheritance of good and evil not only in the eyes of men, but also before God, who guides the destiny of races and in His decrees takes into account both good and evil deeds.

Kahana's relationship to the tribe of Eli is illustrative of the relationship of Mary to the house of David. Just as the devout Kahana was descended from Eli and knew of his descent, so Mary knew of her descent from David. Just as the tribe of Eli was immortalized in the Scriptures as having some special importance in the history of the people, so the race of David was among those tribes whose deeds were recorded in detail in Holy Writ. Indeed, the house of David attained the greatest importance and was intimately bound up with the history of the people; for many centuries the history of the Jews was identified with the good and evil deeds of members of the house of David. According to the prophets, this close connection would never be dissolved, for out of this family the Redeemer, the "Son of David," would come forth.

Mary's attitude toward the house of David may be compared to that of Kahana toward his ancestors in the house of Eli. Although retired within the sanctuary of her own piety, she did not hold herself aloof from the past and the future of her race. Whenever she read the Scriptures and entered into their spirit, she learned the history of the house of David, especially of her great ancestor David, the king, prophet, and penitent. More than the pious Kahana, she was urged by religious motives to study the deeds of her family, principally because, according to the sayings of the prophets, the Redeemer was to issue forth from it.

Great was her joy when she, the daughter of David, read of the many manifestations of grace that God had showered upon her house; and great was her sorrow when she read of the base ingratitude with which God's great favors had been repaid. Yet God had not withdrawn His promises to her people. He had indeed permitted the house of David to lose the throne; He had permitted it to sink into poverty and insignificance; but He continually declared that out of the house of David, even though it had been so deeply humbled, would come forth the Redeemer.

Mary's relationship to the house of David had a deeper effect upon her soul than Kahana's relationship to the house of Eli had upon his. She who was without sin and was full of grace felt grievously the weight of the burden of sin that rested upon her race, and within her burned an ardent desire to make atonement; she wished to cleanse her people from their guilt that they might be worthy to receive unto themselves the Savior from heaven.

Popular messianic expectation

Religion and piety in the Old Testament are fundamentally different from religion and piety in the New Testament because of their relationship to the Redeemer. The faithful of the Old Testament looked upon the Redeemer as one who was to come. St. John the Baptist directs his disciples to ask: "Are you he who is to come?" For the faithful of the New Testament, even for the Apostles, after the Ascension, Jesus is the Redeemer who has appeared and has returned into heaven. In those faithful of both the Old and the New Testaments with a deep and lively faith in the Redeemer, this difference is still more remarkable. By their faith the Old Testament believers were led to look constantly to the future, to the fullness of time, and with their faith in Him who was to come their desire for His coming grew. This longing for His coming led the devout of the Old Law to search out how long they must still wait, and they tried to picture to themselves how His coming would be. The deeper their insight into the nature of sin and therefore into the nature of the redemption, the closer they were to approaching a knowledge of the Redeemer as He would one day be manifested.

Because, in the ages after Christ, the faithful look back to events enacted in the past, we find extreme difficulty in understanding a people who lived by faith in a Savior and Liberator to come, a faith able to inspire men and lead them to God, who had announced His coming beforehand and had determined the time of His appearance among men.

Because of our fundamentally different viewpoint, we may easily lose sight of the actual state of things. We can without difficulty picture to ourselves those people in the generation before the birth of Christ. They carried in their hearts a false hope of the Messiah, were in rebellion against the overlordship of the Romans, and were straining to make every effort against the tide of paganism, which threatened on every side. We can understand their impatience and their pointing to the promises of the coming Redeemer. Thus the leaders and many among the people themselves expected a powerful and resplendent ruler who would drive the Romans from the land and confer on Jerusalem the worldwide mastery then held by Rome. Just at this time when Jesus was born, a popular religious book appeared, called the *Ascension of Moses*. The author, looking forward to the days of the Messiah, exulted as he said: "Then shalt thou rejoice, O Israel, and tread upon the neck of the [Roman] eagle, for the days of the eagle are full."

By such misinterpretation of the Messianic prophecy a political and religious tension was created, and certain demagogues took advantage of the situation to form a following and declare themselves the expected Messiah. Such was that Theodas, mentioned in the Acts of the Apostles, who arose and gathered a following about himself. After him, at the time of the census, came the Galilean Judas, also mentioned in the Acts, who stirred up a revolt. The air was charged, the scepter had gone from Judah, the alien monarch Herod ruled the land by the favor of the pagan

29

Romans, the weeks prophesied by Daniel had passed, and the suspense in the minds of the people grew from year to year. Yet these distorted hopes for the coming Messiah do not give a complete picture of the uninterrupted union of God with the people by means of His revelations, nor do they supply an understanding of Mary's attitude before the Annunciation. To understand these things fully, we must know the spirit in which the devout among the people, illumined by God's grace, awaited the "days of the Messiah," since they for whom God had vouched must be considered as the only bearers of the true Messianic hope.

Mary's desire for the Savior

He has helped his servant Israel, in remembrance of his mercy, as he spoke to our fathers, to Abraham and to his posterity for ever (Lk 1:54–55).

During this time, when earthly-minded men of all classes expected a redeemer who would be a political leader instead of a religious savior, among the people of Israel was to be found a leaven of devout persons who cherished and preserved in their hearts the true and undistorted Messianic hope. These expected a Messiah who would be a deliverer from spiritual bondage, from the misery of sin. By their longing was enkindled the lively faith that the days of the Messiah were close at hand. The Gospel speaks of these men whose lives were spent in praying for the advent of the Messiah and in anxiously awaiting His coming. The angel said to Zechariah: "Your prayer is heard"; and this prayer must have included the petition for the coming of the Messiah. Simeon had prayed earnestly, and the Spirit of God revealed to him that he would not die until he had seen the Redeemer. The same is true of the prophetess Anna, whose life was spent in continual prayer and fasting.

Yet none of these possessed Mary's ardent longing for the Redeemer. More than Simeon and Anna, she suffered because men were separated from God and lived under the law of sin, and, more than they, she longed for the time when peace would be established between God and men and when men would live at peace with one another. All this, she knew, would be accomplished in that great hour when the Savior would appear, and so all her longing and loving was transmuted into the desire for the

Redeemer. Great would be her joy when she would no longer be so lonely, when others would think more of God and speak of Him and do His will. So deeply was she immersed in this longing that she herself did not realize how her whole being was absorbed in it.

In what manner and to what extent was she able to satisfy this longing by learning all that had been foretold of the Messiah and the redemption? At hand were two sources to satisfy this desire: one was Holy Scripture; the other was the worship in the Temple, which was closely dependent on the revelations of Holy Writ.

In these modern days, when we are so boastful of the great number of our schools and the low percentage of illiterates, the question will immediately be asked: Was Mary able to read? Could she afford to buy copies of the Scripture? We are at first inclined to answer "No" to both questions. But perhaps the following considerations will cause us to hesitate before answering. A few centuries ago, the educational opportunities existing among us were not greatly different from those in the time of our Lord. From discoveries made in old German farmhouses, even in remote Alpine villages, it has recently come to light that pious men and women set themselves to learn how to read merely because of their faith, although they did not at the same time learn to write. Mary was related to the priestly family of Zechariah, which, in all likelihood, possessed some books; from the Gospel we know that some members of the family were able to read and write. That Mary had inherited some manuscript rolls is not impossible. In an itemized list of the personal possessions of a certain woman of the time, we find enumerated: "A coverlet, a Book of the Psalms, a Book of Job, and a Book of Proverbs, all rather old and worn." This instance is most probably not unique. We may suppose as likely or at least possible that some books of Scripture or excerpts from them were in the house at Nazareth. Furthermore, if we give full credence to the words of Flavius Josephus, very many people, especially young men, learned to read principally that they might be acquainted with the Law. The customary privilege accorded every man and even every boy to read to the congregation in the synagogue presupposes that many learned how to read.

Quite apart from the supposition that members of Mary's family were able to read, she had opportunity to satisfy her desire for knowledge of the things of God by the public readings of the Scriptures in the services of the synagogue. We can scarcely appreciate how much faith and devotion are handed down from generation to generation by means of oral tradition, even when the women, the mothers among the people, are unable to read and write. Sometimes the memory of young people who are religiously inclined, although deprived of the opportunity of going to school, is remarkably accurate and retentive. Even today we find some persons who after forty years are able to repeat, in great part verbatim, the sermons preached at a mission. Others, after hearing a sermon, can return home and write it down almost word for word. Certain scholars, searching for an old religious drama, came upon an old woman in the Alpine country who at the age of eighty was able to repeat not only her own role but the words of the other characters in a play in which she had taken part sixty years before. Some people who have never seen a page of music have an amazing memory for folk songs.

Similar conditions prevailed in the land of Israel. Scriptural narratives and prophecies lived on in the memory of the people. Speaking of the people's religious education, Josephus points out that, besides the reading of the written word, memorizing of the sacred text played an important part; in one passage he remarks that the men of Israel knew the Law more fluently than they did their own names. For the devout among the people, this knowledge of the Law and the prophets was the measuring rod and the guiding star of their acts, their beliefs, and their hopes. By this knowledge their souls were nourished and strengthened.

This close attachment to the words of divine revelation and this immersion in the spirit of these words was present in an especially high degree in Mary's life. Filled with great longing and the most delicate feelings, Mary took to herself whatever she heard of the things of God in the Scriptures or in the synagogue worship. To her had been given the grace of religious understanding to master and retain all she learned; according to St. Luke, Mary "kept all these words in her heart."

Rock crystal, lying in a mountain stream, grows according to a law peculiar to itself by the deposit of secondary quartz about each grain. A similar growth took place in Mary's secluded and hidden life. Her soul rested in the sacred waters of all those things which the Scriptures and the Temple worship told of God, of the divine decree of the redemption, of the coming Redeemer Himself, of the time of His coming, and of the manner in which He would redeem the world; according to a law peculiar to herself, because she was without sin, her soul grew steadily and quietly. It was comforted to see rising above the fall of Adam and Eve the bright promise of the coming Savior, the promise of the woman and her Child who would crush the head of the serpent. In the books of the prophets and in the Psalms the vision of the Redeemer became ever clearer and more radiant, and into these sacred prophecies she penetrated ever deeper with all the longing of her soul.

To Mary had been given an extraordinary insight into the nature of sin, and even now she was extraordinarily endowed to enter into the mystery of the redemption and to live only for Him who was about to come into the world. For her, full of grace, there were no longer any thoughts, resolves, or actions that were not directed in some way to the coming manifestation of divine grace to mankind. Her consecration of her virginity to God was also influenced in some way by the coming redemption. So expectant of the Savior had some men become that they vowed themselves to the performance of good works in order to "hasten the coming of the Messiah." Perhaps it was with such sentiments that Mary had vowed her life to God; in silence and solitude she gave herself in sacrifice for the house of David in preparation for the redemption. With these sentiments she received the grace to become worthy to be the mother of Him who as the Son of God was to give Himself in sacrifice for mankind.

By this consecration of herself to God she had completely withdrawn herself from the world so that, like the aged Simeon and the prophetess Anna, or perhaps in a more perfect manner, she might spend her life praying for the advent of the Messiah and preparing herself for his coming.

Mary and the Psalms

In order the more fully to comprehend Mary's life, we must know the influence that the spirit of the Scriptures had on her soul. We may here consider Mary's attitude to the Book of Psalms, that most popular book of the Old Testament. It was the Jews' official and private prayer book and also their hymn book. Thus it came to pass that many psalms were especially current among the people, like those prayers that are handed down among us from one generation to another. We may suppose that Mary was better acquainted with the Psalms than with other parts of Scripture; this supposition will be strengthened by what we will have to say later about the *Magnificat*.

The psalms are prayers full of mystery. They wither away into skeleton forms when we say them with dry and barren hearts; they expand and give rise to the most sublime thoughts when we recite them with devout and loving sentiments. In the quiet house at Nazareth, Mary recited these psalms, and on the great feasts she followed their meaning as they were recited in the Temple. For her the words became transparent; and we too, when we hear the psalms from her lips, seem to understand them better.

Psalm 110, which at that time was universally known, had a special importance for Mary, for it came from the pen of her ancestor David, the king and prophet:

> The Lord says to my lord:
>   "Sit at my right hand:
> till I make your enemies your footstool."

> The Lord sends forth from Zion
>   your mighty scepter.
>   Rule in the midst of your foes!
> Your people will offer themselves freely
>   on the day you lead your host
>   upon the holy mountains.
> From the womb of the morning
>   like dew your youth will come to you.
> The Lord has sworn,
>   And will not change his mind,
> "You are a priest forever
>   after the order of Melchizedek."

> The Lord is at your right hand;
>   he will shatter kings on the day of his wrath.
> He will execute judgment among the nations,
>   filling them with corpses;
> he will shatter chiefs
>   over the wide earth.
> He will drink from the brook by the way;
>   therefore he will lift up his head.

In Mary's time this psalm was received by all as Messianic; and Jesus before the supreme council of the Jews declared, in the words of this psalm, that He would soon "sit at the right hand" of God.

Mary was accustomed to the picturesque language of the Scriptures, which expresses ideas with a wealth of imagery. These figures, however, were differently interpreted according to the mind of the individual. Many Israelites read from this psalm that the Messiah would conquer the enemy, that is, the Romans, and inflict on them a crushing defeat. For them, the significant words of the psalm were those describing the battlefield covered with the enemy's dead and foretelling the defeat of the enemy and the way he would be compelled to bend his neck beneath the foot of the victor. Other passages were intentionally or carelessly overlooked. When, for instance, the psalm described the Messiah as the "priest after the order of Melchizedek," who had offered bread and wine, and that he had been begotten from "the womb of the morning," little or no impression was made on them. Much less were they able to understand the puzzling words: "The Lord says to my lord: 'Sit at my right hand.'" They failed to understand who these two Lords were. The faithful, on the other hand, in their ardent longing for the Messiah, paused precisely at these passages, which seemed to contain the mysterious and the divine. They did not, of course, completely grasp their meaning, but in these words they seemed to hear a heavenly melody to which they listened with rapture, although the words remained obscure.

Others psalms told of the Messiah; but the men learned in the Scriptures were blind to the inference; these psalms were too sad and plaintive, they were filled with sobs and cries of anguish. There was that song of David (Psalm 22):

My God, my God, why hast thou forsaken me?
    Why art thou so far from helping me, from the words of
        my groaning?
O my God, I cry by day, but thou dost not answer;
    and by night, but find no rest.

Yet thou art holy,
    enthroned on the praises of Israel.
In thee our fathers trusted;
    they trusted, and thou didst deliver them. . . .

But I am a worm, and no man;
    scorned by men, and despised by the people.

All who see me mock at me,
  they make mouths at me, they wag their heads;
"He committed his cause to the Lord; let him deliver him,
  let him rescue him, for he delights in him!"

Yet thou art he who took me from the womb;
  thou didst keep me safe upon my mother's breasts.
Upon thee was I cast from my birth,
  and since my mother bore me thou has been my God.
Be not far from me,
  for trouble is near
  and there is none to help.

Many bulls encompass me,
  strong bulls of Bashan surround me;
they open wide their mouths at me,
  like a ravening and roaring lion.

I am poured out like water,
  and all my bones are out of joint;
my heart is like wax,
  it is melted within my breast;
my strength is dried up like a potsherd,
  and my tongue cleaves to my jaws;
  thou dost lay me in the dust of death.

Yea, dogs are round about me:
  a company of evildoers encircle me;
  they have pierced my hands and feet—
I can count all my bones—
  they stare and gloat over me. . . .

But thou, O Lord, be not far off!
  O thou my help, hasten to my aid!

What were Mary's thoughts when she read this lament? With her religious spirit she entered much more deeply into the world of suffering, of loneliness and dereliction, than did the learned scribes who dismembered each verse and studied it.

We will again speak of these psalms, and we will show how these words of Scripture in the course of Mary's life changed their meaning in a mysterious though glorious manner; how these prophecies were at first something that referred to the much desired but yet unknown Redeemer, then something that foretold the fate of her own Son, and, finally, something that expressed what had been enacted in her life and in the life of her

Son. Her relationship to the writings of the Old Testament was unique.

Espousals among the Jews

The preliminary arrangements preceding an espousal were a matter of barter between the fathers of the young people. Each sought to come away from the "trading" with advantages for his own family. The father of the groom set out to obtain from the bride the highest possible dowry under the most lenient conditions. Among the poorer classes, the dowry consisted principally of household furnishings and clothing; among the wealthier classes, it included land and slaves, money, and valuables such as jewelry. The use of these goods belonged to the man and were called "milking" goods; thus the wool of sheep, which often formed part of the dowry, belonged to the husband, while the natural increase, the lambs, belonged to the woman.

Besides this dowry, properly so called, there was another marriage portion called the "iron herd," which was regulated by other legal provisions. The husband possessed the right freely to dispose of this marriage portion; its increase was to his benefit; in case of the marriage being dissolved, he was obliged to return it merely in its original condition. Because of this characteristic of unaltered condition, it was called the "iron herd," that is, figuratively, iron sheep and cattle. The same expression was used centuries ago in connection with certain pious foundations, which were to secure a definite return for each year.

The distinction between the dowry proper and the marriage portion rose principally when there was question of slaves. The slaves forming part of the dowry proper belonged to the wife; if they died, the loss was hers, and the husband was not bound to replace them. But, if a slave of the marriage portion died, the loss was the husband's; and, in case of a dissolution of the marriage, he was bound to replace the slave.

Still another marriage portion was called the marriage assignment. It was the amount of money the husband was obliged to pay from his own possessions to the woman if he dismissed her. The sum to be paid was arrived at by adding to a basic tax, which had to be paid in every instance, a kind of surtax proportionate to the amount of the dowry and the marriage portion. Frequently, the prospective husband had to mortgage his property or give a bond for this sum. In the marriage preliminaries, the father of the bride tried to fix this sum as high as possible.

These provisions of the antenuptial agreement were important, not only from the financial point of view, but also morally, for they were obviously powerful motives to prevent the husband from hastily dismissing his wife in an outburst of anger. This custom of making a marriage assignment seems to have been generally observed at the time of our Lord. A certain man once complained, when he had been advised to dismiss his wife, that he had nothing with which to pay the large marriage assignment to which he had obligated himself. Soon after the introduction of the marriage assignment, an abuse arose: the husband would allow himself to be divorced and would then declare himself bankrupt. When the surety had paid the obligation for him, he remarried the woman and took possession of the money paid to her: a counterpart to the insurance and compensation manipulations of modern times.

Since the preliminaries of a betrothal were so much concerned with these business matters, the young people were not permitted openly to show any inclination toward each other; it might have had a prejudicial influence on one or the other negotiator. The preliminaries were followed by the betrothal itself, which had the same legal effects as the marriage. The betrothal ceremony consisted in the groom giving the bride some object worth at least a penny as a pledge of fidelity, and saying: "You are hereby betrothed to me." A blessing was given, and thereafter the bride was known as the man's wife, just as Mary, in the Gospels, is called the spouse of Joseph.

Frequently, though not always or in all localities, the transaction was put down in writing. If the matter was arranged orally, witnesses were brought in. Custom had decreed that a year should elapse between the betrothal and the marriage.

Besides this normal course, provision was made in extrabiblical writings for unusual circumstances, including the breaking of the engagement. In the event of a dissolution, the discontinuance of visits between the parties or the angry discussion among the relatives were not the important things; both sides gave more attention to the financial details and sought advantageous conditions about the return of the dowry, marriage portion, and marriage assignment, if these had been paid to the groom. If the groom unduly delayed the marriage, the woman could remonstrate and, according to many, could demand a bill of divorce, as was customary for married women, so that she could marry another. If the groom died, the woman was considered a widow. This fact indicates that the betrothal was very much like marriage in the eyes of the law; and the woman's father or her representative demanded the return of the marriage assignment and whatever else may have been paid to the groom.

Underlying this custom of solemn betrothals preceding the marriage was probably more wisdom than is at first apparent. The woman was to be bound early to her future husband; at the same time, she was not to be burdened too early with the responsibilities of married life. Therefore an early espousal was entered into, which was definitely binding; and the marriage was delayed for some time in order to spare the woman. Betrothals as observed in the Middle Ages arose from similar considerations. With the increasing tendency to weaken their binding power, these espousals became empty formalities. In Egypt, people became betrothed with the understanding that the legal effects would be in abeyance until the marriage; and thus the effectiveness of the espousal was reduced to the position it now has among us.

Marriages were generally solemnized on Wednesday, because this day was almost midway between Sabbaths. The solemnity began when the bride was brought to the home of the groom.

Mary's espousal to Joseph

The angel Gabriel was sent from God to a city of Galilee named Nazareth, to a virgin betrothed to a man whose name was Joseph, of the house of David (Lk 1: 26–27).

At the time of Mary's espousal to Joseph, her life came within the provisions of these laws and customs with but few deviations from the normal course of things. From all indications, it appears that Mary's parents were dead; thus she came under the guardianship of one of her relatives, who exercised his office either by legal appointment or perhaps even without such formal authorization. According to a popular legend, Mary was reared in the Temple; if this be true, she may have come under the direction of her relative the priest Zechariah. We must, however, dismiss this pious legend as unauthentic, because, at the time the Gospels speak of her, she was living at Nazareth, probably with some other relative.

39

When the time came for Mary to contract marriage, the relative who stood in her father's place began to plan these things for her. Theoretically, every young woman had the right to refuse the husband who was proposed to her, although frequently in practice her refusal was not taken into consideration. If the guardians of a girl who had come of age entered into an agreement without consulting her, the contract was not binding; if the agreement had been made in behalf of a girl still under age, even though she consented, she could afterward refuse to be bound by the contract.

Under circumstances similar to these, Mary was espoused to Joseph. The first advances probably came from Joseph, or perhaps relatives made the first approaches. An important consideration was that both parties be of equal birth, a custom that had a religious and a social background. From a somewhat later period, several proverbs have come down to us that probably had considerable influence upon the lives of the people: "If a man marries a woman who is not of his social standing, he is considered in the eyes of the law as having plowed up the whole world and having sown salt in the furrows," that is, as having destroyed it forever; "If a man marries a woman for her money, he will beget children that are not worthy of him"; "Grapes belong to grapes, and not to thorns: like and like belong together." The prophet Elijah was looked upon as the guardian of the genealogical tables of the people; and a belief commonly held was that he would cast out all illegitimate offspring when he should return again. Especially among the more prominent classes, for example, the priesthood, it was considered a duty to marry a person of equal birth. There was a saying that if the daughter of a priestly family married beneath her station, she should be considered as though she were a widow or a divorced woman or as being childless. At all events, such a marriage was thought to have no promise of future happiness; and many doctors of the law forbade their disciples to participate in the solemnizing of such marriages.

The families of nobler extraction likewise were insistent that the parties to a marriage be of equal station; and this custom was especially binding upon Mary and her relatives. Further, if she had inherited anything, if she had some personal property, custom obliged her to marry within her own relationship. In general, marriage to a man within the relationship, but outside the forbidden degrees, was considered praiseworthy; in the case of a woman of some property, the spirit of the law dictated that she marry a close relative, but not within the forbidden degrees. The obligation to make such a choice was almost religious, and the story of Tobias shows that the more devout families conscientiously observed the custom. The archangel Raphael, speaking to the younger Tobias of his cousin Raguel, said: "He has an only daughter named Sarah. I will suggest that she be given to you in marriage, because you are entitled to her and to her inheritance, for you are her only eligible kinsman" (Tob 6: 10-11). After Tobias had asked for Raguel's daughter in marriage, Raguel said: "You are her relative, and she is yours. . . . Take her according to the law of Moses" (Tob 7: 12-13).

The Bible does not tell how Mary and Joseph came to be espoused; and Mary's anguish before the espousal is hidden from us. Many things contrived to cause her suffering and anxiety; when her relatives made known their intention to arrange a marriage for her as soon as possible, the serious conversations and the lighter talk about the marriage, all caused her pain and anguish. Nor was this all; because she was such a retiring and modest maiden, her relatives impressed upon her that there was a religious obligation to enter into marriage. Perhaps before her espousal to Joseph, other attempts had been made to marry her to one of the young men of the relationship who might appear a likely husband. Possibly the resolve to promise herself to Joseph was the last resort out of these difficulties.

Reflecting on these things, we should also like to know how Mary and Joseph declared their intentions to each other. The most natural opportunity was presented when Joseph came to ask for Mary in marriage. We have already spoken of the vows connected with an espousal and consequently with marriage; they had to be made known before the espousals were concluded. Mary knew that she must tell Joseph of the vow she had made, and in telling him she must have regarded him as a "just" man, as a holy man in whom she could repose these sacred confidences.

While Joseph listened to her, perhaps he had a similar intention, perhaps the desire of his heart was to live a life of virginity and give himself entirely to God. Perhaps, too, only the urging of his relatives had brought him to these espousals, their insistence that he should marry someone, perhaps Mary, in particular.

In such case, Mary's declaration that she had consecrated

herself to God and that she would enter the espousals and the marriage only on condition that she could remain faithful to her resolve, must have seemed like a voice from heaven to Joseph. Perhaps then he too made a similar vow. We have, of course, no way of knowing how far Mary and Joseph, revealing the most intimate secrets of their souls to each other, were in agreement.

To admit that the urging of relatives or the pressure of public opinion played any part in Mary's marriage with Joseph is sometimes offensive to traditional religious sentiment. Traditionally, we are loath to suppose that the motives and influences present in ordinary marriages were present in this holy union. The attitude arises from that narrow point of view which denies that God makes use of natural things for supernatural purposes and builds the supernatural on the natural. The early Christians of the East invented a fantastic tale of Mary's espousal, according to which this merely private concern of one family became a concern of the whole people of Israel.

The following is the old popular legend of Palestine. Mary lived in the Temple and there, like a dove, she was fed by the hand of an angel. When she was twelve years old, the priests came together in council and said: "Behold, Mary is now twelve years old (i.e., a young woman); What shall be done with her? " And they said to the high priest: "Thou standest at the altar of the Lord; go in to the Holy of Holies and pray for her, and whatsoever the Lord shall reveal to you, that let us do." Then the high priest took the amulet with the twelve bells and entered into the Holy of Holies and prayed for her. And behold, an angel of the Lord came to him and said to him: "Go out and assemble the widowers of the people, and each one shall bring with him a staff, and she shall be the wife of him to whom the Lord shall give a sign." The heralds went out into all the country of Judea and sounded the trumpets of the Lord, and immediately all came together. Joseph threw aside his ax and hurried to meet with the others, and when they were assembled they took their staffs and went to the high priest, who took all the staffs and went into the Temple and prayed. After he had finished his prayer, he took the staffs and went out and returned them, but no sign appeared on them. Joseph received the last staff and, behold, a dove came out of the staff and rested on Joseph's head. The priest said to Joseph: "Thou hast been chosen by lot to take the Lord's virgin under your protection." But Joseph remonstrated, and the priest said to him:

"Fear the Lord thy God, and remember what God did to Dathan, Abiram, and Korah, how the earth opened up and they were swallowed up because of their refusal. Now, Joseph, fear the Lord, that such things may not come upon thy house." And Joseph was filled with fear and he took Mary under his protection, and he said to her: "Behold, I have received you from the Temple, and I leave you now in my house while I go to finish my buildings. The Lord will keep you until I return."

The real event was much simpler than the legend would have us believe. It all happened in the ordinary course of everyday life in a small Eastern village. As later Jesus was to spend years in obscurity, so now Mary and Joseph were living in obscurity; all that was unusual in their lives, all that was divine, was hidden beneath the appearances of ordinary human living.

The usual property transactions also took place in this espousal. Here again we are inclined to deny that Mary and Joseph were concerned with their trivial possessions: yet all such matters belong to this earthly life. Mary received a dowry, which consisted of clothing and household furnishings; she received a marriage portion, which was very likely some additional clothing and household ware and perhaps a little plot of ground; she received a widow's portion, a small sum of money that she would inherit on Joseph's death. Perhaps it was all of small value, but among the poor these small possessions are as important as great wealth among the rich. The arrangements were made either by Joseph himself or by some authorized agent. Perhaps these events were so completely concealed beneath the fabric of ordinary occurrences that the relatives congratulated themselves on their cleverness in arranging this betrothal to everybody's satisfaction.

In Nazareth, if not immediately, at least later, the saying was: "Mary has betrothed herself to Joseph the carpenter." And they added their comments on the matter. Very probably they said: "Those two belong together." Perhaps it was not always said with the best of good will: "Those two!" Mary, this insignificant maiden, who because of her retiring disposition was in the eyes of many really a nobody. And Joseph, this quiet workman; he was, after all, very much like Mary.

II.

From the Annunciation
to the Nativity

In the sixth month the angel Gabriel was sent from God to a city of Galilee named Nazareth, to a virgin betrothed to a man whose name was Joseph, of the house of David; and the virgin's name was Mary (Lk 1: 26-27).

After her espousal to Joseph, a feeling of security came upon Mary's soul; for the Lord had given her in Joseph a spouse who respected her resolve to lead a life consecrated to God. During this time her soul was filled with peace and joy; when she reflected on the circumstances in which God had placed her, she offered Him her fervent thanks. It would be only a short time now, and then she would go to Joseph's house and live there with him. She felt that God had signified His approval of her wish to live for Him alone and to spend her life awaiting the Messiah and preparing herself for His coming. Joseph was there, protecting her from all that was without, and she knew that he shared her sentiments. Like all the devout in Israel, she could now pray with him for the coming of the One who had been promised. Together with Joseph, in longing for the Messiah, she could lift up her heart in prayer in the morning and in the evening, during the prayers on the Sabbath, and during the sacrifices on the great feast days for which they went every year to Jerusalem; and when they had returned home, with him she could speak of the words of Scripture and the sayings of the prophets. Mary saw stretching before her a life such as the prophetess Anna had lived, a life full of prayer and surrender to God, a life filled with longing for the Messiah and preparation for His coming.

During this time, between the espousal and her entrance into Joseph's house, occurred, according to God's decree, the Annunciation by the angel, by which the whole plan of her life, which she had thought was definitely secured in its consecration to loneliness and simplicity, was disturbed and robbed of its security. From now on her life was intimately bound up with God's mysterious plans, and she was able to know the direction of her life's course only insofar as these divine plans were revealed to her.

Mary was now prepared for her great hour. In her longing for the Redeemer she had surpassed all others, both in intensity and in the purity of her love. And now her longing had so increased that she was prepared in a special manner to receive the divine message. Pure and sinless, she had suffered as no other had suffered beneath the weight of the sins of the house of David, the sins of her people Israel, and the sins of the whole human race. In short, she suffered because of mankind's defection from God, a defection with tragic consequences often spoken of in the Scriptures. Conscious of no sin of her own, she constantly saw before her the overwhelming accumulation of mankind's sins, which only the Redeemer could take away; with inexpressible longing she awaited the Redeemer's coming that He might destroy the works of the devil, cast sin out from the lives of men, lead them back to God, and renew the life of the world. She desired the Redeemer not for herself, but for the guilt-laden human race. This pure and unselfish longing completed her preparation for the Annunciation.

Mary's intense longing was, as it were, the last inducement for the Savior's descent into the world. Many among the people believed that the Messiah's coming would be hastened by the prayers and good works of the saints, and many, like Simeon and Anna, prayed and fasted for His coming; but nothing hastened His coming so much as Mary's praying and ardent longing. In early times, the Church and the faithful cherished the thought that Mary had induced the Savior to come from heaven to earth by her purity and holiness and by her love of God and men. They gave expression to the thought in fables and parables. An old fable told of an unconquerable unicorn, against which the strength and swiftness and strategy of the hunters availed nothing, although, strangely enough, the unicorn always became tame and docile in the presence of a virgin. The fable was interpreted as referring to the Redeemer. Christ was the unicorn, and no human power or human strategy was able to bring Him down from heaven, but He was content to become man in the womb of the Virgin Mary and to abide with her.

The angel's message

And he came to her and said, "Hail, full of grace, the Lord is with you! " But she was greatly troubled at the saying, and considered in her mind what sort of greeting this might be. And the angel said to her, "Do not be afraid, Mary, for you have found favor with God. And behold, you will conceive in your womb and bear a son, and you shall call his name Jesus. He will be great, and will be called the Son of the Most High; and the Lord God will give to him the throne of his father David, and he will reign over the house of Jacob for ever; and of his kingdom there will be no end" (Lk 1: 28-33).

In the dimly lighted interior of a poor house in Nazareth, the most decisive conversation in the world's history took place, the conversation between the angel Gabriel, whom God had sent as His spokesman, and the Virgin Mary, whom God had chosen to be His Mother. It may have been that when the angel came she was at prayer or in meditation, but even when she was not at prayer her soul remained recollected.

"And he [the angel] came to her." Clearly, then, the angel appeared in visible form, assuming the form of a man. And as men do, he came in with a greeting; but the Gospel indicates that, in spite of his human form, Mary recognized a spiritual being. Perhaps the angel appeared to her enveloped with some heavenly light; such an appearance would have been especially effective in the darkened rooms of a Palestinian house. The angel addressed her: "Hail, full of grace, the Lord is with you!" This was the first time since Adam's expulsion from Paradise that a human being was addressed with deference by an angel. He spoke to Mary as to the woman who was under God's special guidance and who has received signal graces from Him.

Mary was troubled; not, indeed, with a physical terror, such as men experience when startling things occur in nature, during catastrophes, or in the presence of death. Her fear was of a different kind, and the Evangelist seems to indicate that it was very great.

Mary remained silent and thought of this salutation, poising her soul and making it secure in the presence of this mysterious event which had now occurred to her. She knew that she stood in a special relationship to God by having vowed her virginity to Him, but this being from another world went far beyond this in what he was saying; he called her "full of grace." All during her life she had felt that she stood alone in the world, and now, if it were true, the angel had said something that might explain this loneliness. She did not yet know whether this angel who spoke to her in words of highest praise was an angel of light or of darkness. Sinless and in constant horror of sin, this unresolved doubt alarmed her soul, especially when she heard these words of praise.

The angel himself came to her relief. He disclosed the meaning of his greeting: "Do not be afraid, Mary, for you have found favor with God." To have "found favor with God" meant much more than "the Lord is with you," when the words refer to men whom God has chosen for some special purpose. Thus in the Bible it is said that Noah, the second ancestor of the race, Abraham, the father of the people of Israel, and David, the father of the royal house, had "found favor with God." This favor was their call to participate in the work of salvation. Solemnly the angel continued: "And behold, you will conceive in your womb and bear a son, and you shall call his name Jesus. He will be great, and will be called the Son of the Most High; and the Lord God will give unto him the throne of his father David, and he will reign over the house of Jacob forever; and of his kingdom there will be no end."

The great hour had come. For centuries Israel had looked for the days of the Messiah; each generation had handed on to its successor the promise and the hope that the Redeemer would arise in their midst out of the house of David. Now the long expected event had taken place. The angel of the Lord came to Mary, bringing her a message from God that she had been chosen to be the Mother of the Redeemer.

Was Mary prepared to receive this divine message? Had she, by her reading of the prophets, been sufficiently prepared to grasp the full import of the angel's words? Did she understand that the angel was announcing the coming of the Redeemer?

As a simple maiden, she had already had ample opportunity to know the Scriptures and their prophecies concerning the Messiah. She knew the many passages that spoke of the coming of the Redeemer; and her interpretation of these prophecies was free from all those common misunderstandings which distorted the idea of a Messiah and expected Him to be an earthly potentate. Her knowledge of these prophecies was eminently helpful in enabling her to comprehend the angel's message.

Which among these prophecies stood out in her memory as she heard the angel's words? She had done more than preserve the words of Scripture in her heart, she had also meditated upon them, she had compared them with one another, and from them she obtained a picture of the coming of the Redeemer. Now that vision of the Messiah vouchsafed to her under the direction of the Holy Spirit was vividly recalled.

Probably the angel's words had reference to certain prophecies and recalled them to Mary's mind. One prophecy especially dear to Mary must now have come to her mind:

But there will be no gloom for her that was in anguish. In the former time he brought into contempt the land of Zebulun and the land of Naphtali, but in the latter time he will make glorious the way of the sea, the land beyond the Jordan, Galilee of the nations. The people who walked in darkness have seen a great light; those who dwelt in a land of deep darkness, on them has light shined. Thou hast multiplied the nation, thou hast increased its joy; they rejoice before thee as with joy at the harvest, as men rejoice when they divide the spoil. For the yoke of his burden, and the staff for his shoulder, the rod of his oppressor, thou hast broken as on the day of Midian. For every boot of the tramping warrior in battle tumult and every garment rolled in blood will be burned as fuel for the fire. For to us a child is born, to us a son is given; and the government will be upon his shoulder, and his name will be called "Wonderful Counselor, Mighty God, Everlasting Father, Prince of Peace." Of the increase of his government and of peace there will be no end, upon the throne of David, and over his kingdom, to establish it, and to uphold it with justice and with righteousness from this time forth and for evermore. The zeal of the Lord of hosts will do this (Is 9: 1–7).

The prophecies of Isaiah were not unknown to the people. When, in the synagogue at Nazareth, Jesus arose and read from Isaiah a prophecy closely related to the one quoted here, the way He spoke to the people indicated that they already knew these passages of Scripture. Indeed, the prophets were read during synagogue service and, according to the Evangelists, Isaiah was better known than were the other prophets.

On this occasion, the people listened with special interest. Most of the incidents of the sacred story took place in Judea. There stood God's temple. How comforting it was now to hear at last something said of Galilee, to hear the prophet say that some day Galilee too would become famous and that joy would come to their despised country and that a light would rise upon it! Certainly they could not forget this prophecy.

Mary habitually listened to the reading of the Scripture in the synagogue with greater attention and with deeper insight than others. Keeping all these words in her heart and meditating on them, assuredly she did not forget this comforting prophecy. She attended to these words about the birth of a child who was to bring about this great change and announce the dawn of a new kingdom. She thought upon the child's names: "Wonderful Counselor," "Mighty God": the child would manifest the power of God; "Everlasting Father": although only a child, he had a place in eternity; "Prince of Peace": he would therefore be a king, but a king who did not depend upon physical might. To this child had been promised an empire that would last eternally; having ascended the throne of David, he would retain it forever.

Mary heard these words repeated again and again, and each time her longing increased for the Messiah's coming, and she hoped that in the days of the Redeemer God's light would illumine obscure Galilee and shine upon her poor homeland and perhaps even upon herself. It could not now be long until the much-desired Savior would come.

It was no mere coincidence that these words of the angel echoed what Isaiah had foretold centuries before, echoed also what Mary had cherished as a sweet comfort to her soul. Isaiah's prophecies spoke of a glorification of her country Galilee coming with the birth of a child who would ascend David's throne, not as a warlike hero, but as a prince of peace, and would establish his reign forever. The angel echoed the prophet's words when he foretold the miraculous birth of a child who would receive a new name and would be called the "Son of the Most High," and to whom God would give the throne of David his father and whose reign would last forever.

Mary understood much more readily than we who belong to another age that the angel was speaking of the birth of the Redeemer for whose coming she longed so ardently. Now He was about to come, and she from among the daughters of David's house had been chosen by God to be His Mother.

Mary's reply

And Mary said to the angel, "How can this be, since I have no husband?" And the angel said to her, "The Holy Spirit will come upon you, and the power of the Most High will overshadow you; therefore the child to be born will be called holy, the Son of God. And behold, your kinswoman Elizabeth in her old age has also conceived a son; and this is the sixth month with her who was called barren. For with God nothing will be impossible." And Mary said, "Behold, I am the handmaid of the Lord; let it be to me according to your word" (Lk 1: 34-38).

"And behold, you will conceive in your womb and bear a son, and you shall call his name Jesus. He will be great, and will be called the Son of the Most High; and the Lord God will give unto him the throne of his father David, and he will reign over the house of Jacob forever; and of his kingdom there will be no end." Thus the angel announced the solemn message he had brought from heaven to earth, to the Virgin Mary in Nazareth. Now Mary saw as if by intuition that it lay within her power to bring about the fulfillment of what had been the sole desire of her heart.

She was ready to become the Mother of the Redeemer, but she did not yet understand how God wished this to be accomplished. Only a short time before she had, under divine guidance and illumination, consecrated her virginity to Him forever, and by that act she had sacrificed all that the daughters of David held dear, motherhood and the blessing of children. She felt certain that what she had done was pleasing to God, and before the espousal she had told Joseph of her resolve; and they had agreed to live together as brother and sister. Now she heard the angel's announcement that she was to be the Mother of the Savior. She asked him therefore to explain the apparent contradiction between God's guidance in the past and this His present will. She asked: "How can this be, since I have no husband?"

Mary's question is often understood as an expression of concern for the preservation of her virginity at all costs. If this interpretation were correct, Mary would not have been the simple and humble handmaid of the Lord, and her question would not have been different from that of her relative Zechariah. Mary and Zechariah, it is true, asked questions of the angel that are outwardly similar; but the motives prompting them were essentially different. Zechariah's question was the question of one who doubts the truth of a statement, the question of one who does not believe: "How can this be? This is impossible." Mary's question came from a humble and inquiring mind seeking further direction.

The angel rebuked and punished Zechariah for his doubt. Mary's question, on the other hand, was a magnificent manifestation of her faith, an expression of her willingness to be further initiated in the great mystery. Continuing his announcement, the angel explained the divine decree to her: "The Holy Spirit will come upon you, and the power of the Most High will overshadow you; therefore the child to be born will be called holy, the Son of God."

The angel revealed to her that in some miraculous manner, by God's almighty power, she would become the Mother of His Son; and as a pledge for the truth of the message, the angel added that another miracle had occurred in a family to which she was related. This miracle was to attest the truth of what he said. Hence the angel concluded the announcement of the Incarnation by saying: "And behold, your kinswoman Elizabeth in her old age has also conceived a son; and this is the sixth month with her who was called barren. For with God nothing will be impossible."

"The Holy Spirit will come upon you, and the power of the Most High will overshadow you; therefore the child to be born will be called holy, the Son of God." These words explained to Mary why Jesus was to be called the Son of the Most High; not in the sense in which holy men in the past had been called the sons of God, because of their intimate relationship with Him; Jesus was to be called the Son of God because God was really His Father.

The divine decree that the veiled prophecies of the past had presaged was now clearly revealed to Mary. Now she understood all of the great mystery that was necessary for her to understand that she might give her free and considered consent to become the mother of God.

The angel paused to hear from her lips the expression of her consent. In that moment, when the fate of the world hung in the balance, Mary accepted God's will with the same humility and resignation as she had always done throughout her life. She answered: "Behold, I am the handmaid of the Lord; let it be to me according to your word." She gave her consent without inquiring whether her decision would bring her joy or sorrow, honor or disgrace, exaltation or humiliation; her will was directed to one thing alone, to further the work of the Redemption. When she humbly gave her consent, she made a decision that affected not only her own life, but that of the whole human race.

The angel departed from her, and she was alone. In the silence of that house in Nazareth, Jesus the Son of God became man. God came down to earth and, like other men, He began to live as a child.

The Mother of the Savior

In devout Catholic communities, many young women, perhaps more than we suppose, cherish a desire to be the mother of a priest. They are conscious of this desire at the time of marriage or sometimes even earlier; so deeply is it hidden within their souls that often they do not express it in words even to themselves. Sometimes such young women have considered seriously whether or not God had called them to the religious life before this desire arose in their souls. They realize that God has not called them to the convent, but from these meditations often comes a wish to be the mother of a priest. They tell no one of this most intimate secret of their hearts; even later, when their wish has come to fulfillment, it is only under extraordinary circumstances that they make known what was their secret desire.

Again and again occasions will arise to reawaken this longing for a son who will enter the company of God's priests. When such a mother attends Mass, when she hears the priest praying in church, when she is present at a baptism, when she hears a sermon, she thinks: "If I had a son and he became a priest, then he too could offer this holy sacrifice, he too could preach the word of God, he too could administer the sacraments." This mother's longing does not stop with the thought: "If I had a son"; it goes on to what she wishes her son might do. She considers more what her son's work will be in the future than she does her own motherhood.

The sentiments and longings of this mother may lead us to an understanding of the thoughts and sentiments of Mary's heart when she heard the announcement of the angel. She did not desire a son in order to have a child upon whom to shower her love. All the powers of her soul had been so absorbed in the love of God that nothing existed or could exist for her that was not a part of this love. Indeed, in the very beginning, the angel did not ask whether she would consent to become the mother of a son. He spoke immediately of the Redeemer, who would do the will of God: "He will be great, and will be called the Son of the Most High; and the Lord God will give unto him the throne of his father David, and he will reign over the house of Jacob forever; and of his kingdom there will be no end." The angel made known to her at once that her Son was to accomplish the salvation of mankind in obedience to God's will.

All the years of her life, Mary had desired the salvation of the human race; day after day she had prayed that the Redeemer would hasten His coming; and she was constantly intent to prepare herself for that coming. Now, her heart full of longing and love of God, in complete accord with the divine plan for the salvation of fallen mankind, she gave her consent that the Redeemer should descend to her and abide with her. She dedicated her life entirely to the redemption of mankind when she said: "Behold, I am the handmaid of the Lord; let it be to me according to your word."

In that moment, when her actual motherhood began, her spiritual motherhood was also established; indeed this spiritual motherhood already had its inception in her great love for all mankind and her ardent desire for man's redemption. Nay, more, this spiritual motherhood was the preparation and the reason for her selection as the Mother of the Redeemer.

The Church has always believed that by her motherhood Mary was united to Jesus not only by an external bond, but more intimately by her participation in His mission of redeeming mankind. Though in different ages the expression of this belief may have altered, the belief remained unchanged. In early times, the Church writers taught that it was by no compulsion, but by a free act of her will, that Mary consented to become the Mother of God. St. Thomas expresses the same thought when he says that at the Annunciation Mary represented the human race, and that her refusal or consent decided whether or not the human race should be saved. In another passage (*Summa* IIIa, q. 26, a. 1) he holds that others besides Christ may rightly be called mediators between God and man, because they cooperate in the work of uniting men to God. Such were the angels and saints of heaven and the prophets and priests of the Old and New Testament. Without doubt, however, the title of mediator belongs in a higher sense to the Blessed Virgin, for there is no other who contributed so much as she to the reconciliation between God and man. When by her consent she accepted the message of the angel at the Annunciation, she brought the Redeemer to mankind, which lay under the sentence of eternal condemnation. Of her was born the Savior; she is truly His Mother and therefore she is the mediatrix of the mediator, acceptable and pleasing to God.

These thoughts have been repeatedly expressed in the dogmatic constitutions of the Church during the last few centuries. They teach that Mary cooperated in the work of the redemption according to the divine decree and point out that she conceived the Son of God not merely that He might become man, but also that He might be the Savior of the human race. Upon her consent, freely given, to serve as God's handmaid in the miracle of the Incarnation and, as we shall see, by her union in suffering to accomplish the redemption, Mary's eminent position in God's kingdom rests secure.

The visit to Elizabeth

In those days Mary arose and went with haste into the hill country, to a city of Judah, and she entered the house of Zechariah and greeted Elizabeth. And when Elizabeth heard the greeting of Mary, the babe leaped in her womb; and Elizabeth was filled with the Holy Spirit and she exclaimed with a loud cry, "Blessed are you among women, and blessed is the fruit of your womb" (Lk 1:39-42).

Soon after the Annunciation by the angel, Mary went to the southern hill country to visit her cousin Elizabeth. The deciding motive for this visit was the angel's announcement: "This is the sixth month with her who was called barren." The sixth month was the time when pregnancy became publicly known and when it could be spoken of without embarrassment. Had the angel not indicated the time, Mary would very likely not have gone at once, for she might thus have made the visit before the expected birth of John was being spoken of. She did not, of course, know that the birth of John had been foretold to Zechariah in the Temple and that John was to be the precursor of the Redeemer. She learns this in the house of Elizabeth.

Mary did not make the journey alone. If the time was shortly before Passover, she probably joined a group of pilgrims going to Jerusalem. At all periods of the year, however, perhaps every week, people went up to Jerusalem for religious purposes or on business. Traveling companions had to be chosen cautiously. The following advice of a later day, in spite of its obvious exaggeration, no doubt illustrates this necessity. "If a good man is making a journey and you intend to go by the same road, begin your journey three days earlier in order to travel in his company; for the guardian angels accompany him according to the saying: 'He will command his angels that they should guard thee in all thy ways.' If a wicked man is going by the road which you intend to take, begin your journey three days later in order to avoid his company."

It is unlikely that Joseph accompanied Mary. However, if he did go with her, we must suppose that he left her before she came to Elizabeth's house. It is possible that Joseph came with her to Jerusalem and that she continued her journey from there alone.

We should note that St. Luke says Mary went "with haste" into the hill country to Elizabeth. The words are used in the same sense by St. Mark when he tells how Salome returned to Herod "with haste" to ask for the head of St. John the Baptist. The expression denotes some urgency to impart information. Since the Gospels are sparing in the use of words expressing strong emotion, we should give them their full meaning whenever they occur.

What were the motives impelling Mary to go "with haste"? The joy that filled her heart arose from the fact that the Messiah was already on earth, not from the fact that she was His Mother. But she could not impart these good tidings without revealing that she had become His Mother. Who besides Elizabeth was better prepared to receive her confidences? Elizabeth was a woman who had been in some way drawn into the mystery of the redemption. The angel had announced: "And behold your kins-woman Elizabeth in her old age has also conceived a son; and this is the sixth month with her who was called barren. For with God nothing will be impossible." From the angel's express words, it was clear that this was a miraculous conception; it was also in some way related to the coming of the Redeemer, because the angel had joined its announcement immediately by the word "also" to the announcement of the miraculous incarnation of the Messiah.

With these considerations in mind, Mary left Nazareth. On the journey, which lasted four or five days, her mind dwelt on the mystery that abode within her. During these days the senti-ments of the *Magnificat* were awakened in her soul, for she went with joyous exultation, such as we find expressed in the *Magnificat*.

As she approached Elizabeth's house, she abandoned any in-tention she may have had to tell the things that had happened to her; it would have been contrary to the feelings of a retiring woman of the East. Elizabeth should be let speak first; God's gracious gift to her was already apparent. Mary entered the house and respectfully greeted her cousin Elizabeth, the priest's wife; she bowed before her, embraced her, and spoke the customary greeting: "The Lord be with you."

During this greeting the miraculous thing happened; the Messiah revealed His presence. The angel had announced to Zechariah that Elizabeth's son would be filled with the Holy Ghost even from his mother's womb. Elizabeth did not know how or when this would be accomplished. But now, as Mary stood before her, the child leaped in her womb, and she saw in spirit how all these things were related to one another: Mary was the Mother of the Redeemer, and John was to be His precursor; and now, at Mary's approach, her child was sanctified in her womb.

Elizabeth exclaimed: "Blessed are you among women, and blessed is the fruit of your womb. And why is this granted me, that the mother of my Lord should come to me? For behold, when the voice of your greeting came to my ears, the babe in my womb leaped for joy. And blessed is she who believed that there would be a fulfillment of what was spoken to her from the Lord."

This address is indeed most surprising. Custom gave to Elizabeth, because of her advanced years, a right to be greeted respectfully by her young cousin, and we may be sure that Mary did not fail in this mark of respect. But then Elizabeth solemnly declared that Mary was elevated far above her, speaking to her as a subject might address her queen: "And why is this granted me, that the mother of my Lord should come to me?" And she congratulated Mary because of her faith: "And blessed is she who believed."

The Lord Himself had relieved Mary of the burden of making known His presence in the world; and now she broke forth in a hymn of praise, giving full expression to all the feelings that had been rising in her soul since the time of the Annunciation.

The Magnificat

And Mary said,
"My soul magnifies the Lord,
And my spirit rejoices in God my Savior,
for he has regarded the low estate of his handmaiden.
For behold, henceforth all generations will call me blessed;
for he who is mighty has done great things for me,
and holy is his name.

And his mercy is on those who fear him
from generation to generations.
He has showed strength with his arm,
he has scattered the proud in the imagination of their
    hearts,
he has put down the mighty from their thrones,
and exalted those of low degree;
he has filled the hungry with good things;
and the rich he has sent empty away.
He has helped his servant Israel,
in remembrance of his mercy,
as he spoke to our fathers,
to Abraham and to his posterity for ever" (Lk 1: 46–55).

The *Magnificat* is Mary's hymn of praise offered to God for His wonderful works. It breaks forth from her lips like a suddenly released flood when Elizabeth says to her: "Blessed is she who believed that there would be a fulfillment of what was spoken to her from the Lord." This jubilant song pouring out from her heart was more than a variation on the theme of her spiritual experiences. From the *Magnificat*'s theme, which we may paraphrase thus: "God has exalted me because I was humbled," we may infer that Mary had experienced humiliations that are in contrast with the exaltation expressed in the words: "Behold, henceforth all generations will call me blessed." What these humiliations were we do not know, but tribulation and spiritual suffering may have come to her, arising from the circumstances of her life: her saintly living among unsympathetic relatives within the narrow confines of an Eastern village, her tender years and retiring disposition, about which we can only surmise. It seems certain that an estrangement had arisen between Mary and her relatives, which will show itself later. Now Mary rejoiced because God accepted her, the one who had been despised, and exalted her.

Mary sings of God's wonderful works. His grace is not limited to those to whom the world has given great power; the riches of grace may be showered upon souls to whom the wealth of the world has been denied, and all the wealth of the great ones cannot purchase even one of God's graces. The miracle of grace may appear in a man whom the world would judge to be entirely unfit and unworthy. Now the harsh domination of the world has been shattered.

The man who depends upon his own resources strives to

convince himself and others that nature and grace are one and the same, that a man's position in this world is an indication of his position in the realm of grace, or that grace may be supplanted by nature, if not for everyone, at least for gifted and cultured people. All this leads finally to the belief that those men who have combined in themselves great power, wealth, and unusual gifts are instruments indispensable for the operation of God's grace. Against this belief in man and this trust in human power Mary joyfully contrasts her faith in God and in His might.

To enumerate the passages of Holy Scripture that resemble the verses of the *Magnificat* will give us some insight into the formation of the thoughts of that beautiful canticle. Passages similar to the first verse ("My soul magnifies the Lord, and my spirit rejoices in God my Savior") are found in the Psalms (69: 30; 34: 3); in the prophecy of Habakkuk (3: 18); and especially in Psalm 95, which was composed by Mary's royal ancestor David. Its first verse is as follows: "O come, let us sing to the Lord; let us make a joyful noise to the rock of our salvation!"

"For he has regarded the low estate of his handmaiden." Similar expressions are found in other Scripture passages (1 Sam 1: 11; Ps 31: 7; Prov 11: 2). "For he who is mighty has done great things for me" (Ps 71: 19); "and holy is his name" (Ps 111: 9). "His mercy is on those who fear him from generation to generation" (Ps 103: 17); "he has showed strength with his arm, he has scattered the proud in the imagination of their hearts" (Ps 89: 10). "He has put down the mighty from their thrones, and exalted those of low degree" is similar to Sirach 10: 14 and Psalm 147: 6. Evidently, most of the expressions of the *Magnificat* come from the Psalms.

We must likewise note the expressions that are not foreshadowed in the Old Testament. Such are the words: "For behold, henceforth all generations will call me blessed"; and the conclusion: "He has helped his servant Israel, in remembrance of his mercy, as he spoke to our fathers, to Abraham and to his posterity for ever."

In the first of these sentences, Mary announces that the Mother of the Redeemer will be called blessed by generations and that the chant of praise begun by Elizabeth, "Blessed is she who believed," will never be silenced on earth. The other sentence ("He has helped his servant Israel . . .") is in a sense the conclusion of the Old Testament. The great promise given to Abraham and his posterity that all peoples should be blessed in him was fulfilled by the coming of the Redeemer. Both these sentences may be expressed in the words: "The Redeemer is here."

This dividing of the *Magnificat* into parts and attributing them to other persons may seem irreverent to some people, who may ask: "What part remains that may be attributed to Mary?" We should remember that the idea of literary ownership as we understand it today was not yet developed in the East; everyone adopted from others whatever pleased him. It is more important, however, to remember that in this canticle Mary was praying and offering her praise to God; she did not intend to compose a literary piece, and therefore she made use of such terms and expressions as she had learned from the Scriptures.

We must not suppose that Mary was like those Scripture scholars who, whenever they use the language of Holy Writ, cannot rest until they quote chapter and verse. Mary immersed her soul in the spirit of the Scriptures; she absorbed their meaning; she did not master their words in order to use them as material for her own compositions; rather, she was formed and influenced by their language. Her holy soul was endowed with a special faculty that enabled her to comprehend the true meaning of the inspired words, for that same Holy Spirit who had given His special assistance to the authors of the Bible was present in her soul from the first moment of her being and was ever engaged in educating her to be the Mother of the Redeemer.

Some sixty years elapsed between the time Mary pronounced her canticle of praise in the hill country and the time St. Luke recorded the *Magnificat*. With great probability, almost certainty, we can say that St. Luke depended, not merely on oral tradition, but also on some written record. Internal evidence of this chapter dealing with our Lord's youth reveals to the scholar that the record used by St. Luke was written, not in Greek, but in Hebrew; and that in this record the events were written down according to a plan—the announcement of the birth of St. John and of Jesus—and the birth of St. John and of Jesus are narrated as related and corresponding events.

St. Luke in his Gospel expressly states that he sought out those who had witnessed the events in our Lord's life; he also remarks that the happenings at the birth of Jesus attracted wide interest among the people of the hill country. In these circumstances it devolved upon the men among the relatives of Zechariah and

Elizabeth to make a record of these unusual occurrences. The things that had come to Zechariah's knowledge and that he had experienced were far more important than a great many matters contained in the Scriptures, and the angel Gabriel had told him in the Temple that this boy John, the precursor of the Messiah, would bring great joy not only to his father but to many people. It was quite natural and proper for Zechariah to make a written record of these wonderful events that were happening to his house and in his relationship for the benefit of those many people of the future for whom, according to the angel's words, these events would have the greatest significance. Indeed, as a priest of the Old Testament who habitually read the Scriptures, Zechariah might very well have considered it his duty to record these sacred happenings.

The way the *Magnificat* may have been composed is illustrated by an event in the life of a certain Miriam of Abellin, a village in the neighborhood of Nazareth. This young woman, who died in the odor of sanctity as a lay sister in the Carmelite convent in Bethlehem, composed religious chants while she was in her ecstasies. She could neither read nor write and had scant knowledge of any foreign language. Thus she remained very much a child of her own people. But when she began these spoken canticles in her ecstasies, sentences followed each other so quickly as to make it difficult to write them down. These recorded effusions of her heart show that even now pious women from the ranks of the common people are able to compose psalms and canticles. The following is a canticle describing the refreshment of the soul after receiving Holy Communion:

> The Lord hath visited His land,
> Which before was arid and unfruitful,
> But in His presence it became fruitful.
> The dew of the Lord hath descended;
> Flowers and herbs budded forth;
> The tree against which I leaned
> Became sweet as a palm.
> My strength returned to me,
> My hands and feet were again able to carry me.
> My flesh became as that of a child,
> My nerves became soft and pliable again,
> My limbs were strengthened,

The marrow of my bones became soft as dough.
My hair became soft
And lay gently upon my head,
My ears were opened
To hear the sweet words of the Lord.
My tongue was loosed to sing His praises.

This canticle seems to be derived from the Psalms of the Bible in the same manner as Mary's *Magnificat*, and, although it contains unmistakable traces of the style and imagery of the Psalms, it is a new and original composition.

As Miriam's exultant soul expressed itself in these inspired verses, so, too, Mary of Nazareth sang her canticle of praise in Elizabeth's house. And as someone wrote down the verses of Miriam of Abellin, so someone in Zechariah's family recorded the words of the Mother of our Lord.

Mary's humility

"Henceforth all generations will call me blessed" (Lk 1: 48).

After Elizabeth's greeting, Mary poured out the jubilation of her soul and said: "For behold, henceforth all generations will call me blessed." In these words she showed how deeply conscious she was of her incomparable dignity as the Mother of God. Some persons, when they hear this song of jubilation from Mary's lips, may ask whether in this hour Mary remained faithful to that perfect humility which is one of her greatest glories.

Much has been said and written about Mary's humility, but we do not always see clearly in what this humility really consisted. Perhaps the source of the confusion lies in this, that we do not understand the true nature of humility.

Some believe that humility consists in a kind of modesty that, in the presence of other people, becomes a sort of self-abasement. Such a feeling may indicate a fine trait of character, but it is far from Christian humility because it does not enter into man's relationship with God. Others think that humility is abasement before God, such as we find in the lives of some of the saints who, after a more or less worldly life, strive with the help of God's grace to regain the spirituality they have lost. Doubtless such men possess humility in the true Christian sense; but here too, the essence of humility is obscured by unessentials. The essence of humility consists not in abasement before God but, rather, in a disposition to conform to what we recognize to be the will of God, our Creator and our Father. The eyes of the humble man, therefore, are first of all turned toward God; the more saintly he is, the more he is cleansed from sin, the more will other beings be excluded from his view of God his Creator, upon whom he realizes that he is entirely dependent.

A saint may be altogether oblivious of the difference between his life and the lives of other men. This knowledge might endanger perfect humility, and God often protects those whom He has called to perfection by allowing them to remain unaware of how much more perfect they are than others and of how closely they approach to Him.

But Mary was not left in ignorance as to her condition, and her humility was as unique as her dignity of divine Motherhood. God had called her to be His Mother. But before her consent to accept this dignity, God made known to her the unusual character of her relationship to Him and the reasons why He raised her to such an eminence. She was "full of grace"; she had become the Mother of the Son of God. In this exalted position, her humility was accompanied by the highest regard for that position which she held among all other women. Without this knowledge she could not have entered upon her sublime office with fitting reverence and esteem.

The expectation of Mary and Elizabeth

Mary remained with her about three months (Lk 1:56).

The events of the next three months, while Mary lived with her cousin Elizabeth, were such as will never occur again. Both had entered upon motherhood in an unusual manner, each understood the vocation to which God had called her son, and each knew that from the beginning her child would not belong to her but to the office for which God had predestined him. John's vocation was closely bound up with the office of the Savior; one of these children was the precursor of the Redeemer, and the other was the Redeemer Himself. Even as these children had been called before they had seen the light of day, so too God had made known their names beforehand: "You shall call his name John"; "You shall call his name Jesus."

As in the case of other mothers, the thoughts of Mary and

Elizabeth in these days dwelt on their sons' future. In other mothers, love is narrowed by their interest in their offspring, but Mary and Elizabeth became mothers whose loving hearts were concerned with the future of the whole human race. Elizabeth, by long years of childlessness, and Mary, by her resolve to conse-crate herself to God, had been schooled to accept all mankind into their hearts.

The days before John's birth were spent in prayer and medita-tion, from which everyone was excluded. The only man who had been initiated into these mysteries was Zechariah, and he was mute, unable to converse with the two women. During these days, Mary found poise and meditated upon the profound myster-ies into which, as a virgin and a spouse, she had been drawn by God's will. From the Gospels it appears that Mary had told Joseph nothing of the mysterious conception that had taken place within her; perhaps it was here, in the retirement of Zecha-riah's home, that she decided to remain silent about it. Undoubt-edly, she had told him how long she intended to remain with her cousin Elizabeth; now she saw the time near at hand when she must return to Nazareth. How often during these days did Mary and Elizabeth pray to God that He might enlighten them both and show Mary the way in which He wished her to walk! They knew well the Eastern world in which they lived, and they were apprehensive of the harrowing possibilities awaiting Mary when she returned to Galilee.

Mary's marriage to Joseph

Now the birth of Jesus Christ took place in this way. When his mother Mary had been betrothed to Joseph, before they came together she was found to be with child of the Holy Spirit; and her husband Joseph, being a just man and unwilling to put her to shame, resolved to send her away quietly. But as he considered this, behold, an angel of the Lord appeared to him in a dream, saying: "Joseph, son of David, do not fear to take Mary your wife, for that which is conceived in her is of the Holy Spirit" (Mt 1: 18–20).

After about three months, Mary returned to Nazareth. She knew that before long Joseph would be aware of her condition of pregnancy. Of these days, which would be so trying for Mary and Joseph, the Evangelist speaks briefly and with reserve. The diffi-cult situation that had arisen and caused Mary and Joseph so much anguish was one affecting them alone. In those days betrothal was almost equivalent to marriage; if now Mary was expecting a child, no one would think anything amiss, because of Mary's blameless reputation, unless Joseph himself were to accuse her. We can go no further than the simple narrative of the Evangelist: Mary remained silent about the miraculous conception, and Joseph considered dismissing her privately.

During these anxious days, Mary remained silent. During her months with Elizabeth, she had come to understand how God Himself makes known His mysteries. She remained silent, too, because the angel had not directed her to make known to Joseph what had taken place. Yet she felt herself bound to Joseph by the betrothal. The motives that finally prompted her to be silent remain hidden from us, for she found herself in circumstances in which no other human being had ever been before. We know only the simple fact: Mary maintained an unbroken silence about her miraculous motherhood.

The unusual thing that had happened to Mary remained hidden from the eyes of others. For Joseph, her spouse, Mary's silence had a special significance. All thought that she had been the victim of some outrage was excluded from his mind; his bride would have told him of it immediately. Her attitude of silence left him completely without an explanation, although he felt that she was guarding a sacred secret that placed her in this difficult and unexplained situation. Before the angel came to enlighten him, he considered how he might dismiss her privately, because, as the Evangelist says, he was a just man.

The language of the Gospel implies that Joseph had intended to let the matter pass unnoticed; but it could not be disposed of so simply. By the espousal the marriage had already been legally concluded, and if Joseph wished to give Mary her freedom, for such would have been the purpose of a private dismissal, he would have to give her a bill of divorce. In the Gospels a "dismissal" always means a separation accompanied by a legal bill of divorce.

In cases of dismissal, the procedure was precisely determined by the law and was intended to prevent hasty dismissals. To make a divorce legal, a document had to be drawn up by the husband or by someone whom he appointed to act in his stead. The law required that the document set forth the names of the man and woman, the date and place of the action, the declaration of the divorce, and the signatures of two witnesses. The declaration of the divorce was generally expressed in these words: "Behold, any man is now free to marry you." She was now free, therefore, to remarry if she so desired. A bill of divorce, once it was given to the woman, could not be revoked.

The Gospel records that, since Joseph was a just and conscientious man, he was "unwilling to put her to shame" and thought of dismissing her privately. What is meant by "unwilling to put her to shame" and by a private dismissal? Apparently the two things are mutually exclusive, for the public exposure was to be prevented by a private dismissal. The public exposure may be supposed to mean an accusation of infidelity made before the court; Joseph was unwilling to make such an accusation in court and wished to dismiss Mary without formal complaint. According to the provisions of the law of the time, Joseph would not have had sufficient grounds to begin an action for divorce because of adultery, for which the death penalty still remained in force, because the courts required as evidence the testimony of two witnesses to the adultery. This legal practice is reflected in the scene narrated in St. John's Gospel about the woman taken in adultery. The Pharisees stated the case clearly: "This woman has been caught in the act of adultery." There were, therefore, witnesses to the crime.

If Joseph had intended to accuse Mary before the court, he would have been obliged to bring witnesses. But, since no witnesses were available, the public exposure spoken of in the Gospel cannot mean such formal accusation in court. The public dismissal, which Joseph wished to avoid for Mary's sake, may have been a dismissal by a bill of divorce in which the reasons for the divorce were mentioned, and, accordingly, the private dismissal would have been a divorce without mention of the reasons for the action. We may even go a step farther and describe the private dismissal as the procedure in which the bill of divorce made no mention of any definite date and was not signed by witnesses: a document, therefore, of a purely private nature. In all these considerations, we must remember that Joseph had not yet decided what course to follow; he was simply considering what plan would be wiser. His principal concern was to keep from others, including Mary's relatives, the reasons for which he was dismissing Mary, his spouse.

An instance of a private dismissal, in case of the dissolution of a betrothal, is found in a non-biblical writing. A certain description of the Last Judgment says that God will not make the sins of the wicked publicly known, but that He will remain silent about them in the presence of the just; only when the just have ascended to heaven, will He accuse the wicked and pronounce sentence upon them, thus, in a sense, dismissing them "privately."

What were Joseph's thoughts and feelings as he pondered these things? Did he believe that here was an instance of divine intervention or, at least, the possibility of a miracle? These questions we are unable to answer. We are not certain that Joseph excluded the possibility of a miracle; as he beheld Mary, unperturbed in mysterious calm, he could not think evil of her. Her unbroken silence and her mysterious serenity may have caused him to surmise that something miraculous had occurred to her; once the possibility of the miraculous had entered his mind, the private dismissal would have been a logical step.

Apart from this question of Joseph's belief in a divine intervention, did he think that Mary was guilty or innocent? Apparently he was unable to believe her guilty because of her imperturbable calm; yet, because of her condition, how could he believe her guiltless? In these circumstances, Joseph wished to follow that plan which would not compel him to make a decision: he would dismiss her privately.

It was important that Joseph act quickly; delay would simply make the situation more difficult for both of them. But, as often as he decided upon a plan, he felt unable to carry it out. Amid these doubts and uncertainties, an angel appeared to him in his sleep and said to him: "Joseph, son of David, do not fear to take Mary your wife, for that which is conceived in her is of the Holy Spirit; she will bear a son, and you shall call his name Jesus, for he will save his people from their sins."

The angel acknowledged Mary's marriage; he acknowledged Mary as Joseph's spouse, and he enjoined Joseph as the husband to call the child Jesus. The angel's words were of great importance for Joseph, not only at this moment, but also for the rest of his life. God Himself had now confirmed him in his position as Mary's spouse and had recognized him as the legal father of the family into which the Christ Child was to be born. Later, when Joseph submitted the Child to the Law, when he brought Jesus to be circumcised, when he accompanied Mary to the Temple for the ceremony of purification, in short, whenever he appeared as the father of Jesus, he acted on the authority of these words of the angel.

The angel said to him: "Do not fear to take Mary your wife." These words seem to support the opinion that Joseph believed a miracle had been worked in Mary, and therefore he "feared" to bring her to his house. Joseph's fear can best be explained by his belief that the miraculous had occurred to Mary. Now, since God had commanded him by the angel, Joseph ventured to go to Mary's house and bring her to his home. All his anguish and anxiety were gone, and his soul was filled with reverence and awe and love for Mary's secret.

When Mary saw him, she knew that God had revealed her secret to him, as He had also made it known to her cousin Elizabeth; and the anguish of those days was lifted from their hearts. Now Mary was able to tell Joseph of the wonderful things that had taken place in her home at Nazareth, how the angel had announced to her that she was to be the Mother of the Son of God, and how he had commanded her to name Him Jesus. And Joseph related how the angel had instructed him to take unto himself Mary his spouse, and had commanded him likewise to give the name Jesus to the Child she had conceived by the power of the Holy Spirit. Knowing now that God had commanded them both to name the child Jesus, they realized that God had brought them together and had selected them as the guardians of the holy Child. The name Jesus became the seal of their union and a sign that God had chosen them to serve in the accomplishment of His plan.

Now Mary could tell Joseph about what had occurred as she entered the house of Zechariah and about Elizabeth greeting her as the Mother of the Lord. Joseph learned too that John, the son of the aged Zechariah, had been appointed the precursor of the Messiah and, like Jesus, had received his name from God Himself. The depressing clouds of uncertainty had vanished, and Mary and Joseph became conscious of that divine world into which their lives had been drawn. Seeing clearly now that God had chosen them as the depositaries of a great mystery, their hearts full of a pure and holy love such as the world had never known, Mary and Joseph began the immediate preparations for their marriage.

Tradition, relying on dubious legends, has pictured Joseph as an old man. The husband, it is true, was generally somewhat older than his wife, and possibly Joseph was considerably older than Mary, but in order to be Mary's support and the provider for the Holy Family, he should have been in his best working years. It would indeed be quite false to represent Joseph as a very aged man, merely to provide a better explanation of his vow of virginity. Christian art has contributed its share in popularizing the notion of Joseph as an old man.

III.

The Nativity and the Flight into Egypt

The journey to Bethlehem

In those days a decree went out from Caesar Augustus that all the world should be enrolled. This was the first enrollment, when Quirinius was governor of Syria. And all went to be enrolled, each to his own city. And Joseph also went up from Galilee, from the city of Nazareth, to Judea, to the city of David, which is called Bethlehem, because he was of the house and lineage of David, to be enrolled with Mary his betrothed, who was with child (Lk 2: 1-5).

At this time, when Mary and Joseph were married, notices were posted in the villages and towns of Palestine that Emperor Augustus had ordered a census to be taken up in the land. The wording of the decree probably resembled that of a decree recently unearthed in Egypt: "Gaius Vibius Maximus, Governor of Egypt, issues the following edict: Since the appraisal of household property is about to be made, all who, for any reason whatsoever, are living outside their own districts are hereby commanded to return to their homes in order that the usual appraisal of household property may take place."

To outward appearances, Israel was an independent kingdom enjoying the favor and friendship of Rome. In fact, however, Herod was obliged to carry out the wishes of Rome at every turn; to do otherwise would have invited his own dethronement. He was not even free to make his last will and testament without first ascertaining what dispositions would be acceptable at Rome. Rome reserved to itself the right to deal with the land as it saw fit after Herod's death.

One day the imperial edict was promulgated also in Nazareth. All the inhabitants gathered about; those who were unable to read stared at the lettering; some could decipher the more familiar words, but others were able to read out the sentences that fell like blows on their national spirit.

The most bitter, angry feelings were aroused by the decree.

Racial revolt and religious rebellion were stirred up: this idolatrous emperor wished to count the children of Israel, the sons of the chosen race, like sheep. But the Romans had already experienced difficulties with the Jews, and doubtless they made sufficient military preparations to put down any uprising that might develop.

Mary and Joseph also heard the news. Joseph may have heard it while he was away from home working at his trade, or perhaps some indignant neighbor had rushed in from the street to tell them. They understood what the decree meant for them. They came from the house and family of David; their genealogy pointed to Bethlehem, where Joseph must go in obedience to the imperial order.

In this decree of Emperor Augustus we can now clearly see an act of Providence; by it Mary and Joseph were brought to Bethlehem, and there Jesus was born. Augustus, desiring to measure the extent of his imperial power and to number the subjects in his empire, became an instrument in the service of Almighty God.

Whether or not Mary and Joseph looked upon the imperial edict in this light depends on whether the people expected the Redeemer to appear on earth in Bethlehem. Later on, certain persons, hearing our Lord preach, declared: "Is the Christ to come from Galilee? Has not the scripture said that the Christ descended from David, and comes from Bethlehem, the village where David was?" (Jn 7:41–42). They believed that Jesus was born in Nazareth, and their objection indicates that at least some among the people believed that the Messiah would be born in Bethlehem. If such traditions existed among the people, they would have been preserved especially by the descendants of David, and thus Mary and Joseph would have known them. Perhaps it was because of this tradition that Mary accompanied Joseph to Bethlehem where, as we shall see later, they intended to remain after the birth of the Child.

The journey to Bethlehem took them to Jerusalem. No Jew from Galilee came to the Holy City without going up to the Temple and there worshipping the Lord. Mary and Joseph also went up to the Temple; afterward they left the city and continued south on their journey. At a sharp turn of the road, Bethlehem with its scattered houses came into view. There in Bethlehem, in the city of David, the Redeemer, the Son of David, was to be born. Mary recalled the solemn words of the angel: "The Lord God will give to him the throne of his father David; and he will reign over the house of Jacob for ever; and of his kingdom there will be no end." The Mother of the Messiah, her humble spouse by her side, was about to enter the ancestral city of her royal ancestor David. How greatly things must change before the angel's prophecy would be fulfilled, and the eternal kingdom of the Messiah could be established!

The birth of Jesus

And while they were there, the time came for her to be delivered. And she gave birth to her first-born son and wrapped him in swaddling cloths, and laid him in a manger, because there was no place for them in the inn (Lk 2:6-7).

In Bethlehem, Joseph intended to lodge at a *khan*, a public inn, as he had done on the preceding nights of the journey. A *khan* consisted of a courtyard surrounded by a high wall; in the center of the courtyard there was generally a cistern, around which the camels and donkeys were tethered. Along the wall were erected shelters, beneath which the travelers lodged for the night. Frequently, spaces were walled off to make what might be called private compartments between the posts supporting the shelter; these were rented to guests. Such an inn is referred to in the words: "And while they were there, the time came for her to be delivered. And she gave birth to her first-born son and wrapped him up in swaddling cloths, and laid him in a manger, because there was no place for them in the inn."

In all probability, Mary and Joseph could have found a place in the inn; we can hardly suppose the host of such a caravansary would declare that his inn was filled with guests. Even if the *khan* were filled to excess, the innkeeper would assure late arrivals that he could take care of them comfortably for the night. While on the journey, Mary and Joseph had lodged in these *khans* among strangers. But now, when Mary's time was approaching, Joseph sought a place for themselves, a place apart, for Mary, who was expecting the birth of the Child. The only suitable place in the public inn would have been one of the private compartments, and in Bethlehem such rooms were not to be had, or they were already occupied, or perhaps Mary and Joseph were refused because they were poor people.

71

The expression "a place for" is often used in the Bible to mean "a proper place." Our Lord said to Peter: "Put your sword back into its place," that is, into the scabbard, the proper place for it. In Revelation it is said of the wicked angels that "there was no longer any place for them" in heaven, that is, they had lost the places that formerly belonged to them. The construction is similar in the expression: "there was no place for them in the inn." In this instance "place for them" was such a place as Joseph sought for Mary, who was expecting the birth of the Savior.

Here popular legend has inserted the touching scenes of Mary and Joseph seeking shelter in an inn. Mary and Joseph are pictured as going from door to door, asking for shelter, and being everywhere refused, until at last they were compelled to seek shelter in a stable outside the city. Although the Gospels say nothing of such a search, something similar to this must have taken place between the time of their arrival in Bethlehem and their inquiry at the inn. Mary and Joseph were both descendants of the family of David; therefore the members of the race of David residing in Bethlehem would naturally be expected to receive these kinsfolk from distant Galilee. Moreover, the Israelites, like all Easterners, were conscious of the obligations of hospitality. But this natural and ordinary courtesy was, according to St. Luke, what their relatives in Bethlehem neglected. There is question whether the relations between Mary and Joseph and their kinsfolk in Bethlehem were already strained or whether the estrangement was only now developing. Perhaps it had already arisen in Nazareth. The Gospel narrative seems to imply that Mary and Joseph made the journey to Bethlehem alone. Certainly there were relatives in Nazareth who were also obliged to go to Bethlehem, and in normal circumstances all the relatives would have gone together to Bethlehem for the census. But, according to the Gospels, we must infer that the others from Nazareth went separately; and perhaps these relatives were to blame that Mary and Joseph were not well received and were compelled to seek a place in the public inn.

In ancient times—for example, in the time of Jeremiah—the *khan* or inn at Bethlehem was situated outside the city. The district now occupied by the Church of the Nativity was also, at the time of our Lord's birth, outside the city. Probably the inn spoken of by Jeremiah (Jer 41: 17) and the inn at which Joseph inquired are the same. It is a well-known fact that these inns in the East existed on the same sites for thousands of years.

In the neighborhood of this *khan* are found many natural caves, and it was quite in keeping with the customs of the East for the innkeeper to make use of such caves for his own purposes. Sometimes he sheltered his animals in them or stored wares and fuel there; sometimes he even rented them as lodgings to certain of his guests. It was, therefore, not out of the ordinary if the owner of the caravansary directed Mary and Joseph to spend the night in such a cave; in fact, he might have congratulated himself on his shrewdness in thus finding a way out of a difficult situation.

But for Mary and Joseph this "happy" solution of the difficulty was a heartrending blow; step by step they had been driven into desolation and loneliness. First they had been driven from their home in Nazareth by the edict of Emperor Augustus; then the ill will of their kinsfolk had closed the doors of Bethlehem against them; and then they had been turned away from the public inn, either because of lack of room or because of their poverty. Finally, they had taken refuge in a stable. Such was often the lot of the poor, and such "stable-dwellers" were thought to be no better than rabble by those who lived in houses. Perhaps Mary and Joseph had presentiments that all these happenings were symbolically significant and that all this desolation was a proper beginning of the life of Jesus the Savior.

On one of the following nights the Savior came into the world. The Gospels say expressly that the birth did not take place immediately after their arrival in Bethlehem. Mary herself was obliged to do the services generally rendered by the kind and loving hands of helping friends. She wrapped the Child in swaddling clothes and laid him in a manger, a trough formed of clay and stones and resting on the ground. And she knelt before it.

Mary's faith was more perfect than that given to any other human being. Every movement of her body, every gesture of her hands, was an expression of her faith and of her love. Her faith inflamed her love, and her love, in turn, increased her faith. She beheld the Child wrapped in His swaddling clothes, His arms bound to His sides, and as she looked on Him there arose within her soul not only the feelings of motherhood—"You are mine"—but also a stronger realization—"I belong to You."

She laid the Child in Joseph's arms, not as a gift that belonged to her, but as the Supreme Good before which they both sank away into nothingness.

She laid the Child before her in the crib; the ends of hay and straw pointed from beneath the swaddling clothes. In these caves, frequently uninhabited, swarms of vermin awaited those who entered; and in the winter they were quickly attracted by anything that radiated warmth. It was no different on that night. The vermin were the first to greet the Savior in the crib.

While Mary's hands were busy in the service of the Child, she was thinking of the future lot of the Redeemer. What would be the end of a redemption of mankind that had such a beginning? Yet, in spite of all these things, Mary was happy in that hour, overjoyed because the time of grace, the "days of the Messiah," had come.

The visit of the shepherds

And in that region there were shepherds out in the field, keeping watch over their flock by night. And an angel of the Lord appeared to them, and the glory of the Lord shone around them, and they were filled with fear. And the angel said to them: "Be not afraid; for behold, I bring you good tidings of a great joy which will come to all the people; for to you is born this day in the city of David a Savior, who is Christ the Lord" (Lk 2: 8–11).

Together with Joseph and the Child, Mary entered into a heavenly mystery, which effectually isolated them from the rest of the world; and they were unwilling, under any circumstances, to divulge to others what God had revealed to them. But God Himself was leading men to their threshold, simple men who would not take offense because the Redeemer had come into the world in a stable.

These shepherds, homeless men, approached the cave and asked for permission to enter. They said that they had come at this hour because an angel had announced to them that the Messiah had come into the world on this night; the angel had said: "Be not afraid; for behold, I bring you good tidings of a great joy which will come to all the people; for to you is born this day in the city of David a Savior, who is Christ the Lord. And this will be a sign for you: you will find a babe wrapped in swaddling cloths and lying in a manger." They had started out immediately and sought the cave with the crib; and now they were here and asked to see the Child.

The Mother lifted the Child, who had been born that night, from the trough, and held Him that they might see Him and give

Him their greetings. They were simple people who, like children, wanted to touch the things they saw, and very likely they took the Child in their arms. They were used to carrying the little lambs of their flock, and now, in the silence of this night, they carried the Lamb of God in their arms.

The shepherds had not come without remembering to bring gifts for the newborn Savior; it would have been unthinkable in that world to come into the presence of the great ones without a gift. They had, of course, very little from which to choose; of the products of the cattle industry, such as cheese, butter, milk, and wool, they had only the bare necessities. Now, in the winter, they had lambs that were ready for slaughter. In the eyes of the Israelites, all lambs shared somehow in the symbolism of the paschal lamb, and it is likely that the shepherds offered one or more lambs to the newborn Savior, whom St. John the Baptist would later call the Lamb of God. Of this they knew nothing as yet, but the thought of the lamb of sacrifice may have come to their minds as they presented their little lambs as a token of their worship to the Redeemer. The popular representations of the shepherds kneeling before the crib with their offerings of lambs are, therefore, more faithful to the actual facts than many are inclined to believe.

The shepherds' adoration was, for Mary, another sign that God was watching over His Son, whom He seemed to have forsaken. As at Nazareth, so now again He sent an angel with glad tidings, and this common experience established a bond between Mary and these strange men. The song the angels had sung revealed to Mary how the redemption was to be accomplished: the grace of God, which had begun the redemption in the birth of Jesus, was to continue it in the souls of men. Now she saw more clearly than ever how great was God's love for simple and humble men who had no ambitions to be great in the eyes of the world. In her canticle of thanksgiving for the Incarnation she had rejoiced because:

> He has put down the mighty from their thrones,
> and exalted those of low degree;
> he has filled the hungry with good things;
> and the rich he has sent empty away.

To those humble ones whom God exalts, to those hungry ones whom God fills with good things, belonged these shepherds who were grouped around her to give their greetings to her Child. Her joy at their coming encouraged them to put aside their natural reserve, and so these poor men who counted for nothing in the world were the first to be chosen by God to know His great mystery. Their simple faith and trust and love united them to Mary as later countless simple souls were to be united to her and to Jesus the Savior. The cave became a sanctuary in which the first Christmas matins were celebrated.

The morning came and the shepherds, since they were close to the city, went with joyful hearts to recount to the Bethlehem-ites the wonderful happenings that had taken place. In a cave outside their city, the Redeemer had come into the world, the Redeemer for whose coming they all longed so much. The people of Bethlehem listened with astonishment; they looked at these men, whose clothing showed them to be poor nomad shepherds. And then their skepticism began to show its unlovely side. The Redeemer lying in a manger? It was incredible. And this tale about the appearance of angels was either imagined or invented. One could easily imagine such things, keeping solitary watch in the night. Moreover, these wandering shepherds were aliens, and nobody ought to give heed to what they said. Finally, here in the shadow of the palace of the cruel Herod, it was wise to hold one's tongue.

Mary treasured all the happenings of this night in her heart. All mothers retain, even in old age, a vivid memory of the circum-stances surrounding the birth of their children. Trivial occur-rences are taken to be signs of the future, but never before were the circumstances accompanying the birth of a child so signifi-cant as these in the night when Jesus the Son of God was born and was laid in a manger.

The circumcision

And at the end of eight days, when he was circumcised, he was called Jesus, the name given by the angel before he was conceived in the womb (Lk 2: 21).

Every boy of Jewish parents was looked upon as the recipient and the bearer of the promises God had made to Abraham. For him to participate in these promises, however, not only must he be the son of a Jewish father, he must also be incorporated into the religious society of his people by circumcision. Circumcision was also practiced by the Arabs and Egyptians; but only among the Israelites did it possess a definite religious significance. This rite was of such importance that it "suppressed the Sabbath" and could therefore be performed on that day of rest. For weak children it was not without its dangers, and it was not performed until the eighth day. For the same reason, it was generally performed by one who had experience in the matter. The name given the child at circumcision was chosen by the parents; and during the ceremony, the action was accompanied by a blessing pronounced by those present. In case of necessity, the father was permitted to circumcise the child. According to custom, the ceremony was concluded with a meal. During the first seven days after the child's birth, his mother, because of legal uncleanness, was prohibited from all social intercourse; after the circumcision she was again free to associate with others, being obliged, however, to remain at home until the fortieth day.

Because of motherly affection and the intimate union between mother and child, many a Christian mother has spiritual experiences she is unable to express in language. Such is that moment when the newly baptized child is brought back to her from the church, and she whispers for the first time the name that has been conferred on it. Until then the child was without a name, still remaining, as it were, a part of herself; but now he has become an independent being with a name of his own, and he has already entered into a covenant with God. Love and anxiety course alternately through the mother's heart; she tries to peer into the future. What kind of life stretches before this child? How will other men, his companions, judge him? Will they pronounce his name in love or hatred? How long will he bear this name, and who will be the last to speak it? Emotions similar to those experienced by Christian mothers on the occasion of the baptism of their child were also felt by mothers of the Old Testament when a boy was circumcised.

More than any other mother of Israel, more than any Christian mother, Mary's thoughts on that day of circumcision were of the life that lay before her Son. His name had been chosen by God beforehand. The angel had said: "You will conceive in your womb and bear a son, and you shall call his name Jesus," and he added the reason why the Child should be so named: "He will be great, and will be called the Son of the Most High; and the Lord God will give unto him the throne of his father David, and he will reign over the house of Jacob forever; and of his kingdom there will be no end." To Joseph also had been revealed why the Child should be called Jesus, that is, "God helps": "You shall call his name Jesus, for he will save his people from their sins."

The moment came when, after the circumcision, Mary for the first time called His name Jesus and in doing so she expressed her faith and her surrender to God's will, her joy and her sorrow. All her joy and sorrow, this lodging in strange places, this poverty and loneliness, the message of the angels to the shepherds, the simple greetings of the shepherds themselves, all this was now associated and bound up with the name Jesus, which until then she had borne in her heart. What would become of this Child, whose life as the Redeemer had begun under these circumstances? Who would they be who would later speak His name? With what emotions and passions would His name be uttered? And what would be the consequences for the Child Himself, whose name, "God helps," designated Him as the divinely appointed Redeemer?

When she spoke His name, Mary expressed in it the complete surrender of her own will and declared her readiness to accept whatever God had ordained for her as Jesus' Mother. Outwardly, the circumcision was a sad and pitiful affair. The neighbors and kinsfolk who usually came for such an event to offer their good wishes were absent: the neighbors were in distant Nazareth, the kinsfolk—many of them probably at that time in Bethlehem—for some reason unknown to us held themselves aloof from Mary and Joseph. The others in Bethlehem who may have heard of the circumcision probably thought that this young couple were most unfortunate because the Child was born on a journey, and a proper observance of the circumcision celebration was impossible. The name these poor people had given their Child, "God helps," must have sounded strange. There was indeed very little of God's helping to be seen here.

A long time would pass before that day when the name "Jesus" would be inscribed on the Cross, but there were already veiled indications of that climax of the Redemption. Jesus, who would some day be put to death outside Jerusalem, the chief city of His people, had been born outside Bethlehem, His family's ancestral city. These indications became somewhat more distinct when the Child was presented in the Temple and the veil was withdrawn from that tragic future awaiting Him.

The law of presentation and purification
The Law had further claims on Mary's Son, because every first-born boy belonged in a special way to the Lord and must be bought back. In the Book of Exodus (13:12ff.) it is written: "Consecrate to me all the first-born; whatever is the first to open the womb among the people of Israel, both of man and of beast, is mine." Accordingly, Moses had commanded the children of Israel: "Every first-born of man among your sons you shall redeem with a price. And when in time to come your son asks you, 'What does this mean?' you shall say to him: 'By strength of hand the Lord brought us out of Egypt, from the house of bondage.'"

The law of the presentation, therefore, affected the first-born. If a mother's first child was a boy, he must be bought back by the father, on whom the obligation rested. If a man had several wives, each of whom had given birth to a boy as her first-born child, the father was obliged to redeem each one; the ceremony, therefore, could occur several times in the life of a father, but only once for a mother.

The purchase price for the first-born male child was five shekels in coin of the Temple (about five dollars in our money), to be paid in cash; not a small sum for poor people. The price was to be exacted only for those children who, according to all indications, would survive; if the child lived for thirty days it was believed that it would normally survive. The law provided that if a man paid before the thirtieth day and if the child died before that time, the man could recover his money. However, it was not of obligation to pay the purchase price before the thirtieth day, although most pious parents did not delay long after that day to fulfill the prescriptions of the law.

When Pharaoh refused to let the Israelites depart from Egypt, God commanded the people through Moses that the head of each family should slaughter a lamb and put the blood of the lamb on the side posts and on the upper doorposts of their houses; and the angel of God spared the first-born of those houses on which the blood had been put in obedience to God's command, while all the first-born of the Egyptians died. In consequence of this miracle, Pharaoh permitted the Israelites to go out from the land of their bondage and make their way to the promised land.

As an everlasting remembrance of this miraculous liberation, God decreed that henceforth every first-born in Israel was dedicated in a special manner both to Himself and to His people. He was to serve God in the tabernacle and make atonement for the people and offer sacrifices and prayers for them. Later these first-born were replaced by men from the tribe of Levi, but they had to be bought back, "redeemed." A constant procession of first-born, therefore, appeared before the Lord and were remitted by Him to the people; not, however, in the sense that they were no longer God's special property; they were merely freed from the obligation of serving in the Temple. They were expected to labor zealously for God among the people, to whom they had been returned.

Every devout father thought of his son's future when he bought him back; he vowed to educate his son in such a manner that he would always uphold God's authority in whatever vocation might be chosen for him.

At least in the district about Jerusalem, the mother of the first-born also came to the Temple. According to that custom, the Gospel narrates, Mary made her purification offering in the Temple on the same day on which the boy Jesus was presented in the Temple, since, besides the law of the presentation of the child, another law required the Levitical purification of the mother after childbirth.

The law of purification for the mother of a boy was as follows. A woman who has brought forth a male child shall remain forty days in the blood of her purification (seven days before and thirty-three days after the circumcision). She shall touch no holy thing, neither shall she enter into the sanctuary until the days of her purification are fulfilled. "And when the days of her purifying are completed, whether for a son or for a daughter, she shall bring to the priest at the door of the tent of meeting a lamb a year old for a burnt offering, and a young pigeon or a turtledove for a sin offering, and he shall offer it before the Lord, and make atonement for her; then she shall be clean from the flow of her blood. . . . And if she cannot afford a lamb, then she shall take two turtledoves or two young pigeons, one for a burnt offering and the other for a sin offering; and the priest shall make atonement for her, and she shall be clean" (Lev 12:6 ff.).

The gift offered at the purification of a mother differed according to the means of the offerer; the rich offered a lamb, the poor offered two pigeons. Mary and Joseph, being poor, offered a pair of turtledoves. Instead of making an offering of doves, a person could pay an equivalent tax in money to a priest at the Temple; people who came a long distance very likely made use of this privilege.

This law of purification seems strange to us in these modern times. But if we read the history of ancient peoples, we find that those who lived close to nature observed certain religious practices at the time of pregnancy and childbirth. The law of Levitical purification is to be accepted in the same sense. It was a question of a ceremonial uncleanness, not of any sin, and the offering at the end of the prescribed period signified that the person was leaving a condition in which he was conscious of his own weakness and of his utter dependence on God.

Although in Mary there was no question even of such ceremonial uncleanness, nevertheless, she submitted to the law of purification, not by way of conformity to what others did, but in imitation of Jesus, whom God Himself had placed under the law. The divine revelation that took place on the occasion of her purification was a further sign that she was acting in conformity to God's will.

The Presentation in the Temple

And when the time came for their purification according to the law of Moses, they brought him up to Jerusalem to present him to the Lord (as it is written in the law of the Lord, "Every male that opens the womb shall be called holy to the Lord") and to offer a sacrifice according to what is said in the law of the Lord, "a pair of turtledoves, or two young pigeons" (Lk 2: 22–24).

Since the circumcision, Mary and Joseph had often called the Child by His God-given name Jesus. As often as the name came from their lips, its profound significance became clearer: Jesus, the Savior sent by God; Jesus, who would bring salvation to mankind. As they approached the Temple to present the Child to the Lord, they felt that this Child's entrance into the sanctuary of the most High was especially significant.

They came to the Jaffa Gate, near Herod's palace. Before the gate was the usual crowd of Jerusalem merchants and caravan travelers from various localities far and near. Idlers of Jerusalem stood about, and beggars asked for alms. Camels lying at the roadside stared into the distance; donkeys ambled along or stood tethered in rows. As Mary and Joseph, with the Child, made their

81

way through the crowds, scarcely anyone noticed them, unless perhaps some money-changers, who asked Joseph whether he intended to offer doves or to pay the tax in money.

They entered the precincts of the Temple. Now were fulfilled the words of Malachi: "And the Lord whom you seek will suddenly come to his temple" (Mal 3: 1). Even if Mary did not recall these words of the prophet, by her faith she now saw the actuality the prophet had foretold. Something of this prophecy had indeed survived among the people. A story was current that the Messiah would descend from heaven to the pinnacle of the Temple and thus manifest Himself to the people of Israel. But He did not come in such miraculous circumstances. He entered His Father's house for the first time as a child in the arms of His Mother.

The mothers of Israel usually waited at the eastern gate for the priest, and there Mary, with other Jewish mothers, stood until the priest came and received their offerings of doves or money. Joseph stood by her, prepared to pay the ransom for Jesus.

Outwardly, Mary's purification and Jesus' redemption from Temple service were not different from the ceremonies that usually took place on such occasions; but in this instance the ceremony was so filled with actuality that it ceased to be a mere ceremony. As at the Last Supper, celebrating the paschal meal amid the ceremonies of the Old Testament, Jesus was Himself the Lamb of God who marked the end of the ceremony of the symbolic paschal lamb, so now His presentation as a first-born son signified the end of these presentation ceremonies. He was indeed the only-begotten Son of God, who would institute a new priesthood that would be unconnected with the first-born sons. The paschal lamb had saved the first-born sons in Egypt in view of His death on the cross and thus redeemed the whole people from slavery. Jesus, the true paschal Lamb, had been appointed to save Israel, the first-born among peoples, and thereby bring salvation to all other peoples.

Mary and Joseph offered Jesus to the Lord as a gift and then received Him back again. Now, like other parents, they were to rear the Child for that office and those duties to which God had destined Him. But they knew why their Child had come into the world. He had come to save His people from their sins.

The term "first-born" always had reference primarily to the mother, but here it referred in a special way to Mary because

Jesus had no earthly father: inasmuch as the Child was to be surrendered to the Lord, she was the only one united to the Child by physical bonds. She alone, therefore, had prepared herself to offer the Child to God for that sacred task to which God had called Him. Her surrender of her Son was most perfect, and as she gave Him to God she offered her own life at the same time. Joseph, too, offered his life in the service of that Child to whom had been entrusted the salvation of the world. His sacrifice was also perfect, yet different from Mary's, because he was merely the Child's guardian and foster parent.

As God Himself had made known Jesus' birth to the shepherds, so now a man came to the Temple by divine direction. An aged man, named Simeon, one of the devout men of the people, was inspired by the Holy Spirit to come to the Temple at this very hour. Like one who had known them for a long time, he came to Mary and took the Child in his arms, and in that moment he knew that now the promise God had given him, that he would see the Redeemer before he died, had come true. He spoke, therefore, not to Mary and Joseph, but to God:

"Lord, now lettest thou thy servant depart in peace;
according to thy word;
for my eyes have seen thy salvation
which thou hast prepared in the presence of all peoples,
a light for revelation to the Gentiles,
and for glory to thy people Israel" (Lk 2: 29–32).

"Lord, now lettest thou thy servant depart in peace." Simeon was the first person in the New Testament to speak of death without fear. He would gladly depart from this world after seeing the Messiah and holding Him in his arms, the Messiah sent to the people of Israel, who had so long awaited His coming, the Messiah sent to the Gentiles, who had forgotten the promise of His coming. In solemn prophecy Simeon called him: "The glory to thy people Israel, a light for revelation to the Gentiles." Mary and Joseph hearkened as Simeon began his chant of praise and gave expression to these divinely inspired phrases. Simeon rejoiced because, as he said, "My eyes have seen thy salvation"; but the eyes of his soul were turned also upon the whole pagan world. From him Mary and Joseph learned to look beyond the boundaries of their little country. The reference to the Gentiles was a preparation for the flight to Egypt, that ancient kingdom of idolaters. There the words of the aged Simeon would give them strength and comfort and they would know that the Savior's sojourn among the pagans was part of the divinely appointed plan.

Anna, the daughter of Phanuel, of the tribe of Asher, illumined by God, came and stood by Simeon. The Gospel calls this widow a prophetess, a woman filled with the Holy Ghost and living under His special direction. She was now eighty-four years old, and, after seven years of married life, she had consecrated her widowhood to God's service. Anna lived only for God, spending her days in prayer and fasting. Like other devout Israelites, she looked for the coming of the Redeemer. Now, led by the Spirit of God, she came at that very hour when the Christ Child was in the Temple. Like Simeon, she at once rejoiced and gave thanks to God for His great grace. It must have been a dramatic scene when Mary and Anna stood together in the sanctuary, united in their joy that at last the Redeemer had come into the world: Mary, the virgin, who had sacrificed the retirement of her virginal life; and Anna, the aged widow, who had remained a widow that she might the better devote herself to a life of prayer.

Mary, the Mother of the Man of Sorrows

Now there was a man in Jerusalem, whose name was Simeon, and this man was righteous and devout, looking for the consolation of Israel; and the Holy Spirit was upon him. And it had been revealed to him by the Holy Spirit that he should not see death before he had seen the Lord's Christ. And inspired by the Spirit he came into the temple (Luke 2:25–27).

After the birth of Jesus, things happened with startling rapidity in Mary's life. Jesus had come into the world in a stable. He had been laid in a manger, His relatives and the people of Bethlehem had not concerned themselves about this Savior of Israel. While Mary reflected on these things, in her mind arose the question of how this work of redemption would end, a redemption that had such a beginning. But the question caused her no anxiety or apprehension. With the same resignation to God's will as she manifested at Nazareth when she asked the angel how she was to become the Mother of the Redeemer, she now wondered how the redemption of mankind would be accomplished.

Simeon, inspired by God, revealed to her what the future held in store for her Son and for herself. After greeting the Child with joy and giving thanks to God, he turned to Mary and Joseph. He spoke of their great happiness because they were permitted to see the Child not only for a short while but to behold Him day after day and care for Him always. Taught by the Spirit of God, he saw also that their privilege would be accompanied by infinite sorrow, because Jesus the Messiah would save the world by His suffering and death. Enlightened by God, he saw also that Mary's life was more intimately connected with the life of her Son than was Joseph's. Simeon began now, in this holy vision, to prophesy about those things which were foreordained for Jesus and Mary as if the glory and the fate of the Child and the glory and the fate of Mary were one and the same. Turning to Mary, he said solemnly: "Behold, this child is set for the fall and rising of many in Israel, and for a sign that is spoken against (and a sword will pierce through your own soul also) that thoughts out of many hearts may be revealed" (Lk 2: 34–35). Such was heaven's answer to Mary's act of surrender. Thus Simeon ushered Mary into the depths of the mystery of the redemption and made known to her that God had accepted her sacrifice and had given her a special place in the redemptive sufferings of her Son. From the Gospels we know that our Lord tried to strengthen the Apostles' faith in two things: that He was truly the Son of God, and that He must suffer and thus enter into His glory. Before His death, the Apostles did not yet believe unwaveringly in these two truths. But Mary, even at the Annunciation, accepted with unshakable faith the truth that Jesus was the Son of God. Now, hearing Simeon's prophecy, she accepted with a faithful heart this other great truth, that the redemption would be accomplished through the bitter sufferings of Jesus and that she herself would be drawn into her Son's sorrow.

With this prophecy, something new came into her life and remained alive within her until she stood beneath the cross. From this hour she knew that much sorrow awaited her and that it was associated with the salvation of the world. As each day she looked upon her Child, she was reminded of Simeon's words, and they stirred within her heart like living seeds planted there. The quiet days at Nazareth, which seem so empty to us, and the years of our Lord's public ministry, during which Mary remained in the background: all the days and hours of those years were filled with the secret growing of this seed in her heart; as it grew, it entwined its roots about her heart, which it filled with immeasurable sorrow. Thus her heart was made like the heart of her divine Son.

Mary was not vouchsafed that knowledge by which Jesus foreknew all the details of His suffering and death. But the vision of the future, granted her by God through Simeon's prophecy, was in some mysterious manner comparable to the foreknowledge of Jesus. Mary's entrance within the shadow of her Son's future suffering and death brought her closer to Him than any outward insistence on His dignity. In Nazareth, she had become the Mother of the Savior, and now, by Simeon's words, she was consecrated as the Mother of Sorrows. Mary's glory does not consist alone in the offering of her body as a dwelling place for the Son of God, where He might be made ready as the victim for mankind's salvation; she also accepted the office of watching over the Lamb of sacrifice and, when the time should come, of leading Him to the altar of sacrifice.

The Magi

Now when Jesus was born in Bethlehem of Judea, in the days of Herod the king, behold, wise men from the East came to Jerusalem, saying, "Where is he who has been born king of the Jews? For we have seen his star in the East, and have come to worship him" (Mt 2: 1–2).

After bidding farewell to Simeon, Mary and Joseph began the journey home. They passed by the magnificent palace of King Herod. Its towers rose arrogantly to their heights, built of huge blocks of stone, each stone two and one-half yards long and more than a yard wide. They walked along the great wall enclosing the beautiful gardens; cedars, cypresses, and pines could be seen above the walls. People in Jerusalem told of the magnificence of the fountains, which flowed during the heat of the summer. They told of the two great halls of the palace, the emperor's hall and the hall of Agrippa, in which hundreds of guests could be served, and of the vessels of gold and silver; they spoke of the gorgeous arcades where the guests walked. Flocks of pigeons flew from the scaffoldings that had been built especially for them. A certain kind of pigeon is still called the Herod pigeon in Palestine after King Herod, who had a liking for these birds. Many grumbled about the lofty tower, which reared itself to a height of a hundred fifty feet. The foundation of the tower was filled with rock and could withstand any attack by a battering-ram. In the upper stories were halls and baths such as were usually found in a great palace.

Innumerable tales were abroad about the scandalous happenings within the palace. From day to day, old King Herod became more arrogant and more cruel. Antipater, the son of Doris (one of Herod's ten wives), had gone to Rome to obtain the ratification of Herod's last will and testament, which named him as his father's successor. While at Rome, he sent to Jerusalem poison intended for his aged father. Becoming aware of his son's treacherous intentions, Herod affectionately urged him to return, and on his arrival cast him into prison. This villainy he now reported to the emperor and asked for permission to execute his disloyal son. The city was rife with rumors, while within the palace a silent contest for the throne was being waged among Herod's other sons and certain influential favorites. Each plotted against the other, but Herod watched them all, occasionally removing a contender when he seemed too dangerous.

Mary and Joseph had heard these rumors while they were still in Bethlehem, but they did not in the least suspect that within a short time the tyrant's wrath would be directed to the Child that Mary now carried back to Bethlehem.

After the census, Mary and Joseph remained for some time in Bethlehem. No doubt, as soon as possible, they moved from the cave to a rented dwelling. The Evangelist, speaking of the visit of the wise men, says that the star stood over the "house" where the Child was. We cannot insist upon the word, because it could also refer to the cave. Some probability exists, however, that a house was meant, since later the Evangelist seems to indicate that, after the return from Egypt, Joseph intended to reside in Bethlehem. Joseph thought that the Son of David should grow up in the city of David.

One day a caravan of camels was seen approaching the house. The saddles and harness showed they had come from a distant land. The distinguished-looking men in command of the caravan came to the house. Like the shepherds on Christmas night, they asked permission to present their greetings to the Child; and, like the shepherds, they said they had received a message from heaven. They told how in the East, in their homeland, they had seen a star and recognized it as the sign that a great king was born in Israel. Immediately they set out on their journey; day and night they had traveled across the desert, coming at last to Jerusalem, the chief city of Israel. There they were at first disappointed because everyone was unaware of the new King and was frightened when asked about Him. Only old King Herod seemed to understand; he had received them in private audience and told them that the newborn King of the Jews was to be found in Bethlehem. They resumed their journey, and on the road from Jerusalem to Bethlehem the star they had seen in the East appeared again. It preceded them until it stood over the place where they now found the Child.

The Magi told of the promise they had made to King Herod in Jerusalem: that they would return and report to him as soon as they found the Child, for Herod also wished to come and do reverence to the new king. In their unsuspecting simplicity, these men were happy to bring the news of such an important birth.

Mary and Joseph listened attentively as the Magi recounted these events. They observed how the visitors reverently worshiped the Child as the King who had been sent by God. Servants unloaded the packs from the camels and brought forth treasures: gifts of gold, frankincense, and myrrh for the Child. The scene was a most unusual one, as this young mother, the wife of a carpenter, sat holding the Child while these dignified Magi from the East prostrated themselves and laid their gifts at the Child's feet.

Artists often picture Mary seated on a throne, in her arms the divine Infant, who holds the orb in His hand. When the Magi bowed in reverence, their homage was intended not only for Jesus the King, but also for the Mother who held Him in her arms. Mary was the royal Mother of her royal Son. St. Matthew wrote the legend for the picture: "And going into the house, they saw the child with Mary his mother, and they fell down and worshiped him. Then, opening their treasures, they offered him gifts, gold and frankincense and myrrh."

At the same time, Mary was able to comprehend the profound significance of this event. "The Lord God will give to him the throne of his father David, and he will reign over the house of Jacob for ever; and of his kingdom there will be no end." Thus the angel had announced in Nazareth. And now something had occurred that recalled the throne room of a king.

Soon these Gentiles from strange lands concluded their act of worship; but its effect remained for Mary. Two things had taken place according to God's will, transcending the laws of nature: the adoration of the Jewish shepherds and the homage of the Magi, representatives of the Gentiles. Simeon's prophetic words, acknowledging Jesus as "a light for revelation to the Gentiles, and for glory to thy people Israel," were now confirmed. Mary herself perceived the double fulfillment of these words, and now she saw in Jesus not only the Redeemer of Israel, but also the Redeemer of the Gentiles of the whole world who still served idols. Whenever she thought of Simeon and recalled his words, the picture of these pagan Magi came before her mind. Legend has it that the Magi were again present at the death of Jesus; they were, indeed, present there in Mary's remembrance. She was able to understand the world-embracing significance of Jesus' death on the cross partly because, at His coming to earth, these pagan observers of the stars had come from afar with their homage and their gifts of gold, frankincense, and myrrh.

The flight into Egypt

Now when they had departed, behold, an angel of the Lord appeared to Joseph in a dream and said, "Rise, take the child and his mother, and flee to Egypt, and remain there till I tell you; for Herod is about to search for the child, to destroy him." And he rose and took the child and his mother by night, and departed to Egypt (Mt 2: 13-14).

Sometime during the night Mary was awakened by Joseph. He told her of the command he had received from the angel: "Rise, take the child and his mother, and flee to Egypt, and remain there till I tell you; for Herod is about to search for the child, to destroy him." Immediately they sensed the danger that threatened Jesus. Herod had deceived the Magi, requesting them to return and report to him where the newborn King was to be found; his intention was to kill Him. When the old tyrant became suspicious, he acted with characteristic promptness and cruelty.

The angel commanded the Holy Family to go to Egypt. Escape to the north was impossible, and escape eastward through the interminable desert was equally impossible, with Mary and the Child. The only escape from Herod's jurisdiction was to Egypt, and even this involved a journey of several hundred miles.

Did Mary and Joseph know that the Magi had been commanded by God in a dream not to return to Herod? The dream must have occurred while the Magi were still in Bethlehem, since the journey to Jerusalem was a matter of merely a few hours. If, therefore, they were warned in Bethlehem, they most probably spoke of it to Mary and Joseph when they bade farewell. Of course, both Joseph and the Magi may have been warned during the same night. In any case, within a comparatively short time occurred these four events: the Magi's audience with Herod, the adoration of the Child, the departure of the Magi for their homeland, and Joseph's flight into Egypt. Bethlehem was only two hours journey from Jerusalem; as soon as Herod became suspicious, the danger for the divine Child grew hourly. In obedience to the angel's command, Joseph and Mary fled that very night in which they were apprised of the danger.

In pictures and legends, the flight into Egypt is somewhat fantastically described. We are told of palms that bowed as the Holy Family passed by, of fountains that sprang up to give water, and of bandits that became gentle. All this obscures the actual horrors of the flight. Until Mary and Joseph had reached the desert beyond Gaza, they were in constant danger of being discovered by searchers. Whenever they heard the hoofbeats of a donkey behind them, whenever a face suddenly appeared from behind a vineyard wall, whenever some passing traveler looked at them intently, their fears increased that they would be apprehended. Indeed, the flight had more terrors for Mary and Joseph than are found in the highly imaginative tales of the journey.

Little mention is made of the dangerous roads that Mary and Joseph had to traverse at the beginning of the journey. From Bethlehem, which lies about two thousand feet above sea level, the way descended to the lowlands. There was no highway, only a steep path, which for centuries had been trodden by man and beast. Part of this path they were obliged to travel by night.

When morning came, they looked down upon the land of the Philistines, lying beneath the early morning sky. On the second day they may have reached Gaza, the last of the larger cities before the desert, and here they purchased provisions for the journey across the desert. Then they entered the desert.

Travelers crossing the arid regions of the desert were obliged to observe a time schedule that brought them to certain stopping-places for the night. In the morning, groups of travelers started out together and remained together during the day. Probably, therefore, Joseph did not cross the desert alone with Mary and

Jesus. In the beginning, when the journey took them through districts that were still sparsely settled, the members of a traveling group changed sometimes, but afterward, in the depth of the desert, no newcomers joined the group.

Day after day, the landscape remained monotonously the same, so that no progress in the journey was evident. In the west, the yellow sand dunes glowed against the low horizon, undulating softly into each other; and beyond the dunes lay the sea. Coming too close to the dunes would make travel more difficult because of the deep sand; leaving them out of sight was dangerous, because the direction might be lost in the arid waste. Along the edges of the road, stretching like a broad ribbon across the desert and marked by the traces of other caravans, lay the bones of animals that had been left, exhausted, to die by the roadside, unable to continue the journey. Bleached by the merciless sun and polished by the fine sand of the desert, these bones glistened like ivory. In the heart of the desert the sand became as fine as flour.

This desert, which lay between the mountains of Israel and the Nile, appears again and again in Scripture. Abraham, the great father of Israel, had come this way. Mary recalled, too, the story of Joseph of Egypt. Did not her spouse, who traveled beside her, bear the same name? Was not that first Joseph also suddenly snatched from the mountains of his homeland and delivered up to this same desert? Did he not also go ignorant of the fate awaiting him in Egypt? Later, in the time of the famine, Joseph's brothers came the same way; and Benjamin, the youngest son of their father Jacob, soon followed; lastly, the aged Jacob himself journeyed through this desert.

Across these endless plains, Moses, the man of God, had roamed as a shepherd; and, after leading the people of Israel out of Egypt's bondage at God's command, he had wandered with them for the span of a lifetime through these same desert lands.

Mary, the daughter of her people, conscious of her religious heritage, had often accompanied her holy forebears in spirit through the desert. Now she herself was crossing the great waste, and in her arms she carried Him whom God had promised to her fathers, to Abraham, Isaac, and Jacob—the ruler of the house of Jacob, the true Redeemer who saved His people not merely from an Egyptian bondage, but from the bondage of sin, the promised Redeemer in whom all the history of the people seemed to be gathered up.

The sojourn in Egypt

Joseph departed to Egypt, and remained there until the death of Herod. This was to fulfill what the Lord had spoken by the prophet, "Out of Egypt have I called my son" (Mt 2: 14-15).

After the long and wearisome journey, Mary and Joseph came to the broad valley of the Nile. At that time many Israelites lived in Egypt; some had indeed formed separate communities there; and Joseph probably joined such a community of his fellow Jews. Mary and Joseph were merely two poor immigrants among many who came to Egypt from their homeland. Some of these had fled their own country to escape the revenge for some bloodshed, and their compatriots did not, therefore, insist on questioning them about their past. But Mary and Joseph gave the impression of being peaceful people, and their appearance did not arouse any suspicion of past adventures.

Mary's feelings on coming to live in an alien land can be best understood by one who for long has lived in the intimacy of a Catholic parish in the country and is then obliged to live in a large industrial city. Such a person is indeed not alone in the great city, but he is spiritually lonesome, a grievous suffering for those who are naturally sensitive.

Everything was strange for Mary in this land, and she did not know how long the exile would last. She could not look forward to some definite time when the period of banishment would be over. "Remain there till I tell you," such were the angel's indefinite words. Every sight and every sound reminded her that she was in a strange country. The sky seemed to stretch so far from desert to desert across the green valley of the Nile. From the south flowed the Nile, with its varying shades of red; the water was poured or pumped into canals, and man and beast drank it; above, strange birds, such as the ibis, winged their silent flight.

Stranger yet than the land upon which she looked were the people among whom she lived. The mighty Pharaohs, the ancient kings of Egypt, lived no more, but the old spirit of paganism that had actuated them still ruled over the country with much splendor and power. Idols were still erected in the magnificent temples: idols with human bodies and the head of a cow or a bird, some idols representing a ram or a hippopotamus. Besides these idols, the Egyptians worshiped demons and evil spirits, from whom they sought what they could not obtain from the good spirits. In addition to these public acts of religion, there were various secret practices and magical rites, which were observed in secret both by the cultured and by the common people. While she lived in this fruitful valley of the Nile, Mary suffered from the oppressive atmosphere of paganism surrounding her.

In this confused world of Egyptian paganism, Mary entered more deeply into the Sacred Scriptures; now more than ever she understood the significance of Simeon's prophecy that Jesus, her Son, was to be the light for a revelation to the Gentiles.

At home, in Nazareth, Mary had listened with wrapt attention to the history of Israel as it was told again and again in the Scriptural readings in the synagogue. Those events of ancient times, commemorated annually by all the people at the time of the great feasts, had made a deep impression upon her soul. Each year the religious climax was reached in the celebration of the Passover and the sacrifice of the paschal lamb. This feast was closely associated with the land where she now dwelt with the Redeemer. Here, on the banks of the Nile, her forefathers had suffered slavery and persecution; here the first paschal lamb had been sacrificed, and so the people were delivered from bondage and misery; here the people of Israel had been selected as the chosen people of God. Thus, while she dwelt in Egypt, the beginning of Israel's history became alive again for her.

Westward, the pyramids were silhouetted against the sky. Mary thought of the mighty kings, their builders, who had so grievously oppressed her people. The water of the Nile flowed gently through the land and covered the soil it had deposited the year before. Here, in these level fields, where now the slaves were mixing clay and making bricks, her ancestors had been forced to toil to the point of utter exhaustion. In lonely places, the rushes grew exuberantly and stemmed the flow of the stream. In such a spot Moses, whom God chose as the savior and liberator of Israel, had been placed as an infant in a wicker basket.

Everything recalled those far-off days. As once the first great liberator had rested unknown in the basket by the water's edge, so now the last of the liberators, the promised Redeemer, was a child by her side. Moses' sister, who had saved the child, was also called Mary; as the Israelites of that time longed for the day when they could set out for the promised land, Mary now longed for the day when her banishment would be over.

She never forgot that Jesus had come into the world to save these pagans also; in spirit she saw them included in His labors. She met the Egyptian women carrying their water jugs, and they asked the name of her Child. What a strange name! But, after all, they had no concern with this Child or with His Mother. Yet, as Mary knew, all these people were in need of redemption by Jesus, and some day they would participate in the fruits of His sacrifice. Even now she received them into her maternal heart.

The return to Nazareth

[Joseph] rose and took the child and his mother, and went to the land of Israel. But when he heard that Archelaus reigned over Judea in place of his father Herod, he was afraid to go there, and being warned in a dream he withdrew to the district of Galilee. And he went and dwelt in a city called Nazareth, that what was spoken by the prophets might be fulfilled, "He shall be called a Nazarene" (Mt 2: 21-23).

An angel appeared to Joseph, the guardian of Mary and of the Child, and said to him: "Rise, take the child and his mother, and go to the land of Israel. For those who sought the child's life are dead." Joseph prepared to depart from Egypt. Once more they looked upon this strange country, and then they traveled eastward to the desert. The last of the temples disappeared in the green countryside behind them. Soon they came to the sand, and the donkeys found no more fodder. Again they plodded on, day after day, and, when the heat became unbearable, at night. Here and there along the road they recalled sights they had observed on their journey to Egypt. At last they saw fertile fields again and flocks grazing in the pastures. In the caravansaries, traders were busy, offering beverages and provisions for sale; in the evening, natives of the district joined the travelers and narrated events of the past and the present. Gradually, Mary and Joseph learned what had happened in their homeland since their flight.

Shortly after their flight from Bethlehem, Herod died. The news of his death was received with great rejoicing throughout the land; many hoped that his son Archelaus would not imitate his father's cruelty. Soon, however, it became evident that he would continue his father's reign of terror. After Herod had been buried with unexampled pomp, and Archelaus had been proclaimed king, the people came together in great numbers and demanded satisfaction for the death of two doctors of the law whom Herod had commanded to be burned in the days of his last illness. In reply to their demands, Archelaus sent his cavalry among the populace and dispersed them. He then went to Rome to obtain the royal dignity. But before the matter was decided there in his favor, the people of Israel sent a deputation to the emperor asking him not to appoint Archelaus king. In the meantime, a new revolt broke out in Judea. The emperor thereupon chose a middle course; he established Archelaus as the ruler of Judea, but refused to confer upon him the title of king.

Mary and Joseph soon heard about the cruel murder of the children in and about Bethlehem, and now they realized how great had been the danger that threatened the life of the Child. They were, however, obliged to remain silent about their escape lest they expose Him to other dangers. Within herself, no doubt, Mary recalled Simeon's words: "Behold, this child is set for a sign that is spoken against." The words were now being fulfilled, even before the Child had left her arms. What indeed was the fate awaiting Him when He should reveal Himself as the divinely sent Messiah, the Son of David and King of Israel?

Mary and Joseph had intended to reside in Bethlehem, the city of David. But upon learning the state of affairs in Judea, they were at a loss where to go. Then an angel again appeared to Joseph and directed him to go to Nazareth.

Thus one day Mary and Joseph went up from the plain of Esdrelon to the hill country, where lay the village of Nazareth. They saw their native village lying before them, a confusion of houses and narrow streets. The return home was not an unmixed joy. They knew that their relatives in the village would now inquire why they had not returned after the census and why they had gone off to Egypt. If Joseph, before departing for the census, had announced his decision to remain in Bethlehem, these relatives would be curious to know why he had then gone to Egypt. Mary and Joseph could not divulge the true reason for their actions—that they had acted in obedience to the angel's command—for then they would have had to divulge the mystery of the Child. The inquisitive neighbors may have wondered at the change in Mary and Joseph after their marriage: they had lived here so long as simple, quiet people; they had regularly attended the synagogue; and then, suddenly, they had gone to Egypt.

We are now able to understand the part that the journey to Bethlehem and the flight to Egypt played in the life of Jesus. By their absence from Nazareth, Mary and Joseph were removed from their inquisitive relatives, and the mystery, known to them alone, remained hidden. True, it had been revealed, according to the laws of grace, to the shepherds, to the Magi, and to Simeon and Anna. After the flight to Egypt, these witnesses of the miraculous events, like the relatives at Nazareth, lost all connection with the Christ Child. Thus Jesus grew up in Nazareth in obscurity, although Mary and Joseph were well known there in the days before His birth. Jesus' miraculous conception and birth remained mysteries, of which no one in the village knew anything.

IV.

The Hidden Life at Nazareth

The life of women in Israel

Consciously or unconsciously, we are accustomed to visualize Mary's outward appearance as we see her represented in pictures, in which she wears a veil such as is still worn today by women in the East. From both biblical and non-biblical writing, we are led to suppose that women always appeared in public with their heads covered or veiled. Of what material these coverings or veils were made, we are not certain. The headdress and, especially, the hair, which was generally braided, were often ornamented with small plates, clasps, circles, or stars, which, according to the wearer's means, were made of glass, silver, gold, or some other metal. All women, even the poor, wore some ornament. Perhaps then, as now, a woman fastened to her head-covering some coins from her bridal dowry, which were her personal property, and the number and value of these coins indicated her wealth.

A favorite ornament was the "golden city," a circle or wreath on which a picture of the city of Jerusalem was engraved. Solicitous men brought these wreaths for their wives or daughters as a remembrance from Jerusalem, where the sale and manufacture of souvenirs was a profitable industry.

The custom of appearing in public with the head veiled was especially binding on married women. If a woman disregarded this custom and appeared in public without the veil, she was considered to have dishonored herself and her husband. In the time before Christ, a matter of some legal importance was the question whether the offense had been committed and whether a man had the right to divorce his wife because of it.

The doctors of the law once raised the question whether a woman should be considered as having her head covered if she wore her spinning basket or, as we might say, her sewing basket. Many, but not all, considered such covering sufficient about the house. The question is not as academic as appears at first sight, since women who were able to carry water jugs on their heads could also carry such baskets on their heads. Later the custom of appearing in public with veiled heads was imposed on Christian women by St. Paul. Writing to the Corinthians, he said: "That is why a woman ought to have a veil on her head," that is, a sign that she is subservient to and dependent upon her husband.

Apparently, besides thus covering the head, a custom arose of drawing the veil over the face. The custom is presupposed in the following tragic incident: A high priest was about to sit in judgment on a woman accused of adultery; when the veil was raised from her face, he was horrified to see that the woman standing before him was his mother. If this custom existed at the time of our Lord, it was probably observed only in the larger cities, such as Jerusalem, and in the winter resort of Jericho, but not in such small towns as Nazareth. The practice was never adopted in the country because it was impractical for women at work. We may conclude, therefore, that Mary wore a headdress similar to that worn by women in the East today.

Like the men, the women wore an undergarment and an outer garment, with this difference, that the women preferred finer materials and more brilliant colors and often ornamented their garments with borders and embroidery. The garment was held in at the waist by a girdle, and custom required that the garment reach down to the ankles. For practical reasons, the men's garments were short; only the wealthy and the learned appeared in public in long flowing robes.

Because of the hot climate, the foot-covering consisted usually of sandals, which had soles of wood or tanned leather that were sometimes polished and blackened. By most people of the ordinary classes sandals were not worn for the greater part of the year, since at home men, and especially women and children, went barefoot. Footgear was worn mainly for attendance at Sabbath services and for long pilgrimages. Mary and Joseph belonged to that class which is obliged to be sparing of expense, and accordingly they followed the prevailing custom in this matter.

A strong contrast existed between those women who retained the traditional garb of the people and those who followed the latest trend of fashion, which at that time was a mixture of old Eastern customs and newer ideas in dress imported from Greece and Italy.

Practices still in use for the care of the hair were already known at that time: the hair was dyed, false hair was braided with one's own, and the braids were worn in various artistic arrangements. A slave or a close friend was ordinarily employed as hairdresser, and we hear of complaints that such hairdressers violated confidences reposed in them. Combs and mirrors, ointments and pomades, were in general use, and the hair was dressed and arranged according to plans and styles decreed by the current mode.

Many kinds of accessories and ornaments were added to the ordinary articles of clothing. Some women placed small vials of aromatic balm in their shoes so that the air might be perfumed at each step, and some wore thick cork soles to add to their height.

The news of the latest occurrences was spread, even as it is today, from the large centers of population out into the countryside. Peddlers traveled about the rural districts "so that the daughters of Israel might more easily come by the articles needed to enhance their beauty." As a rule, life in the country was simpler and stricter. Because of the higher moral standard observed in the country, it was remarked that the veiling of the face need not be so strictly observed as in the cities.

This account may appear irrelevant, but it is of some value. Mary is often presented in vague generalities as the model of women, and the impression is given that, in her time, life in general, and especially for Mary herself, was utterly different from what it is today. But in fact she lived in a world that was not so different from our own as we would at first imagine.

In his first epistle, St. Peter describes the model woman in the following words: "Let not yours be the outward adorning with braiding of hair, decoration of gold, and wearing of robes, but let it be the hidden person of the heart with the imperishable jewel of a gentle and quiet spirit, which in God's sight is very precious" (3:3-4). Certainly no woman has fulfilled this ideal as perfectly as Mary.

The father and mother in the family

The Holy Spirit selected and prepared not only a mother, but also a family, for the Incarnation of the Son of God. Thus the Incarnation was not accomplished in a virgin who was still unattached, or in a woman who was the mother of a family, but in a virgin who was espoused. Nothing shows more clearly the importance

God attached to the family than the fact that Jesus spent thirty years of His life in the midst of a family.

In the religious life of the people, the men were without question the leaders; but generally they accepted certain duties along with their rights and privileges. Thus, for instance, it was agreed that certain religious obligations, especially the more arduous, rested upon the man; the man alone was obliged to know the Law, to recite twice daily the profession of faith, and to make the annual pilgrimages to Jerusalem.

The man's preeminence was strikingly shown in the religious services. St. Paul, in his first epistle to the Corinthians says: "The women should keep silence in the churches. For they are not permitted to speak, but should be subordinate, as even the law says. If there is anything they desire to know, let them ask their husbands at home" (1 Cor 14: 34–35). Thus the woman's position in the synagogue is briefly described; instruction is exclusively the duty of the man, and the women shall listen attentively and shall humbly receive the doctrine and its explanation.

This position of the man in religious life had a potent influence on the education of the children. A boy must have been deeply impressed when he heard his father recite the profession of faith twice every day and later, when his father taught him the prayer, reminding him that this prayer was recited by the men only. So, too, the boy's religious consciousness must have been stirred when he saw his father preparing to go to Jerusalem for the celebration of the Passover and heard him explain that all the men of the nation were assembling in Jerusalem in God's presence.

This practice did not imply that the woman should be without religion. It was quite well understood that if the men gave a good example in word and deed, the women too would be religious, and that, after all, a good man was a good mother's gift to the people. The exclamation, "Blessed is the womb that bore thee," is an expression of that sentiment.

The woman, like the man, was obliged to recite the ordinary prayers, in the morning and evening and at table, and pious women undertook the arduous pilgrimages to Jerusalem as Mary did. For the rest, certain duties connected with the home and the family were considered a woman's important obligations, and neglect of them would bring misfortune on the home. Thus, for instance, it was the woman's duty to tend the Sabbath lamp and keep it lighted; but her most sacred duty was so to train and educate the children, especially the men of the coming generation, that they would be zealous for God's revelation.

The Gospels give but few indications about the relations between Mary and Joseph and their relations with the Child. Joseph was, indeed, the responsible head of the family who appeared in public as Jesus' legal father. On the first occasion when he was obliged to act in this capacity, he had been expressly authorized by the angel, "You shall call his name Jesus," and in this command was included the direction to submit the Child to the rite of circumcision. By appearing in this way as the legal father of Jesus, Joseph assumed the other obligations of the Law. The messages that God sent about the protection of the Child were always imparted to Joseph: "Rise, take the child and his mother, and flee to Egypt"; "Rise, take the child and his mother, and go to the land of Israel"; "Being warned in a dream, he withdrew to the district of Galilee."

Outwardly, the order in the family according to rank was: Joseph, Mary, and the child Jesus; inwardly, however, it was: the child Jesus, Mary, and Joseph. On only two occasions did this inner order appear externally. The aged Simeon, holding the Child in his arms and speaking of the conflict that would be waged in Israel because of the Redeemer, passed by Joseph, the foster father, and addressed the Mother directly, "And a sword will pierce through your own soul also." Both Mary and Joseph must have noticed that Simeon said nothing to Joseph, but Joseph's holy soul, which bowed humbly in the presence of Mary's preeminence, was incapable of taking offense. Even this silence of Simeon was prophetic—Joseph would be of service in the work of the redemption by departing from this life before Jesus appeared publicly as the Messiah.

This external order in the family was disregarded for the second time when the family was reunited in the Temple. It was Mary, the Mother of Jesus, and not Joseph, His legal foster father, who asked the Boy, "Son, why have you treated us so?" Perhaps Joseph had yielded to her, but in the next sentence Mary acknowledges Joseph as the head of the family when she mentions him in the first place: "Behold, your father and I have been looking for you anxiously."

On the same occasion. Jesus also disregarded this external order and revealed the true order of persons: "How is it that you sought me? Did you not know that I must be in my Father's house?" As the Son of the Father in heaven, He stood above Mary and Joseph whenever the Father required anything of Him.

Life in the home

In Palestine, even now, the home is not so much a dwelling place as a place for lodging and sleeping. Since Mary and Joseph, as their offering at the presentation indicated, belonged to the poor, we must visualize their home as being very simple. The following is a description of a traditional home as we might find it in Palestine in the early twentieth century. Crossing the threshold, we come into a room on the ground floor, generally used as a stable for sheep, goats, and the donkey. A step leads to the principal room, which is about a foot and a half higher than the first room. Here the family eats and sleeps. In one corner we find the fireplace, a portable affair made of clay, with several openings through which fuel is placed on the fire, on which food is cooked in pots and pans. Along the walls, which are pierced sometimes by one window and sometimes by none at all, are arranged oil jugs, clay vats for holding wheat and figs, and the bridal chest containing the feast day clothes. Sieves and pouches hang from the walls, wooden vessels and cooking pots stand on the window sill, while spoons, other utensils, and lamps are placed on shelves. Straw mats, spread on the floor, are the beds.

May we suppose that Palestinian houses in our Lord's time were similar to present-day houses in that same country? Some writers have pointed out that the incorporation of the country into the economic and commercial system of the Roman Empire brought with it a new culture and new customs. The point is, no doubt, well made with regard to the upper classes and, in prosperous times, for the middle classes also; but for the poor classes, to which the Holy Family belonged, few important changes have been made. This is evident from the Gospels and other contemporary writings. In one of the parables, our Lord tells of a man replying to his importunate neighbor: "Do not bother me; the door is now shut, and my children are with me in bed" (Luke 11:7). Elsewhere we read: "A father is permitted to recite the official evening prayer in bed when his small children sleep with him under the same cover; but it is forbidden when adults sleep under the same cover." Such scenes could take place only in dwellings similar to the flimsy houses of modern Palestine; as also the scene described by our Lord of the woman who lost a piece of money and lighted a lamp so that she might see to sweep the dark room.

Even the rainy season has many sunny days, and the people of Palestine are not often obliged to seek the indoor shelter of comfortable rooms. The family living quarters are frequently not a room in the house, but the courtyard, surrounded by a fence or wall, in front of the house. When visiting a family, one went from the street into the courtyard, and from there into the house.

For the people of the Middle East, the courtyard was at least as important as the house itself. Here the ordinary life of the family took place; here in the summer they found relief from the heat in the shade, and in the winter they could be warmed by the sun. As in other countries sheds and outhouses are attached to the house, in Palestine they were attached to the courtyard wall. There was a shed for fuel and another for grain and dried fruits; here, too, poultry was kept. The women sat on the ground in the courtyard to grind their wheat; and the noise of their hand mills belonged to the everyday life of Israel just as the clanking and groaning of the water wheels were a part of the life of Egypt. It was a welcome sound when it announced a coming wedding, but it was not so agreeable when a neighbor began to grind early in the morning close to the dividing wall; sometimes the vibration of the mill loosened the plaster. To avoid such mishaps, it was agreed to keep the mill three handbreadths from the wall. Fruit trees, such as the shady fig tree, and climbers, such as the luxuriant grapevine, were planted in suitable places in the courtyard. This was the workplace for the family; for a carpenter it was an ideal workshop.

Certain rules of conduct for women show that the courtyard was considered the first room of the house. Women were permitted more liberty in the courtyard than on the streets. It was said that if a woman was bound to veil her head in the courtyard, not a single daughter of Abraham could have remained with her husband. To appear in public with uncovered head was something that touched her honor, and for this offense her husband could divorce her. Accordingly, the courtyard was legally regarded as a part of the house. It was also considered the common living room for one or more families. For this reason, if a man owned a house that opened on a court used by other families, he was not permitted to rent it to a doctor, a blood-letter, a weaver, or a teacher, because in these instances so many people would have come into the courtyard that it would lose its character of living room.

Hence we may, with considerable likelihood, describe the house of the Holy Family as follows. In front was an open space used in common with one or more families whose houses also opened upon this yard. Among these neighbors may have been relatives of the Holy Family, perhaps some of those mentioned in the Gospel. Actually, life in the little house at Nazareth was not the glamorous idyll portrayed in pictures and in poems. In their courtyard life went on, as it did in the yards to the right and the left of it.

The work of the mother

Soon Mary saw how Jesus, her Child and the Son of God, began to discover the world about Him in the house of Nazareth. He gazed long at the ceiling, He looked toward the door through which light streamed in; when the door was closed, the room was so dark at first that nothing could be distinguished in the gloom. In the corners of the room were various chests and containers, earthenware jars containing dried figs and grapes, peas and beans. The most wonderful container was built into the wall; its opening was closed with a stopper. Every morning Mary placed a vessel before it and, drawing the stopper, allowed as much barley to flow out as she needed for the day; and each time, the Child observed the operation with evident interest.

Jesus knew what came next. He took His mother's hand and together they went out into the courtyard. Here were the mill-stones, one upon the other. Mary sat down and turned the upper stone while she poured grain into the funnel, and Jesus watched for the white flour to flow from between the stones.

Then Mary took a shallow bowl and poured a measure of flour into it. She took some leaven left over from the last baking and, dissolving it in water, mixed it into the flour and made a new dough, which she then allowed to rise. It was like a recollection of His childhood days when in later life Jesus said: "The kingdom of heaven is like leaven which a woman took and hid in three measures of meal, till it was all leavened" (Mt 13: 33).

Then Mary went to the bakehouse, a kind of clay hut, which she probably used in common with other families. Into the fire-box of the oven she placed brushwood, hay, and waste material from the workshop. The fir box was covered with potsherd and tiles, and above the oven was placed an arched cover made of clay or metal to prevent any impurities from falling on the tiles where the dough would be placed later.

If Mary used more than two quarts of flour in making bread, she was obliged by the law to send some of the bread to the priests. What was done in those places where there was no priest is not clear; but in the mind of the people a neglect of this duty brought misfortune on the home.

After an hour, if the fire had burned down to embers, Mary pushed the ashes aside and, dusting her hands with flour, she took the dough, which was now ready, and drew it out to form flat cakes about the size of a plate. Lifting the cover from the hot tiles, she laid the flat cakes in the oven and covered them with the lid. When the bread was properly baked, she removed it from the oven. This bread supplied the family for several days and formed the principal part of their meals, which consisted also of olives preserved in salt, figs pressed in the earthenware jars, and, on rare occasions, dates, which had to be bought because they did not ripen every year here in Nazareth.

Every day the mother went to the village well to draw water for the home. The water jug was always carried on the head. At the well she met the other women of the village. Here Jesus sometimes heard the women speaking of the water supply being exhausted in other villages. He saw that the well was a fountain of living water, the most precious treasure of the village.

Baking bread and carrying water were an important part of a woman's work; in a sense, they were her special duties. Among the ordinary people this conception still remains. In some localities a bride, when entering her new home, takes leaven and touches her forehead and the lintel of the door with it; she then puts the water jug on her head and enters. These actions are intended to symbolize that henceforth the bride's duties in this home will consist of baking bread and carrying water.

The spinning of wool and flax was exclusively the work of the housewife. In the Book of Proverbs we read among the words of praise for the thorough housewife: "She puts her hands to the distaff, and her hands hold the spindle" (Prov 31: 19). Spinning was such an important duty that even the wealthier women were not exempt from it if they wished to be considered accomplished housewives. Sheep wool and flax were the materials used for the spinning of thread. Since for this work the arms had to be unencumbered, for a woman to spin in public was considered improper, although probably then, as now, some women did their spinning on the streets. For the poor women, the natural place for spinning was, of course, the courtyard. When in pictures of the Holy Family Mary is represented with the distaff, the detail is in accord with things as they were.

Some of the thread and yarn was used for mending, but most of it was used in the loom. The products of weaving were intended partly for use in the family and partly for sale. Because clothing at that time was in such form that the whole cloth could be used, the cloth was not woven into bolts and then cut according to patterns and sizes. Clothes were woven, that is, the entire garment was completed on the loom.

St. John tells us that Jesus had such a seamless garment, for which later the soldiers at the Crucifixion cast lots because they did not wish to divide it. Legend has it that Mary herself wove this garment. We may quite reasonably suppose that such was the fact. Undergarments were made of linen, which was widely used in Galilee, more so than in Judea, where wool was replacing linen. According to an old saying, one should buy linen cloth from the women of Galilee, and woolen cloth in Judea. Our Lord, in the Sermon on the Mount, referred to the work of spinning and weaving: "Consider the lilies of the field, how they grow; they neither toil nor spin; yet I tell you, even Solomon in all his glory was not arrayed like one of these" (Mt 6: 28–29).

The boy Jesus watched His Mother when she mended the clothes. She was careful to save all old patches, and, when a garment was torn, she looked for a piece to match the cloth of the garment. Perhaps He once asked her why she did not use a new piece of cloth to mend the tear, and she told Him that the new piece would shrink when it became wet and that old pieces were better for patching. Perhaps this scene may have come to His mind when He said: "No one puts a piece of unshrunk cloth on an old garment, for the patch tears away from the garment, and a worse tear is made" (Mt 9: 16).

The new garments were kept in chests, and Mary laid herbs and spices between them and often took them out into the light to see whether the moths had eaten little holes in the fabric. Valuables were also placed in the chests to keep them safe from thieves. Later Jesus taught: "Do not lay for yourselves treasures on earth, where moth and rust consume and where thieves break in and steal" (Mt 6: 19). As a child, He had seen the chest where the best clothes and valuables were put for safekeeping.

Mary was occupied also in other tasks, which varied according to the season of the year. If Joseph, like many other workingmen, kept goats or sheep, they were entrusted to a shepherd who took them to pasture in the morning and brought them back in the evening. Jesus Himself, at least occasionally, may have been the shepherd who led the little flock to pasture.

Judging from modern conditions and also from ancient records, we may suppose that Joseph owned or rented a small plot of ground on one of the stony elevations outside the village. Our Lord, in the days of His childhood, saw how the new grain sprang from the seed, how the weeds soon threatened it, how it grew quietly and steadily for several weeks until harvest time. These details come to life again in the parables: "A sower went out to sow. And as he sowed, some seeds fell along the path, and the birds came and devoured them. Other seeds fell on rocky ground, where they had not much soil, and immediately they sprang up, since they had no depth of soil, but when the sun rose they were scorched; and since they had no root they withered away. Other seeds fell upon thorns, and the thorns grew up and choked them. Other seeds fell on good soil and brought forth grain, some a hundredfold, some sixty, some thirty" (Mt 13: 3-8).

Nourished from within, the grain grows silently. Having observed it at Nazareth, Jesus describes it later to his listeners in a parable: "The kingdom of God is as if a man should scatter seed upon the ground, and should sleep and rise night and day, and the seed should sprout and grow, he knows not how. The earth produces of itself, first the blade, then the ear, then the full grain in the ear" (Mk 4: 26-28).

Another of Mary's household duties was to provide sufficient fuel without any expenditure of money. Groups of women went out on the barren hillsides and gathered thorns, thistles, dried grass, and small branches from the hedges, bound them in bundles, and carried them home on their heads. In the spring, they gathered wild herbs, which were prepared for food, and in the summer they gathered figs and grapes and dried them for winter use. Thus there was always work to be done.

On one day of the week, the Sabbath, Mary rested. Preparations for the Sabbath were begun on Thursday, for then it was customary to wash the clothes that were to be worn to the synagogue. Soda and potash were already known as cleansing agents, but it is doubtful whether Mary made use of these means. She soaked the clothes, rubbed them, and hung them in the sun to dry. Linens were bleached, and sometimes clothes were ironed to give them a glossy finish.

Mary, the spiritual guide of the boy Jesus

Jesus, who was truly the Son of God, assumed human nature and was therefore truly man, like us in all things except sin, as St. Paul says. As a human being, Jesus experienced a spiritual development; He grew from childhood to boyhood and from boyhood to manhood; like other men He gathered new experiences of life. This experimental knowledge existed in Him side by side with that infused knowledge which He possessed from the beginning. Hence we may rightly speak in general of His human development, and in particular of the religious development of His human nature, keeping in mind at all times that the veil of mystery will never be entirely removed from the life of His soul.

The spiritual awakening of an ordinary child is filled with mystery. In the life of a child a moment comes when we think we can discern in his eyes the first stirring of the soul, as though he were returning his mother's look, or as though the soul had ventured for a moment to come to the threshold of his house. The child learns to sit up, he tries to stand; thrusting his hand uncertainly into the air, he holds the edge of a chair and makes his first step, surprised and frightened at his own daring. He makes the first step alone, then perhaps another, and falls into his mother's arms.

The child tries hard to read the faces of those about him; he watches the posture of others, especially of his mother, and tries to imitate them. Observation is the child's first school, imitation his first lesson; and these are the most important activities during the first months of his development.

In trying to picture to ourselves the relations between Mary and her divine Son, we are always in danger of falling into error by minimizing either Mary's motherhood or the childhood of Jesus. Sometimes Mary is pictured as though she were not really His Mother but, rather, a woman who, knowing indeed that He was the Son of God, beheld His divinity as do the saints in heaven. On the other hand, Jesus is pictured as though He were not really a child, but merely acted as one. He was truly a child,

He did not play at being a child; and His Mother's face was a mirror reflecting the world about Him.

How mysterious was the life of Jesus and Mary during those years when the Child was awaking to its own spiritual life! Jesus was that Child who, more than any other of the children of men, lived in the most intimate union with God; His divinity was united to His humanity, filling all the phases of His human life. And Mary, more than any other mother, was created to lead her Child to God. Her whole demeanor and her every movement, which the Child observed in her even before He could think, was a preparation for that moment when He would grasp the spiritual. Whether she stood by the fire or took the water jug from its place to go to the well, there was always something about her that remained the same; indeed no change could be noticed in her as she came from her prayers to her work and returned again from her labors to pray.

No mother ever bent over her child with such faith as Mary did; in Him she saw not only something immortal and eternal, but the Son of God Himself. Every caress was an act of adoration; and each time He surrendered to her fondling a new grace came to her. And yet it is very probably true, as we read in the writings of the mystics, that whenever Mary fondled the Child she maintained a reverent restraint.

Jesus began gradually to understand His mother's attitude, and He desired to serve God in the same spirit. The truths of revelation, the ceremonies symbolizing them, and the usages derived from them all influenced the Child even more deeply and more irresistibly than musical sounds affect a naturally musical child. When at last the day came when Jesus pronounced the name of God for the first time, He had already formed some ideas concerning God. Now, too, the Child began to ask those mysterious questions which children ask of adults. Just as the doctors in the Temple were astonished at His questions and answers when He was twelve years old, so now there were moments in the home at Nazareth when Mary paused and looked at Him and reflected on what He said.

The daily prayers

All Jewish parents were in duty bound to teach their children to pray. It rested principally upon the father to recite the prescribed prayers for his son as soon as the boy was able to learn them. The

Holy Family at Nazareth was a new creation in mankind; they accepted the traditional forms of prayer and divine worship, but now for the first time these prayers were completely understood. With what seriousness Jesus received the announcement of that kingdom which was above the earth, that kingdom from which He had come into the world! With what ready enthusiasm He repeated after Mary and Joseph the verses of the first prayer taught to children, the prayer which began as follows:

> Hear, O Israel:
> The Lord our God is one Lord;
> and you shall love the Lord your God with all your heart,
> and with all your soul, and with all your might.
> And these words which I command you this day shall be
> upon your heart;
> and you shall teach them diligently to your children,
> and shall talk of them when you sit in your house,
> and when you walk by the way,
> and when you lie down, and when you rise.
> And you shall bind them as a sign upon your hand,
> and they shall be as frontlets between your eyes.
> And you shall write them on the doorposts of your house
> and on your gates (Deut 6:4-9).

This profession of faith in the one true God was the foundation of all other prayers. Later, when Jesus rose up as the teacher of Israel, He confirmed this doctrine. When the doctor of the law asked, "Teacher, which is the great commandment in the law?" Jesus countered by asking, "How readest thou?" He referred him to something well known, namely, to this passage which every Israelite knew by heart, since he was obliged to recite it twice every day; the doctor of the law knew at once to what Jesus was referring and he began to recite the opening verses of this daily prayer (Deut 11:13-21).

This first part of the morning prayer, admonishing the people to subject themselves to God in all things, was followed by the second part, which declares that the people's fortune or misfortune depends on their attitude toward God.

"And if you will obey my commandments which I command you this day, to love the Lord your God, and to serve him with all your heart and with all your soul, he will give the rain for your land in its season, the early rain and the later rain, that you may gather in your grain and your wine and your oil. And he will give grass in your fields for your cattle, and you shall eat and be full. Take heed lest your heart be deceived, and you turn aside and serve other gods and worship them, and the anger of the Lord be kindled against you, and he shut up the heavens, so that there be no rain, and the land yield no fruit, and you perish quickly off the good land which the Lord gives you.

"You shall therefore lay up these words of mine in your heart and in your soul; and you shall bind them as a sign upon your hand, and they shall be as frontlets between your eyes. And you shall teach them to your children, talking of them when you are sitting in your house, and when you are walking by the way, and when you lie down, and when you rise. And you shall write them upon the doorposts of your house and upon your gates, that your days and the days of your children may be multiplied in the land which the Lord swore to your fathers to give them, as long as the heavens are above the earth."

Later, when Jesus said: "Seek his kingdom, and these things shall be yours as well" (Lk 12: 31), He gave a summary of these inspired words which He recited every morning, perhaps even to the last day of His earthly life.

The third part of the prayer (Num 15: 37–40) impressed upon every son of Israel that he must keep the commandments out of gratitude for the deliverance from the bondage of Egypt and must openly profess his membership in God's people by wearing a sign on his clothes.

> The Lord said to Moses,
> "Speak to the people of Israel,
> And bid them to make tassels on the corners of their
>   garments throughout their generations,
> and to put upon the tassel of each corner a cord of blue;
> and it shall be to you a tassel to look upon and remember
>   all the commandments of the Lord,
> to do them, not to follow after your own heart and your
>   own eyes
> which you are inclined to go after wantonly.
> So you shall remember and do all my commandments,
> and be holy to your God.
> I am the Lord your God,
> who brought you out of the land of Egypt,
> to be your God."

Even before Jesus learned this prayer, Mary had attached the blue knotted threads to His garment, the sign of the sons of Israel. As soon as a boy was able to dress himself, he was obliged to wear this sign. Mary knew that this incorporation of her Son into

111

the company of the praying men of Israel was significant for Him, as well as for the people of Israel, for He was the Savior of Israel, and Israel was His people.

Jesus memorized these verses even before he completely understood them as a human being. Morning and evening He listened attentively as Joseph chanted this profession of faith of all pious Israelites. A small box was attached to the doorpost, and through an opening one could touch the parchment on which the sacred words of this prayer were written. When Joseph left the house, he raised his hand to touch the sacred parchment (just as a devout Catholic raises his hand to the holy water font), and he often raised the boy Jesus in his arms that He too might touch the parchment.

Mary took part in these prayers recited in the house at Nazareth; but the actual reciting of prayers was the duty of the men. In the Temple, she attended the sacrifices, though she did not herself offer sacrifice.

In the morning, when the gray dawn separated earth from sky and the great dome above was filled with blue, these prayers were said in the house in Nazareth; and again in the evening, like a chant that never ceased.

The Sabbath

For a devout Jewish family, the synagogue service on the Sabbath was the spiritual support of the week. The Sabbath was the sacred day of rest and of public worship, although synagogue services were held also on Mondays and Wednesdays, which were the days when the courts were in session and when farmers from neighboring villages came to town. An opportunity was thus afforded them of occasionally attending public worship if they had no synagogue in their own village.

On the Sabbath, everyone who could do so changed his linen undergarment and his outer garment, except, of course, the very poor, who had only one shirt and one coat. There were instances of a man and a woman possessing but a single garment; one of the two had to remain at home while the other went to the synagogue. We are told also of an instance of two men having the use of one cloak, which they had borrowed from a third man.

The preparation of food on the Sabbath was strictly forbidden. Nevertheless, part of the day's observance was to have better food on the Sabbath; there were three meals instead of the usual two—before and after the morning service, and following the afternoon service. Since, during the week, the poor had scarcely any food except bread and water, to have something extra for the Sabbath was a simple matter.

The service in the synagogue consisted of readings, addresses, and prayers recited in common. In our Lord's time, a plan had been adopted with regard to the readings and addresses: certain appropriate passages were selected for the Scripture reading on feast days, and the books of Moses were read on ordinary Sabbaths.

In general, the pious Jew conducted himself in the synagogue as a good Catholic does in church. For example, the Jews were given this admonition: "Conduct yourself reverently in the synagogue, do not eat or drink there, do not enter the synagogue in the summer merely to escape the heat of the sun or in the winter to come out of the rain; and private obsequies shall not be celebrated there." The ruins of destroyed synagogues were also considered sacred places and were not to be used as places for the drying of figs and grapes.

The seventh day of the week, the Sabbath, was each time an event for the boy Jesus. At sunset on the evening before, trumpets announced the coming of the Sabbath; in half an hour the Sabbath rest would begin. Workmen in the fields round about the town prepared to return home, the merchants in the bazaars gathered up the wares they had been displaying and put away the stands and tables. Joseph cleaned the workshop, and Mary put her household utensils in their places; the food for the Sabbath had been prepared and put aside in a sort of food chest. Now the Sabbath lamp was lighted, and, like a messenger of God, the holy day entered the house and took possession of it.

At last came the day toward which Jesus had looked with pleasure. With Mary and Joseph, Jesus walked to the synagogue through the streets, which seemed now wider and neater. In the anteroom they washed their hands, as we take holy water on entering the church. Within the synagogue, Mary went to the place reserved for the women, while Jesus and Joseph joined the men.

The synagogue was a more pretentious building than their simple home; it possessed an atmosphere of solemnity. In front, on a platform, was a reading desk to which a man went to read from the Law; back of him, but some distance from the wall, hung a great curtain, behind which was the cabinet with the sacred rolls. Before the reading desk were seats for the prominent men of Nazareth, who during the readings sat facing the people. Some of these men considered these places of honor more important than the service itself and seemed to invite the attention of the congregation to themselves.

The president of the synagogue gave a sign to the sexton, who in turn signaled to the cantor to begin.

First a prayer of praise was offered; the cantor began, "Praise the Lord for He is good," and then enumerated the blessings God had given His people. The men and boys answered in chorus, "For His mercy endureth for ever." Then all arose and recited the prayer, "Hear, O Israel," professing their faith in the true God. At the conclusion of the prayer, the sexton called out the names of those men who were to read from the Law.

This reading was by no means the exclusive privilege of the doctors of the law; for that matter, even boys were permitted to do the reading. It was customary on the Sabbath to have several readers, sometimes as many as seven in succession. To insure a dignified reading, the reader was notified beforehand. It is related of the famous Rabbi Ben Akiba that, being called upon to read from the Law, he declined because he had not been able to rehearse the passage two or three times. The readers were called up in the order of dignity, priests were preferred to Levites, and Levites to the ordinary men of the people.

The reading was an official function, accompanied by appropriate liturgical ceremonies. The reader went to the place designated for the reading, unrolled the manuscripts of the Law, and pronounced a formula of praise: "Praise God who is most worthy of praise." The people responded: "Praised be God forever." The reader gave the passage in Hebrew, which was immediately translated into the vernacular Aramaic; and the translation was at the same time an explanation. It was forbidden to recite the Law from memory. Certain passages intended only for adults were either passed over or not translated into the vernacular. Three years were required to complete the reading of the Law. Following the reading came an address by one of the doctors of the law, given in Hebrew and at once translated into Aramaic. The service concluded with a benediction formula intoned by the cantor and answered by the congregation; if a priest was present, he gave his blessing.

In the afternoon service, there was another Scripture reading, probably a continuation from the morning reading, without the solemn liturgical ceremonies of the morning. Certainly we may suppose that Mary and Joseph did not neglect this further opportunity of increasing their religious knowledge. After the service, people often made a little excursion outside the village.

Some also visited the sick and those who were in mourning. Some learned men, basing their opinion on Shammai, a doctor of the law, taught that such visits were forbidden, but in practice people generally accepted the more lenient view of the school of Hillel. We should note that, even from the beginning of His public ministry, Jesus visited the sick and cured them on the Sabbath. Perhaps this custom of thinking of the sick on the Sabbath went back to the days when He accompanied Mary and Joseph on Sabbath afternoons.

Mary's humility in Jesus' company

When Jesus began to wash the feet of His disciples, Peter remonstrated, saying: "You shall never wash my feet." Jesus answered: "If I do not wash you, you have no part in me." Then Peter asked the Master: "Lord, not my feet only but also my hands and my head!" Peter was here manifesting his humility toward the Master, but it was a humility as yet not sure of itself, an unbalanced humility, turning now to one extreme and then to the other.

With regard to Jesus, Mary found herself in a position far more difficult than Peter did when the Lord knelt at his feet; and this position was not for a moment only, but endured for years. Mary was obliged to accept services from Jesus that He did of His own will; as His Mother, she was obliged to give commands to the boy Jesus, obliged to exercise authority over Him. Had she taken Peter's attitude, she would have said, "Lord, I will never give Thee any command." But Mary's humility had reached greater heights than Peter's.

John the Baptist was remarkable for his great humility. When Jesus came to him to be baptized by him, he answered: "I need to be baptized by you, and do you come to me?" But when Jesus said, "Let it be so now; for thus it is fitting for us to fulfill all righteousness," John consented. In this position John found himself only once; but Mary lived thus for many years.

Let us suppose an instance that may have occurred many times. Mary commands the boy Jesus to carry water from the well. If her humility had been uncertain and unbalanced, like that of Peter, she would have thought: "I will go myself. Why should I send Jesus, the Son of God, through the streets with a jug to wait in line with other boys at the well?" We find it difficult to accept duties that outwardly are in opposition to humility and, at the same time, preserve our humility inviolate. Mary's life was an unbroken series of such acts of humility.

When Jesus was twelve years old

In the life of every child a time comes when he seeks to loosen the spiritual ties that bind him to his mother. He does things that he knows will not be pleasing to his mother, although the mother may suspect nothing of this, and he omits doing things that he knows would please his mother. Thus between mother and child an invisible wall rises, which, even after frequent repetition of such acts and omissions, remains hardly perceptible. Not always is the mother intent on the better things and the child inclined to what is less noble; sometimes, indeed, a religious child will be more conscientious than the mother and more careful to refrain from faults that he sees in his mother.

In her inmost self, Mary remained at all times intimately united with Jesus. Like Him, she was ever intent on doing the will of His heavenly Father; for His Father was also her Lord and her God. But, although their sentiments were the same, they did not recognize God's will in each instance in the same manner. That will was made known to Jesus more fully and more directly than to Mary. As compared with His knowledge of the Father's will, hers was imperfect. It was always possible that in certain circumstances Jesus alone understood His Father's will.

At times the Father required something of His Son that Jesus alone had to do. Then Jesus did not make the Father's will known to Mary by long explanations; Mary recognized it when she saw what Jesus did. Thus it was when in His twelfth year He remained in the Temple without telling Mary and Joseph.

At times the Father required of His Son something that affected not merely the life of Jesus, but also that of Mary. Then Jesus made His Father's will expressly known to her, but only when the time had come to do what the Father had commanded. Thus it was when Jesus spoke to her at the wedding feast at Cana. His words in the Temple and His words at Cana are full of mystery. At first glance they appear harsh and unfeeling. But the

116

Gospel narrative does not describe the expression of countenance and the tone of voice that accompanied the words. If we had the complete picture of this event, we would see in the words an evidence of our Lord's conscious divinity.

Jesus remains in the Temple

Now his parents went to Jerusalem every year at the feast of the Passover. And when he was twelve years old, they went up according to custom, and when the feast was ended, as they were returning, the boy Jesus stayed behind in Jerusalem. His parents did not know it (Lk 2: 41–43).

The roads leading to Jerusalem were thronged with people, some on foot, some on donkeys, and some on swaying camels, followed by their servants. Pilgrims from the valleys of the Euphrates and the Tigris, from the mountainous country of Asia Minor, and from the region about Damascus had joined the groups of Galileans. From beneath their plodding feet, the dust clouds rose into the air and descended again on the fields close by, on the silvery olive trees and on the cube-like houses beside the road. As they went along, the pilgrims chanted psalms, the penetrating voices of the leaders hovered over the line of travelers, the melody rose and fell with each verse. The singing in groups warded off weariness. At a bend of the road they looked back to see how much distance they had covered, and they looked ahead to see how much still lay before them.

Children and grownups from villages along the route came out to greet the pilgrims; some, recognizing the psalm that was being sung, joined in the chant and marched along for part of the way or even went on with them to Jerusalem.

Here, in this long train of caravans, Jesus, now twelve years old, walked with the other pilgrims of Israel. Since they had left the well where they watered the animals in Nazareth, His soul had been stirred with deep emotion, which increased as they approached Jerusalem.

The pictures of Jesus on the way to Jerusalem lead us to think of this twelve-year-old pilgrim as a child; but in the East a youth at that age has attained the mental development of a boy sixteen years old among us. Moreover, Jesus was not an ordinary youth; He was, if we may use the term, a religious genius. In His understanding of life—and true religion is primarily concerned with life—Jesus was advanced far beyond those of his age, even apart from His infused divine knowledge.

How He had listened at Nazareth when others spoke of the law of God or of the services in the Temple! It had made a deep impression on His soul; now, on the way to Jerusalem, all these impressions awoke to life, now He saw all these laws and pre-scriptions as a whole.

He observed all that happened on the pilgrimage more care-fully than others, although at the same time His mind was filled with but one thought, the Temple. That was the place where His Father dwelt, there one could pray better than at home or in the synagogue, there alone one could offer sacrifice, there spotless animals were slaughtered and burned at the entrance to the Holy of Holies as a sign that God was the Lord and that the sons of Israel were sinners.

From His human experience, Jesus had no definite notion regarding the consequences of His first meeting with His Father. As yet no thought entered His mind of separating from His parents and staying in Jerusalem; but at every moment as a human being He felt the attraction of the love of God as He had never felt it before.

These mysterious feelings continued when Jesus, the twelve-year-old pilgrim, entered the Temple. He saw not only the exte-rior of the Temple, like an ordinary boy from distant Galilee beholding its glorious structure for the first time. He understood the significance of the whole arrangement. For Him the Court of the Gentiles was more than a place where the animals were bought for sacrifice; it was also a sign that all nations had been called to adore the God of Israel, the Creator of heaven and earth. He stood at the railing and read the warning written on a tablet: "No Gentile may enter within the enclosure. Whoever is appre-hended within must blame himself if he is put to death." Jesus was overcome with holy awe; it was purely by God's grace and not because of any merit of their own that the sons of Israel were permitted to approach closer than others to the Holy of Holies.

What were His thoughts when He beheld the great altar of sacrifice, which overawed even ordinary men? The stream of blood, which had flowed for centuries, was at the same time a confession of man's sinfulness and an admission of man's utter inability to atone for his sins. If the blood of these animals offered in sacrifice had any power to reconcile mankind to God, then certainly what was being done now should be sufficient. Now, on the day before the Passover, thousands of lambs were being slaughtered, and the great courtyard was emptied and refilled several times. It was blood and nothing but blood here at the altar; but all these sacrifices were only symbols and substitutes for a sacrifice that was to come, that sacrifice of which He Himself was both victim and priest.

Jesus stood in the courtyard and saw the fine marble walls of the Temple with their gold ornamentation; He saw the shaded entrance with its curtain; there in the Holy of Holies God dwelt. Only one impulse stirred in Jesus' soul: He must go to Him. It seemed as if His whole life had been only a preparation for this moment. We cannot grasp how His love for God flamed up at that moment. He had now but one wish: to replace all these sacrifices with a better sacrifice, to make all this outpouring of blood superfluous by a more efficacious shedding of blood, to remain here in the Temple always and be sacrificed and consumed for the glory of God, to be the priest who would enter into the Holy of Holies with that blood which was no mere symbol but which would take away the sins of the world.

His Father granted Him one thing: as once He would rest for three days in the sepulcher, He was now permitted to retire from that hidden life of Nazareth into a life in which He was intimately united to God His Father.

All this, which we are only able to indicate, was revealed in His outward behavior. Mary, whose soul was united to Jesus' soul in closest union, observed Him closely and understood unerringly the change that was taking place in Him. She understood how here in the Temple He was attracted by the presence of God; and seeing it she increased her love for God and for her divine Son.

Coming now for the first time on the pilgrimage to Jerusalem with Jesus, Mary recalled the day when she had carried this Boy in her arms into the Temple and the aged Simeon had spoken those words of the conflict that would be waged against Jesus and into which she would be drawn. At the same time, she realized that in the following year Jesus would attain His majority before the Law and would make this pilgrimage as a "son of the Law" and would no longer be so dependent upon her.

During these days in the Temple with Jesus at her side, while she prayed and assisted at the sacrifices, Mary was inwardly bidding Jesus farewell while He was still a minor in the eyes of the Law. The next time they came to Jerusalem He would be a "son of the Law," no longer subject to His parents. While He was still her Child, she offered Him once more to the Most High.

The words of the aged Simeon lived again within her and now, as she beheld Jesus at her side, entirely absorbed in prayer and in God's presence, she offered Him to God. She offered His life with all those fateful things which Simeon had prophesied for Him and for herself. In these moments, indeed, those two were offering themselves to God, and in the sight of God this was the first manifestation of that sacrificial spirit which united the sufferings of Jesus and Mary on Calvary.

But this inner preparation for the redemption was to be followed by a heartrending prelude to those still distant days when her Son would be revealed as the victim of the sacrifice of redemption, and the sword of sorrow according to Simeon's prophecy would pierce her heart. Silently yet swiftly the joys of the feast were changed into anguish and sorrow.

The finding of Jesus in the Temple

Supposing him to be in the company they went a day's journey, and they sought him among their kinsfolk and acquaintances; and when they did not find him, they returned to Jerusalem, seeking him. After three days they found him in the temple, sitting among the teachers, listening to them and asking them questions (Lk 2: 44–46).

During spare time in Jerusalem the pilgrims were occupied with various little tasks incidental to the journey. They sat by the gates of the city and mended their sandals; the sharp stones of the road often cut into the heels and into the soles, which were sometimes made of hemp. Clothes were to be mended also.

Mary and Joseph and the Boy lodged during the feast days in Jerusalem with some acquaintances with whom they had found lodging in other years. The Law did not prescribe that the pilgrims must remain in Jerusalem for the eight days of the feast, but those pilgrims who had come a great distance stayed on in order to rest themselves for the return journey. Thus Mary and Joseph probably remained for the week in Jerusalem. The last day of the festal week was observed as a second holy day, like our second Christmas or Easter Monday. On the following day, the caravans began to depart; not all the thousands of pilgrims, however, could leave at the same time. The departure of the Mohammedan pilgrims after Nebi Musa gives us some idea of the confusion of people, donkeys, camels, sedan chairs, drivers, and traders preparing to depart from Jerusalem. After the feast, the roads leading from Jerusalem were crowded for many miles by caravans following on each other's heels and often mingling together.

Because of these conditions, the people observed a certain method in their travels. On the first day, only a short distance was covered, and the departure was about midday. The rendezvous for the departure, the time of departure, and the place for the first night's lodging were agreed upon beforehand. If anything had been forgotten, or if anyone came too late or had been lost on the way, the mishap could be easily rectified.

In one of these caravans, Mary and Joseph left for their return to Nazareth. Like them, Jesus had heard the announcement of the time of departure, the place where the caravan would assemble, and the place for the first night's stop.

When the caravan arrived at the first stopping place, everyone was present except Jesus. Mary and Joseph went about inquiring among their relatives and acquaintances. No one had seen the Boy during the journey; they must return, therefore, to Jerusalem. Presumably Mary and Joseph returned to the Holy City the same night. The Passover was celebrated in the week after the first full moon of the spring; bright moonlight therefore illumined the road, which was still filled with returning pilgrims. At first they thought that Jesus had been delayed, and they inquired at the place where they had eaten the paschal lamb; they inquired too among their friends and at the shops. As often as Mary saw a boy of Jesus' age, she felt a pang in her heart; she remembered again the words of Simeon: "A sword will pierce through your own soul." Had that hour come so quickly?

"After three days" or, according to our reckoning, on the third day, they found the Boy in the Temple. Until this moment Mary and Joseph believed that not only had they lost the Boy, but that Jesus had also lost them. Day and night they were tortured by the thought that all this time He was trying to rejoin them; now, when they found Him again, the sight that greeted them made them think that it was another Jesus in another world.

During the feast days, the doctors of the law explained the Sacred Scriptures in the Temple. For those living far from Jerusalem, this was the only opportunity to hear the famous expounders of the law. As is still customary in the East, the listeners sat around the teacher on mats with their legs crossed. The teacher sat on a stool, with the roll on his knees. An essential part of the instruction was a dialogue between teacher and pupil. It was said that a good pupil "did not interrupt another, was not precipitate in his answers; he asked questions pertaining to the subject and answered respectfully; he mentioned the first things first and the last things last; if he had not heard of the matter, he answered that he did not know and admitted the truth." Sometimes such ideal pupils were found among the listeners; once a doctor of the law kissed a boy who had answered well and said: "Hail ye, Israelites. You are all most learned from the greatest to the least."

It was like this when Jesus sat among the listeners and heard the doctor of the law. It was wonderful how Jesus asked questions and answered them. The doctor of the law could not resist calling the attention of his fellow teachers to this future teacher of Israel. After the lectures, Jesus was invited into the company of the teachers, and they spoke to Him as if He were a famous man of the law from Alexandria spending some days in Jerusalem. It was thus, after their long search, that Mary and Joseph came upon the Boy.

Mary's first thought must have been: Jesus did not lose us; He left us purposely. She said therefore: "Son, why have you treated us so? Behold, your father and I have been looking for you anxiously." He answered: "How is it that you sought me? Did you not know that I must be in my Father's house?" The Evangelist remarks that Mary did not understand these words. Even today we do not understand their full import.

"How is it that you sought me?" Even this question is not easy to understand. Did Jesus wish to say to Mary and Joseph that they should not have looked for Him at all, or that they should have come directly to the Temple and sought Him there? Furthermore, Jesus said: "Did you not know?" They should have known, therefore, when they began to seek Him, that He "must be in his Father's house." These words indeed tell us that Jesus had remained in the Temple in conformity to the will of His Father, who was the Lord of the Temple.

However we may interpret these words, the fact remains that in Joseph's presence Jesus refers to another Father, to "his Father." In these circumstances any other well-bred Israelite boy would have asked his parents' forgiveness, but Jesus did not. His words, however, were not as harsh as they sound to us. Precisely at times like this the tone of voice and the look of the eyes are very important, especially between a mother and child. The Evangelist refers to Jesus' answer as "the saying which he spoke to them," that is, no ordinary expression, but a saying like the sayings of the prophets.

With regard to this "saying," we may easily lose sight of one thing. It was here in the Temple that Jesus for the first time expressly referred to God as His Father and supreme Lord. Mary and Joseph knew the hidden mystery of the Child, but until now His life had been so hidden that they were unprepared for this manifestation of His divine Sonship and this open reference to it. Here, for the first time, the divinity in Jesus made itself known and in such a way that it was something unapproachable for Mary. The Evangelist says that Mary and Joseph did not understand this saying. The remark is significant, for it tells us that until this time Mary had received no special revelations that might make known to her how she should act toward Jesus, and how she should conduct herself in such unforeseen occasions as this. An incident similar to this one occurred many years later, when Mary at Cana saw her Son rise up as the Messiah announced by John the Baptist.

Mary and Joseph were both consoled and surprised when Jesus joined them again and went down with them to Nazareth. Would it not have seemed natural for Him to attach Himself to one of the doctors of the law and remain in the vicinity of the Temple? But "he went down with them and came to Nazareth."

After the anguish of their search in Jerusalem, other mental sufferings awaited them on their return to Nazareth. What should they say to the inquisitive neighbors who would rush to the doors and besiege them with questions: "How long did you look for Him? Where did you find Him?" What answer should they make, now that they themselves no longer understood the Boy? They could indeed tell how they found Him in the Temple, but not the answer He had given them, that "saying" which they did not understand: "Did you not know that I must be in my Father's house?" They could not tell of these words of their Son, which they themselves did not comprehend, and reveal them to others, who might misinterpret them.

How quickly gossip flew back and forth in the neighboring houses in Nazareth after their return! We must remember how in these small villages everyone is interested in any unusual occurrence and how the matter is discussed and judged again and again. Mary and Joseph were obliged to submit to all this. Jesus' stay in the Temple was not only a manifestation of Himself to the doctors in the Temple; it was also a revelation to Mary and Joseph and to His relatives. For Mary all this was a prelude to that loneliness on Calvary when she could not justify her Son before men because she was too close to Him and knew the mystery of His being.

After the return to Nazareth

And he went down with them and came to Nazareth, and was obedient to them; and his mother kept all these things in her heart (Lk 2:51).

"And he went down with them and came to Nazareth, and was obedient to them." This sentence may lead us to believe that, after the mysterious occurrence in Jerusalem, life continued in Nazareth as before. But it was not so.

After those anxious days of the Passover pilgrimage, life in the home at Nazareth was very different. Nothing changes and intensifies our love for another so much as to lose him for a while. A mother stands at the bedside of her sick child; it is night, and she is alone with him. Beads of perspiration stand on the youthful brow—she does not know whether it is a sign of strength or weakness; the breathing is softer and softer—she does not know whether it is health-bringing sleep or a gradual sinking into death; little sounds come from the child's lips—are they signs that he still lives or are they the last expiring sighs? In the moment when her anxiety has reached the breaking point, the child opens his eyes, and in them is the look of one who has returned to himself. Now a new love awakens in the mother's heart; and from now on her attitude toward the child will be changed.

After Jesus' return to Nazareth, Mary's love for Him experienced this change and intensification. But He did not recover from some sickness that, if it should recur, would be promptly recognized. He had gone from her unexpectedly and, when she found Him, He gave no clear explanation for His act, leaving the future uncertain. Possibly He would again be in similar circumstances—would again separate Himself from Her without giving word beforehand. From this day on, Mary's love for Jesus was mingled with a feeling of anxiety.

124

Mary could no longer feel secure that the morrow or the next year would be as today. The days went by uneventfully, and for Mary and Joseph this itself was incomprehensible and mysterious. Jesus' obedience was as incomprehensible as His remaining in the Temple. The shadow of sorrow that had enveloped Mary during the search at Jerusalem never left her. Her joy in Jesus and her anxiety for Him increased with her love for Him; she could no more cease being anxious for Him than she could cease loving Him.

In pictures and legends, popular fancy has supposed many wonderful events to have happened during the period of the hidden life. Among these the most cherished scene is as follows: Jesus is working in the shop of His foster father, imitating Joseph at work, after the manner of children. He takes some beams of wood and forms a cross, while Mary and Joseph, deep in thought, look on. A similar thing actually happened in the spiritual realm, not once, but daily. And every day Mary recalled the words of Simeon and thought of all the pain and sorrow awaiting her Son.

Mary and the Psalms

As a maiden and, later, as a young woman, Mary had recited the hymns and prayers and psalms of Israel like other pious Israelites, like Elizabeth and Anna, like Zechariah and Simeon. Filled with longing for the consolation of Israel, for the coming of the Redeemer, she had treasured in her heart every word that spoke of the coming Messiah. Now, during the hidden life, she read a new meaning in the psalms, now she knew that Jesus, her Child, was the promised Redeemer. She heard the same psalms chanted, she recited the same prayers; each year she listened to the same excerpts read from the historical and prophetical books. But now all these things were mysteriously changed. While the other worshipers said these prayers as always and chanted the psalms, for Mary they were now changed.

For the others these prayers continued to be all that they knew of the coming Messiah; but for Mary they were no longer the central point. For her these mysterious words of longing and expectation, these lamentations and prophecies, were centered on her Son Jesus. Whenever she prayed, her thoughts turned to Him; and whenever she thought of her Son, she recalled all those things written about Him in the Scriptures. All those passages which had been impressed upon her mind and had been garnered into her soul like the harvest of a lifetime were made alive by an intimately personal interest.

She did not, of course, understand in detail these mysterious words, she did not know yet how these joys and sorrows, these victories and defeats of her Son would be entwined with each other in the compass of a lifetime. To the ancient prophecies, one had been added that referred to her alone, pointing to the days of sorrow and suffering that were to come for her and for the Messiah. "A sword will pierce through your own soul." Thus Simeon had spoken to her after the birth of the Savior. In her soul this prophecy acted like a powerful magnet, attracting to itself all the prophetic passages of Scripture that spoke of "the man of sorrows," and of the mockery and pain, the derision and destitution foretold of Him.

If we carefully read the Psalms that were accepted as Messianic, keeping in mind the new understanding Mary had of them, we can in some way appreciate how their meaning changed for her. What were her thoughts now when she read Psalm 110?

"Sit at my right hand,
till I make your enemies your footstool."

The Lord sends forth from Zion your mighty scepter.
    Rule in the midst of your foes!
Your people will offer themselves freely
    on the day you lead your host
    upon the holy mountains.
From the womb of the morning
    like dew your youth will come to you.
The Lord has sworn,
    and will not change his mind,
"You are a priest for ever
    after the order of Melchizedek."

The Lord is at your right hand;
    he will shatter kings on the day of his wrath.
He will execute judgment among the nations,
    filling them with corpses;
he will shatter chiefs
    over the wide earth.
He will drink from the brook by the way;
    therefore he will lift up his head.

We can only surmise what she thought when she read of her ancestor David: "The Lord says to my lord." She was the first, with the assistance of the Holy Ghost, to understand the hidden meaning of these mysterious lines. She was the first who could say: "This word has come to pass." With great reverence she sought to understand those things that were still veiled in darkness. "You are a priest for ever after the order of Melchizedek." What was hidden beneath these words? When would they be fulfilled in her Son, who was growing up to be a carpenter, cutting and smoothing plow beams and fashioning doorsills and window sashes?

One thing she realized even now. The majestic words with which the psalm opened: "The Lord says to my lord: 'Sit at my right hand, till I make your enemies your footstool,' " referred to the same future event as the words the angel Gabriel had addressed to her: "The Lord God will give to him the throne of his father David, and he will reign over the house of Jacob for ever." Both passages refer to that time when Jesus would ascend the royal throne promised Him by His Father and begin His eternal reign. And as Jesus was to be an eternal king, so His priesthood was to be everlasting: "You are a priest for ever after the order of Melchizedek."

But Mary's heart was filled with trepidation when she recalled the words of another psalm. One passage (Ps 22:9-10) seemed intended especially for her:

Yet thou art he who took me from the womb;
thou didst keep me safe upon my mother's breasts.
Upon thee was I cast from my birth,
and since my mother bore me thou hast been my God.

But before coming to those words, she read these appalling lines:

But I am a worm, and no man;
scorned by men, and despised by the people.
All who see me mock at me,
they make mouths at me, they wag their heads.
"He committed his cause to the Lord; let him deliver him;
Let him rescue him, for he delights in him!"

Immediately after the reference to the mother, the psalm continues with the soul-stirring lamentation:

Be not far from me,
for trouble is near
and there is none to help.

Many bulls encompass me,
    strong bulls of Bashan surround me;
they open wide their mouths at me,
    like a ravening and roaring lion.

I am poured out like water,
    and all my bones are out of joint;
my heart is like wax,
    it is melted within my breast;
my strength is dried up like a potsherd,
    and my tongue cleaves to my jaws;
thou dost lay me in the dust of death.

Yea, dogs are round about me;
    a company of evildoers encircle me;
    they have pierced my hands and feet—
I can count all my bones—
    they stare and gloat over me;
they divide my garments among them,
    and for my raiment they cast lots.

How would it all be when this prophecy would be fulfilled in her Son? What was she to think of those terrifying words: "My God, my God, why hast thou forsaken me?"

"A sword will pierce through your own soul," Simeon had said to her. Did not these words refer to the same future event as the words of the psalm? The emotions thus awakened within her were the same as those awakened by Simeon's prophecy when he spoke of her as the future Mother of Sorrows.

But the lamentation did not end with lamenting, the prayer did not remain a petition. The lament was changed into jubilation, and the prayer was changed into joyous thanksgiving.

I will tell of thy name to my brethren;
    in the midst of the congregation I will praise thee:
You who fear the Lord, praise him!
    all you sons of Jacob, glorify him,
    and stand in awe of him, all you sons of Israel!
For he has not despised or abhorred
    the affliction of the afflicted;
and he has not hid his face from him,
    but has heard, when he cried to him.

From thee comes my praise in the great congregation;
    my vows I will pay before those who fear him.
The afflicted shall eat and be satisfied;

> those who seek him shall praise the Lord!
> May your hearts live for ever!

The psalm spoke of a great sacrifice in which all those who were poor and wretched in Israel would participate. Not only the poor of Israel: the Gentiles too would be present at this great sacrificial meal. Once Simeon had called the Savior the glory of Israel and a light to the Gentiles, and now in the psalm (Ps 22: 27-32) the sons of Israel and the Gentile nations are brought together to the same sacrifice.

> All the ends of the earth shall remember
> and turn to the Lord;
> And all the families of the nations
> shall worship before him.
> For dominion belongs to the Lord,
> And he rules over the nations.
> Yea, to him shall all the proud of the earth bow down;
> before him shall bow all who go down to the dust,
> and he who cannot keep himself alive.
> Prosperity shall serve him;
> men shall tell of the Lord to the coming generation,
> and proclaim his deliverance to a people yet unborn,
> that he has wrought it.

Not only are the barriers between Israel and the Gentiles raised here, but the division between past and present disappears in these mysterious announcements. A vision of a sacrifice appears, in which all will partake forever.

The death of St. Joseph

Nothing is recorded of that period from Jesus' twelfth year until He was about thirty years old. From the account of the subsequent years, however, we may conclude that during this period an event occurred of considerable importance for Jesus and Mary: the death of St. Joseph. The Gospels contain veiled allusions to the event. When Jesus came to preach in Nazareth, the people asked, "Is He not Mary's son?" A son was thus spoken of only when the mother had been a widow for some time. In another passage we are told that the relatives of Jesus wished to bring Him back home. They would not have thought of interfering in this way during the lifetime of His legal father; they would have had recourse to Joseph. Evidently, at the time of our Lord's death,

Joseph was no longer living; otherwise our Lord would not have given Mary into John's care.

When Jesus became twenty years old, He reached His majority. If His foster father had died before that time, Jesus and Mary would have come under the guardianship of one of their relatives or of some person appointed for the office. If Joseph had died after Jesus' twentieth year, Jesus would have been his heir; the house and the courtyard (which was considered a separate piece of property) and the household utensils descended to Jesus. At the same time, the natural duty of caring for His mother now devolved upon Him. Mary received the marriage portion that had been determined as her personal property at the time of the marriage.

While Jesus was living at Nazareth as a carpenter, Mary's legal relationship with her relatives remained unchanged. In reality, much depended upon the influence of the elders among the kinsfolk and their attitude toward Jesus. If they were favorably disposed, He was entirely unhindered; if, however, they were ill-disposed, they would have found many occasions to show their ill will. How matters actually stood, we do not know. The influence of the relatives would have counted for little if the elders were not much older than Jesus Himself. Possibly the male kinsfolk mentioned in the Gospels (Judas [Jude], Simon, James, and John) were the oldest relatives and not much older than Jesus.

Joseph's death also brought about a change in the relations between Jesus and Mary. Until his death, Joseph was the head of the family and Mary's protector. Thus he exercised some influence on Mary's life with Jesus and regulated it to some extent. Now, as a grown-up son, Jesus must support, protect, and represent His mother. Externally, no doubt, their life was much as we find life today in a good Eastern family. Even with regard to his mother, the son becomes the "master of the house," but he is a mild master who clothes his commands in the form of a request. Mary's duties continued to be the ordinary household tasks: cooking and washing, spinning and weaving, grinding meal and baking, carrying water and gathering fuel. But whenever any question arose concerning the family, Mary submitted the matter to Jesus, and He decided it. If the family was invited to a meal, the invitation was addressed to Jesus, and He replied for both. If, as happened at the marriage at Cana, Mary was already invited, Jesus must be invited as soon as He could be reached. During the meal itself, He was answerable for the family honor. These circumstances, as we shall see, were the background for the miracle at Cana.

Mary alone with Jesus

Since Adam's sin, men have been abysmally ignorant of that state in which the race lived before the fall. They are ignorant of all the glorious human possibilities of that state, both for the individual and for the community. Even the spiritual achievements, the ascents to God of which the average man would have been capable, are a mystery to us. Many of those achievements would have seemed quite "natural" to him, just as today some men regard sin as something natural. Our ignorance is still greater when we consider what might have been possible in that state if entire families and communities had lived together in peace and harmony. Then that community of living would have been an actuality, which now appears in fragmentary fashion in sagas and legends. And our ignorance is even greater if we try to imagine what course the development of the race as one great family would have followed if, through the centuries, generation after generation had lived in the state of grace. Then discoveries and inventions would have served the common good, instead of contributing to the misery and destruction of the race.

Mary grew up, as we have said before, as a person who belonged not to this sin-laden world, but to a sinless world that has long ceased to exist. When, therefore, we try to reconstruct her life, we are always confronted with the insurmountable difficulty arising from our ignorance of how life was in the state of grace. We are insensible to what souls like Jesus and Mary meant to each other in the service of God; without needing to speak to each other, they ascended the steps of sanctity together. Part of our ignorance is that we are so little aware of that ignorance. The difficulties in the way of our knowledge are multiplied because Mary and Jesus, belonging to a sinless creation, were placed in a world groaning beneath the tyranny of sin. Therefore we are unable to picture to ourselves how Jesus and Mary lived together after the death of St. Joseph. The only two people in the world who were full of grace lived together in the same house, the only two who knew of the Incarnation of the Son of God and who were part of the mystery. Even during Joseph's lifetime, this spiritual companionship was marked by an intimacy and a harmony such as had never before been known in any family on earth. But between Jesus and Mary there was a still closer union so that, after Joseph's death, when they were alone, a new life began for them.

During all this time Mary was confronted with a mystery: her Son was busy in the workshop, He sawed and planed, smoothed and fitted, delivered the finished work, and received orders for new work. All this was being done by the Son of God, by the Redeemer who had been promised to the people. In what way would the redemption be accomplished, how would the Savior manifest Himself to the people?

And where was John, Elizabeth's son, who, according to the angel's word, was to appear and prepare the people for the Savior's coming? Was the time so far distant that the precursor had not yet made his appearance? When indeed would that come to pass which Simeon had foretold her?

All these unanswered questions did not disturb her. The thought of Jesus' Messiahship, out of which these questions arose, gave her strength to persevere in silence as the handmaid of the Lord.

Of all the virtues with which Mary was endowed, a significant and indispensable virtue was this, that she was free from any kind of curiosity, although no one ever had such legitimate reasons for questioning. Simple curiosity and genuine anxiety might have impelled an ordinary mother in Mary's circumstances to speak. Yet we have no record that Mary ever asked her Son when He would manifest Himself as the Redeemer and in what manner He would do it. The mystery of His life at Nazareth is in the fact that in no way did He reveal to her what the future held for Himself and for her.

In spite of these uncertainties, there was never a home where such peace and quiet reposed. All the cares and anxieties and labors of ordinary life that Jesus and Mary shared with the other inhabitants of Nazareth were the least of the things that absorbed their thinking and planning. Over and above all the passing and changing cares of her household duties and Jesus' labors in the workshop, was always the thought of Jesus, not as she saw Him here before her, but as her soul beheld Him as the Son of God. Every other thought came and went like a stream while this one thought of Jesus remained firm and unchanging.

We are naturally curious to know something of Jesus' and

Mary's outward appearance. Even in ancient times there were so-called "true portraits of Jesus." Mary was a woman with a fully developed personality, which must have been impressed upon her countenance and expressed in her demeanor; Jesus was a man with a unique personality, and the lineaments of His face and His carriage must likewise have been an expression of that uniqueness. At the same time, the thoughts and feelings of Jesus and Mary were more alike than those of any other two persons. The similarity in appearance between Jesus and Mary was based also on the fact that Jesus had no earthly father, and therefore the facial characteristics that He inherited from His mother were not modified by any influence of the father. This mysterious seal of similarity became more marked as the years went by.

Mary's future sufferings

Jesus foresaw His suffering and death with all the accompanying circumstances. He saw how His mother would follow Him on the path of ignominy and be the witness of His agonizing death on the cross. While at Nazareth He did not think of Jerusalem, of the Mount of Olives, and of Calvary without being reminded of the tragic future. He did not see the soldiers or the servants of the Temple without thinking: "These are they who will one day bind me and mock me and scourge me and place the crown of thorns upon my head."

Every day, every hour, Jesus saw His mother before Him, knowing what awaited her in the days to come. He saw her as she sat by the fire; He saw her lowering and raising the spindle, silent and recollected, as though nothing would ever disturb this quiet peace; He saw her carry water and prepare the dough for baking with those familiar movements of her hands. And at every moment He knew that some day she would be torn from this scene of domestic peace and be made to stand before the "many of Israel" and before all the people as the Mother of the Crucified. Thus He carried within His heart as part of His own Passion the foreknowledge of what His blessed Mother would suffer during His coming suffering and death.

However much He may have desired to sympathize with her because of the coming grief, He did not for one moment wish to assuage her pain against His Father's will. He did not desire to lift the burden of sorrow from her; He sought rather to prepare her for that awful hour when the full weight of grief would rest upon her heart. She must learn beforehand to see Him humiliated. For that reason the time of the hidden life at Nazareth was significant. Still more significant is the fact that, during His public ministry, Jesus allowed Mary to remain in the background. He foresaw the end of the jubilation and the acclaim; He knew that of the crowds following Him only a small number would remain faithful.

Jesus saw in Mary not so much the Mother of the celebrated miracle-worker as the Mother of the Redeemer rejected by the people, the Mother of Him who hung on the cross. Even now He was thinking of how, during the great conflict, Mary's heart would be pierced by the sword of sorrow.

Jesus was to die on the cross, within sight of Jerusalem, in the presence of the people who would be assembled for the Passover. That hour was ever present before His mind, and beneath the cross He saw His Mother standing.

During the days at Nazareth and during His public life, He gave His Mother the sympathy that later she would return to Him on the cross. But He seemed to hold her back during the days of His success, preparing her for that hour when, alone and forsaken, she would stand at the foot of His cross.

Mary's retirement, significant during our Lord's public life, was not the result of a love growing cold, but the gift of an increasing love that looked ahead to the cross, which would be set up as the sign of the redemption.

Mary's vision of Jesus' eternal kingship

He will reign over the house of Jacob for ever; and of his kingdom there will be no end (Lk 1:33).

Mary was governed by one desire: to do the will of God; everything that appeared to her as God's will was for her most desirable and most precious. She did not consider whether it would bring joy or sorrow; she accepted both as if they were one. Often we interpret her answer to the angel, "Behold, I am the handmaid of the Lord," too superficially. Beneath that declaration lay a most earnest surrender to God's will; a surrender so complete and so perfect that its consuming zeal did not appear outwardly.

Besides Simeon's words, Mary kept in her heart the words that the angel Gabriel had addressed to her and that seem to be in contrast with Simeon's words: "The Lord God will give to him the throne of his father David; and he will reign over the house of Jacob for ever; and of his kingdom there will be no end."

In this surrender to the divine will, which sprang from her burning love of God, Mary held fast the words of the angel and of Simeon with a constant will, hoping only that God's holy decree would be accomplished. The angel, in his first message, said nothing about suffering, not indeed because he would thereby more readily induce her consent to the Incarnation, but because in God's plan the kingship of Jesus the Son of God was the end and purpose of the Incarnation. Therefore the angel spoke of it alone, and therefore she too looked always for the establishment of the divinely promised eternal kingdom of Jesus her Son.

V.

The Miracle at Cana

The influence of relatives

The family lists given in the Bible may seem to us today simply irrelevant interruptions of the narrative. But, for readers of that day, these genealogies served as outlines of the family history of which the narrative was a part.

In those times the bond of blood relationship had an importance that we can hardly appreciate today. All decisions affecting the welfare of any relative were regarded as the concern of the whole group. This was especially true when the question arose of admitting someone into the circle of relatives by way of marriage. On the other hand, an individual had the right to call upon his relatives for help in times of need. A generally accepted view was that if a person became successful and attained a prominent position, he was in duty bound to raise his relatives to his own level. Accordingly, prominent and affluent members exercised an unrestrained influence over the group of relatives. Herod is an outstanding example of a man who reached a high position and attempted to elevate his brothers and sisters and other relatives to his own eminence. He is likewise an example of a family chief treating the members of the family group as his subjects who, if they value their lives, must render obedience to his commands.

When relatives thus form an organized unit, the individual member may be ostracized if he does not conform. In early times this exclusion was called "the cutting-off from the family." This ostracism occurred, for example, when a member of the group took a wife who was not of equal birth. The casting out of the recalcitrant member was then performed with public ceremony. The relatives shattered on the ground a vessel filled with fruit and announced: "Brethren of the house of Israel! Our brother has taken a wife who is beneath him, and we fear that his posterity will be mingled with our posterity. Come, therefore, and eat of this fruit as a sign to future generations that his descendants shall not mingle with our descendants." The ostracism from the family was decreed for other infractions against the family honor besides marriage cases.

If an impoverished family was obliged to sell its possessions, it was the duty of the closest relative to buy the property; and if, later, the poor member obtained sufficient means, he had the right to buy back his property. In distributing the tithes for the poor, a person was allowed to give half to his poor relatives.

Under these circumstances, the bond of consanguinity might easily become a chain enslaving the spirit. Life was lived at such close quarters in these small villages that a person constantly felt the influence of his relatives' opinions. The different attitudes and viewpoints were manifested in many varied practices. Some recited the prescribed prayers regularly and conscientiously, others neglected them; some said additional prayers, others thought them superfluous; some went always to Rabbi Elias, others adhered to Rabbi Joseph. Some fasted on Mondays and Thursdays, others did not; some gave alms for this good cause, others purposely arranged matters so that their gifts would go for some other cause. Some went up to Jerusalem by way of Samaria, others preferred to go by the road east of the Jordan; some remained in Jerusalem for eight days, others only for the feast day. Some retained the old manner of dress, others adopted the new fashions, with the new cuts and new arrangements of folds and plaits. Some believed the Messiah would come as a worldly ruler, others believed He would come as the Redeemer from sin; some thought He would come soon, others thought He would not come until people were less wicked. Some felt themselves bound by the prescriptions about giving tithes, others ignored these duties but insisted on the prescriptions about legal purifications; some made vows to offer sacrifices, others promised prayers and alms.

As a rebellious relative would be made to feel the pressure of the whole "family" group, so a member who was considered too pious, according to prevailing ideas in the matter, might be exposed to much mental suffering. We can easily understand how this was a constant possibility for Jesus and Mary, living in the midst of their relatives, but especially when He revealed Himself as the Messiah.

At each change in Jesus' life, the relations of Jesus and Mary to their kinsfolk also changed. In accord with the three periods in

His life—the hidden life, the public ministry, and the period of His glorification—there were three different attitudes adopted by His relatives. During the period of the hidden life, the relations between Jesus and Mary and their relatives were normal, since the mystery of the Incarnation was still not made known to all.

In the second period, during the public ministry, Jesus' relations with His kinsfolk were extraordinary. He proclaimed Himself the Messiah sent by God, but His relatives were among those who "did not believe in Him."

After the Resurrection, the relatives adopted a new attitude toward Jesus and Mary. Now they believed in Him and joined the community of the new Church, and the earlier rupture was closed. Indeed, within the Church, the blood relatives of our Lord, "the Lord's people," were given a special rank. The episcopal see of Jerusalem was regarded almost as their hereditary possession. What a glorious title it was in the East to be related to the Lord may be seen from a letter written by Sixtus Julius Africanus, about the year 230, to a certain Aristides. According to the writer, there were still living some Christians who boasted that they were blood relatives of the Lord and that they were competent to settle questions about relationships going back to the time of Jesus.

In the following pages we will consider those relatives of Jesus who are mentioned in the Gospels and those with whom He came into closer contact.

The relatives of Jesus at Nazareth

Is not this the carpenter's son? Is not his mother called Mary? And are not his brethren James and Joseph and Simon and Judas? And are not all his sisters with us? (Mt 13: 55-56).

Such as we have described it above was the circle of relatives among whom Jesus and Mary lived at Nazareth. Since in the course of the sacred narrative the relatives are mentioned only in passing, the infrequent references to them may easily be overlooked. We give, therefore, the passages that mention them.

After the wedding at Cana, "he went down to Capernaum, with his mother and his brethren [relatives] and his disciples; and there they stayed for a few days. The Passover of the Jews was at hand, and Jesus went up to Jerusalem" (Jn 2: 12-13). When Jesus was preaching in a certain house, "his mother and his brethren came to him, but they could not reach him for the crowd" (Lk 8: 19; Mt 12: 46; Mk 3: 31). In connection with our Lord's preaching in the synagogue at Nazareth, we read: "Is not this the carpenter's son? Is not his mother called Mary? And are not his brethren James and Joseph and Simon and Judas? And are not all his sisters [female relatives] with us?" (Mt 13: 55–56). Of the Crucifixion, St. John writes: "But standing by the cross of Jesus were his mother, and his mother's sister, Mary the wife of Clopas, and Mary Magdalene" (Jn 19: 25). St. Matthew records: "Among whom [the women who had followed him from Galilee] were Mary Magdalene, and Mary the mother of James and Joseph, and the mother of the sons of Zebedee" (Mt 27: 56). St. Mark says: "Among whom were Mary Magdalene, and Mary the mother of James the younger and of Joses, and Salome" (Mk 15: 40). Before the Feast of Tabernacles, "his brethren said to him, 'Leave here and go to Judea, that your disciples may see the works you are doing.' . . . For even his brethren did not believe in him" (Jn 7: 3, 5). In the Acts of the Apostles we read: "All those with one accord devoted themselves to prayer, together with the women and Mary the mother of Jesus, and with his brethren" (Acts 1: 14). In his first letter to the Corinthians, St. Paul declares that he possessed the same rights "as the other apostles and the brethren of the Lord and Cephas" (1 Cor 9: 5).

The Holy Family, strictly speaking, consisted only of Joseph, Mary, and Jesus; the "brethren" and "sisters" were not brothers and sisters but other relatives. This is clear from several passages in the Gospels.

From Mary's words to the angel we may conclude that after the birth of Jesus she continued her life of virginity within marriage. She said expressly: "I have no husband." This form of the present tense included past, present, and future. It was as though someone should say: "I do not sing," meaning not only that he does not sing now, but that he does not sing at all.

When Jesus' "brethren" came to Him (Mk 3: 31), they took the position of elder brothers with respect to a younger brother; but we know that He had no elder brothers, since He was the firstborn. These men were, then, not brothers in the strict sense, but close relatives.

When Jesus rose up in Nazareth to preach, the people referred to Him as "Mary's Son." The expression can best be explained if Jesus was Mary's only Son. At the end of our Lord's life, John took the mother of Jesus to himself. This would have been unusual if any brothers or sisters of Jesus were living.

Whenever, therefore, the Bible speaks of "brethren" or "sisters" of Jesus, the expression means relatives outside the Holy Family. That they were called "brethren" and "sisters" was a result of the limitations of the language. The Jews had no proper expression for "cousin"; all close relatives were called "brethren" or "sisters." Thus Abraham said to Lot: "We are kinsmen [brethren]" (Gen 13: 8), whereas they were really cousins; the sons of Cis, Eleazar's brother, are called the "brethren" of Eleazar's daughters (1 Chron 23: 22).

Nor does it militate against this view that in the Gospels Jesus is called the "first-born," since the term was used to designate the boy who must be bought back according to the Law. The expression "first-born" was used whether other children followed or not. In a record discovered in Egypt dating from our Lord's time, a boy is called the first-born even though the mother died at his birth. Clearly, then, the word "first-born" was used even when there were no other children.

Nor is the statement that Joseph "knew her not until she had borne a son" (Mt 1: 25) an indication that Mary had other children besides Jesus. The literal translation does indeed give rise to some misunderstanding, but the Aramaic word here translated "until" is not coextensive with the English "until." This will be clear from a sentence taken from a non-biblical writing. A certain learned man said of a gifted pupil: "This I know, that this man will not depart from this world until he decides questions of doctrine." Did the teacher wish to say that the pupil would die immediately after rendering his first decision as a doctor of the law? No, he merely wished to say that this pupil would some day be a famous scholar. When, therefore, Matthew says: "He knew her not until she had borne a son," he merely wishes to say that, after Joseph had taken Mary to his house, he did not "know" her and that soon afterward Mary brought forth her Son. Nothing is said of Joseph's relations with Mary after the birth of Jesus. Other passages in the Gospels must form the basis for the solution of the question.

How closely related to Jesus and Mary were these relatives mentioned in the Gospels? Of those persons, probably Mary the wife of Clopas is the closest relative of Mary the Mother of Jesus. That two sisters bore the same name may be explained by the possibility that they were half-sisters. Besides Mary the wife of Clopas, four male relatives are mentioned: Simon and Jude, James the younger and Joseph; they are always mentioned in pairs, and the members of each pair were probably more closely related.

What follows is not intended as the result of scientific research in this matter of the Holy Family's genealogy, since, after all, the question of Jude's relationship with Simon is of little importance in Mary's life. The significant circumstance, after all, is that Mary lived in the midst of close relatives.

One theory supposes the relationship as follows: Mary, the wife of Clopas, married twice; from the first marriage (probably with Alphaeus) she had two sons, James and Joseph, whereas Simon and Jude were children of the second marriage. Another theory supposes that James and Joseph were sons of Mary, a sister of St. Joseph, and that Simon and Jude were sons of Clopas, a brother of St. Joseph. During the Middle Ages, the following theory won favor: Anna, the mother of Mary, married three times. Mary the mother of Jesus was a child of the first marriage (with Joachim). From the second marriage (with Clopas, a brother of St. Joseph) was born the Mary who later married Alphaeus, by whom she had four sons (James, Joseph, Simon, and Jude). Of Anna's third marriage was born a third Mary, who later married Zebedee, by whom she had two sons: James the greater and John the Apostle. Besides these relatives who lived in Nazareth, Mary had a relative in the hill country of Judea, Elizabeth the wife of the priest Zechariah.

Jesus goes to John the Baptist

Then Jesus came from Galilee to the Jordan to John, to be baptized by him (Mt 3:13).

Amid such circumstances as we have just described, Jesus lived as a carpenter until He was thirty years old. About this time news came to the village of Nazareth that a man had appeared on the shores of the river Jordan who called himself John and preached: "Repent, for the kingdom of heaven is at hand." Soon afterward, some men of Nazareth went to the Jordan to see the prophet who was so much talked of. They returned so enthusiastic about what they had seen that people in Nazareth formed traveling parties and went to the Jordan. The religious enthusiasm that was spreading from the Jordan valley over the whole land of Israel now took hold of the cities and villages of Galilee. From the greatest doctors of the law to the most obscure beggar sitting by the city gate, everyone was convinced that by the "kingdom of heaven" was meant the time for the coming of the Messiah.

Then the day came when Jesus too left Nazareth to go to the Jordan. The same Jesus who later, after the multiplication of the loaves, was so careful that nothing be lost of what remained after the people had eaten, assuredly maintained good order in His carpenter workshop. Now He put away His tools, said farewell, and began the journey.

He probably told His mother only that He was going to John on the Jordan and revealed to her nothing of what would follow in consequence of this decision. In obedience to His Father's command, He wished to begin the proximate preparation of redemption by being baptized by John.

What were Mary's thoughts as she remained at home alone in Nazareth? The first news she heard of the appearance of John awakened something in her inmost soul. Year after year, she had waited and listened for some news of that John, the son of Elizabeth. Now, at last, what had been foretold and what must come to pass before the Redeemer manifested Himself was happening. The angel had indeed said to Zechariah in the Temple: "He [John] will turn many of the sons of Israel to the Lord their God, and he will go before him in the spirit and power of Elijah, to turn the hearts of the fathers to the children, and the disobedient to the wisdom of the just, to make ready for the Lord a people prepared."

The hour had come at last. With the fulfillment of that first prophecy, the prophecy of Simeon stirred within her: "Behold this child is set for the fall and rising of many in Israel, and for a sign that is spoken against (and a sword will pierce through your own soul also), that thoughts out of many hearts may be revealed." At the same time she recalled the angel's prophecy in her home, which she had left shortly before her marriage: "The Lord God will give to him the throne of his father David, and he will reign over the house of Jacob for ever; and of his kingdom there will be no end." Her faith in the angel's declaration gave her at all times strength to bear the words of Simeon's prophecy and to wait patiently for their fulfillment. This expectancy of some future trial for her Child and herself became tenser each time an unusual event occurred in the life of Jesus, as, for example, when He remained in the Temple at Jerusalem.

When He went to the Jordan and remained away week after week, the words of Simeon's prophecy echoed in the empty stillness of the house. Day and night her thoughts were with her Son; never before had He been away from her so long.

During these lonely days of waiting, an event occurred that may seem to us somewhat strange, in view of Mary's anxious spirit. She had been invited to a wedding in Cana, and she accepted the invitation. It was a hardship for her to go to a wedding feast, now that her soul was filled with anxious expectation. She understood, of course, that as a somewhat elderly woman and a widow she would be expected to assist in preparing the meal and caring for the guests. Had she followed her inclination, she would have remained at home while Jesus was absent; but she made the sacrifice. Her readiness to be of service was magnificently rewarded by Jesus, for there at Cana He came to her. And there He began that outward separation from His mother which would mark His public ministry.

The wedding at Cana

In his Gospel, St. John selected certain incidents in the life of Jesus. Among these was the wedding at Cana. In his account of that event, we draw attention to two circumstances. First, the narrative is so placed as to conclude that period during which Jesus gathered His first disciples about Him; the Evangelist apparently sees a connection between the calling of the Apostles and the wedding feast. Second, in the first part of the narrative, the Evangelist accords Mary a prominent place; but we do not immediately see why she is considered as having been influential in the working of the miracle. Indeed, our Lord's words to her seem at first glance to be a reproof.

Since the miracle at Cana was the first of Christ's miracles, it is significant in several respects. For the first time, Jesus, who until then had been known by all only as a carpenter, appeared as the Messiah before the gathering; among them, besides the other wedding guests, were His relatives, His disciples, and His Mother. His manner of performing this first miracle would determine His attitude toward them all during His public ministry until His Passion. The miracle at Cana was the farewell to His hidden life and the solemn beginning of His public activity. First we will describe the attitude of the eyewitnesses and the customs and usages amid which the miracle took place.

Marriage customs

On the third day there was a marriage at Cana of Galilee (Jn 2:1).

A marriage celebration was a religious feast. Charity prompted attendance at the various marriage festivities, from the adorning of the bride to the joyous gathering in the home of the groom.

The marriage celebration began when the bride was publicly brought to her new home. Wednesday was generally chosen, since it was almost midway between Sabbaths. The celebration frequently lasted seven days, and people spoke of a wedding week rather than of a wedding day.

The wedding customs and usages involved a considerable expense for the bridal couple. But these customs also protected them from the burden of excessive expense, because each guest was expected to bring a gift. These gifts were equivalent to a number of loans without interest. The newly married couple, as years went on, would make a wedding gift of approximately the same value on the occasion of the marriage of anyone belonging to a family that had given them a wedding present. The custom was so strictly observed that in old sayings the wedding gift was expressly called a loan. It was so regarded in the law, and its repayment, as we have just described, could be enforced by legal procedure.

These marriage customs are not, as we may think, peculiar to the East. In certain Alpine villages similar customs are observed. In one district of the Alps the "best man" makes a list of the wedding gifts presented by the relatives and friends, making a notation whether the gifts are "donated" or "given." For those gifts which are "donated," the bridal couple are not obliged to make a return gift; but if the gift is merely "given," the couple must reciprocate with a similar gift at the next wedding in the "giver's" family.

Usually the gifts were not in money; more often they were household articles and food that could be used at the wedding feast. Therefore, wine was a favorite gift to the bridegroom. For festivities attended by many guests who stayed for several days, a considerable amount of wine was needed.

In this matter, we must rely upon ancient witnesses, since

Muhammad's prohibition of wine made some changes in the marriage customs of the East. In ancient times, gifts of wine were important. Each man invited to the wedding generally brought a jug of wine for the bridegroom. Indeed, when a man was seen carrying a jug of wine, he was supposed to be on his way to a wedding.

In the cities, even before the destruction of Jerusalem, special societies were founded to perform such works of mercy as attendance at weddings and funerals. These societies made the customary gifts on such occasions for their members. Later, a rule was made that no one should bring to the house of the wedding a jug filled with water, thus giving the impression that he was bringing a gift of wine. This was permitted, however, for those who were members of the above-mentioned societies, for they had already fulfilled their duty through the society.

Not all the guests arrived the first evening. This is clear from the old regulation, which provided that the bridal blessing was to be given whenever a number of guests arrived. It was understood that late arrivals, like Jesus at Cana, were no less obliged to make a gift to the bridegroom; the only difference was that the guests who arrived at the beginning of the wedding presented their gifts together as a kind of homage to the bridal couple, whereas those coming later presented their gifts individually.

Jesus arrived at Cana after the wedding feast had begun. Since, legally, He was the head of the house at Nazareth, and since Mary had been invited, He was of course invited as soon as He could be reached. The disciples were invited because of Jesus, as members of His following. According to recognized custom, He was obliged to make a gift not only for Himself, but also for His disciples. Because they arrived late and the ceremonious presentation of gifts had already taken place, Jesus was free to present His gift when He chose. For Him to come without making a gift would have been very improper.

Under ordinary circumstances He might have accepted the invitation for Himself alone and allowed the disciples to go elsewhere; but under the present circumstances this was impossible. He came not simply as a relative or friend; He came as the Messiah publicly proclaimed by John the Baptist and accompanied by those whom He had chosen as His disciples. The matter, therefore, stood thus: Jesus had to be invited because His Mother was present at the wedding; and those also had to be invited whom He had designated as His Messianic following. Jesus was the head of the family at Nazareth and as such responsible for it; He was also the head and master of a spiritual family, the family of His disciples, and likewise responsible for them, according to accepted custom. If, therefore, He wished to make the gift usually offered by men, it must be a gift of wine.

The fact that Jesus appeared as the Messiah changed the situation in other respects. As soon as the news went abroad that the Messiah had come, many came, not out of regard for the bridal couple, but to see the Man whom John had declared to be the Messiah. Just as, later, the Samaritans, hearing the news from the woman, went out to Jacob's well, so now several villagers flocked to the bridegroom's house. Consequently, many of the people present were not merely guests of the bridegroom, but in a way Jesus' guests as well; because of Him the number of guests was increased.

The duty of serving the guests belonged to the "steward of the feast," who was usually a relative or friend of the bridegroom. The steward took charge of the festivities and saw to it that sufficient food and drink were provided; his principal duty consisted in mixing the wine, since the heady native wine was never taken without a mixture of water.

The steward performed his duties with dignity; during the days of the festivity he was the official host. The bridegroom was, so to speak, enveloped in a cloud of solemnity and was not to be disturbed by ordinary cares; in fact, the bride and bridegroom were called the queen and the king. Therefore, before the wedding the bridegroom informed the steward about the provisions of food and drink for the guests. If any unpleasantness arose, the steward, if he was tactful, brought the matter to the attention of the bridegroom's relatives without disturbing the bridegroom himself. Thus, when the wine failed at the wedding in Cana, the steward said nothing to the bridegroom, who apparently was one of the last to learn of it.

The steward was assisted by servants and by the women. In some editions of the Bible, servant is translated as "deacon," and the word is to be understood here in its original meaning of "serving at table." The same word is used by St. John when he describes how our Lord was "served" by Martha; this "service" by Martha included the preparation of the food and the serving of the meal. Accordingly, we may conclude that the servants at the wedding in Cana served not only the wine but also the various dishes and, in fact, did everything required for the care of the guests. A family in modest circumstances was not able to have servants of its own, and the relatives of the bride and groom took over these duties. By using the word "deacons," St. John may have intended to show that the waiters were not hired servants or slaves. The matter is of some importance for a correct understanding of what happened at Cana. If the waiters were relatives of the bridal couple, then Mary knew them more or less intimately before they met at the wedding, and they would be more ready to carry out her suggestion and Jesus' direction.

In the country, the women prepared the meal, but in the cities the societies already mentioned undertook this service. It was commonly understood that the women related to the bridal couple would cook the meals when they came to a wedding, especially the older women and the widows. Such, then, was the nature of Mary's participation in the wedding festivities at Cana.

Pictures of the wedding feast at Cana err when they portray Mary as a young woman, more like a sister of Jesus than like His mother. Mary was now approaching her fiftieth year, and at Cana she appeared as a middle-aged matron. She was among the older women who were assisting in the house at Cana, and as such she supervised the work of the younger women and girls. The older women also gave directions to the servants, and thus, even before Jesus arrived, Mary had come into contact with the waiters.

Jesus and His disciples at the wedding

Jesus also was invited to the marriage, with his disciples (Jn 2: 2).

The Evangelist St. John, speaking of the days preceding the wedding at Cana, says that the Baptist, on the day after he had called Jesus the Lamb of God, was again on the banks of the Jordan with two of his disciples, John and Andrew. Seeing Jesus walking, he said: "Behold, the Lamb of God," and the two disciples hearing these words followed Jesus. Jesus turned and said to them: "What do you seek?" They answered: "Rabbi (which means Teacher), where are you staying?" Jesus answered: "Come and see." "They came and saw where He was staying; and they stayed with Him that day, for it was about the tenth hour" (Jn 1: 36–39).

One of the two who had heard the words of the Baptist and followed Jesus was Andrew, the brother of Simon Peter. Andrew, when he saw his brother Simon, said to him: " 'We have found the Messiah' (which means Christ). He brought him to Jesus. Jesus looked at him and said, 'So you are Simon the son of John? You shall be called Cephas' (which means Peter)" (Jn 1: 40–42).

On the following day Jesus wished to go to Galilee. He met Philip and said to him: "Follow me." Philip was from Bethsaida, the home of Andrew and Peter. Then Philip found Nathanael and said to him: "We have found him of whom Moses in the law and also the prophets wrote, Jesus of Nazareth, the son of Joseph." Nathanael said to him: "Can anything good come out of Nazareth?" Philip said to him: "Come and see." Jesus seeing Nathanael coming to Him, said: "Behold, an Israelite indeed, in whom there is no guile!" Nathanael said to him: "How do you know me?" Jesus answered: "Before Philip called you, when you were under the fig tree, I saw you." Nathanael answered: "Rabbi, you are the Son of God! You are the King of Israel!" Jesus said: "Because I said to you, I saw you under the fig tree, do you believe? You shall see greater things than these." Then He said: "Truly, truly, I say to you, you shall see heaven opened, and the angels of God ascending and descending upon the Son of man." Then follows the narrative of the wedding in Cana, beginning: "On the third day there was a marriage at Cana of Galilee" (Jn 1: 43—2: 1).

In this passage is described how Jesus chose His disciples, each one of whom at once told an intimate friend what had occurred. They were fired with enthusiasm for Jesus, and in speaking to Him they began already to give expression to their reverence and devotion for Him. John and Andrew, at their very first meeting with Him, called Him "Rabbi."

But this was not all. As they journeyed to Cana, Jesus revealed Himself to these men who had followed Him because of what John the Baptist had said, so that they no longer needed to depend on the testimony of another. Jesus showed them that He possessed supernatural knowledge of the future: he looked at Peter and said to him: "You shall be called Cephas." To another of them, to Philip, He said confidently: "Follow me," showing that He understood Philip. To Nathanael He said: "Before Philip called you, when you were under the fig tree, I saw you," showing that He also knew the past.

From the Gospels we see that the people considered this knowledge of the mysteries of human life in the past, present, and future no less marvelous than the miracles. When Jesus revealed to the Samaritan woman that He knew her irregular life, she said to Him: "Sir, I perceive that you are a prophet." So too Nathanael in his enthusiastic manner, after Jesus told him He had seen him under the fig tree, exclaimed: "Rabbi, you are the Son of God! You are the King of Israel!" No doubt the other disciples had come to the same conclusion, although they were not so quick in expressing themselves.

The disciples still believed that Jesus had received His calling as the Messiah in adult age, that He Himself had not known much of it before this, just as David had been called away from his flocks to be made king, and Amos had been called away from his sheep to become a prophet. Accompanied by these men who were filled with joyous faith in His mission and inspired by a ready and willing loyalty, Jesus came to Cana and was invited to the wedding.

Many questions concerning the Messiah were being openly discussed in those days, since the solemn announcement by the Baptist had been universally accepted. Everyone who came to know anything about the Messiah felt impelled to spread the news, nor were people embarrassed about revealing personal secrets in order to substantiate what they said. The woman at Jacob's well, for example, hurried back to the city and told everybody: "Come, and see a man who told me all that I ever did. Can this be the Christ?" (Jn 4: 29).

When Jesus arrived in Cana, the disciples spoke readily of their conversations with Him. If the other disciples had remained silent, certainly the spirited Nathanael, who was a native of Cana, would not have held his peace. Thus the news was spread from house to house that Jesus, the Messiah, had come to Cana. Soon everyone knew that some men from John on the Jordan had come for the marriage and that the Messiah was with them. And the people of Cana thronged to the house where the wedding was being celebrated.

Those who wished to know more heard how John, the great prophet by the Jordan whom many believed to be the Messiah, had called Jesus the "Lamb of God" and had directed two of his own disciples, Andrew and John, to follow Jesus. They learned that, on the way to Cana, Jesus had admitted other men into His following, that He had promised all of them that they would see wonderful things, the angels of heaven ascending and descending upon Him. The "days of the Messiah" had come.

The disciples also gave enthusiastic testimony of their faith in Jesus. They called Him "Rabbi" (Master) and showed great deference toward Him.

During the first part of the marriage festivities, the bride and the bridegroom were the center of the feast. Now, after Jesus' arrival as the Messiah, that position was occupied by two other persons: Jesus and His Mother.

Today things would follow the same course in the East. Let us suppose that during a wedding a famous sheik from Arabia, a relative of the groom, arrived. Immediately the news would travel about the village that the famous man had arrived, and all the villagers would come together to see him. If the sheik's mother came with him, she too would have a prominent place. A similar thing happened to Jesus and Mary.

Thus the honors accorded to Jesus were partially reflected upon His Mother. If He was the Messiah, then the expression "Mary the mother of Jesus" came to have a new meaning; it was equivalent to "Mary the Mother of the Messiah." Now Mary began to be covered with a great dignity in the eyes of all who were present. To become the mother of the Messiah had for centuries been the ardent desire of countless women. As the mother of the Messiah, Mary would, in the mind of the people, have a share in His power or, at least, she would have great influence with Him. Most people expected the Messiah to be a man of God with great worldly power. It would be prudent, therefore, to be in the good graces of this elderly woman, His Mother.

Among the numerous guests in and about the house were some who held themselves aloof: Jesus' relatives who had also been invited to the wedding. As St. John remarked later, they did not believe in Jesus; even now, when Jesus first appeared as the Messiah, they showed their disbelief. With others who thought as they did, they stood in the dark corners of the house, looked at one another knowingly, shook their heads, and wrung their hands. "What was to be said about this latest turn things had taken in Jesus' life? This relative of theirs had always been a peculiar person, and now He has come to this. He had said nothing of all this to anyone beforehand; He had not asked permission of His mother or of them. It was indeed a matter that concerned them." One thing alone, the testimony that the Baptist had given, restrained their opposition.

Mary greets her Son as the acknowledged Messiah

The mother of Jesus was there; Jesus also was invited to the marriage, with his disciples (Jn 2: 1-2).

This assuredly was not the first time Jesus had been present at a marriage. During the years at Nazareth, if He wished to gain a livelihood as a carpenter, He was obliged to accept such invitations and bring a gift. Had He tried to ignore a custom of such strict obligation as that of attending weddings and bringing a gift, He would soon have lost all His patrons in that small village where all the walls had ears and all the doors had tongues. Instances like this one at Cana had often occurred before. Then Mary had asked Him, as the head of the house, what she should provide as a gift; and they had consulted together about the matter. The conversation between them at Cana had a resemblance to such earlier consultations.

At Cana, however, the situation was different, because they had been unable to speak to each other before the marriage and because Jesus came to Cana not as the "carpenter of Nazareth" but as the Messiah.

After leaving the retirement of her home in Nazareth and meeting Jesus, now with His retinue of disciples, amid the festive confusion at Cana, Mary remained ever the same mother. But, from the reports brought by His disciples, she realized that He had laid aside His carpenter trade like a garment; proclaimed by John the Baptist, He now appeared openly as the Messiah. What had been foretold to Zechariah in the Temple had now come to fulfillment: John had prepared the people for the coming of the Messiah. Jesus was about to manifest His glory. He had told His disciples they would see angels ascending and descending upon Him. That time spoken of by Simeon must be at hand, when the Messiah would become a sign round which the conflict would rage. Those mysterious words of the Baptist: "Behold the Lamb of God, who takes away the sin of the world" (Jn 1: 29), awakened in Mary thoughts of coming sorrow.

If Jesus was manifesting Himself as the Messiah, then He would also reveal the mystery of His divine Sonship. She could not have known that He would reveal this mystery gradually during the course of years; she thought that now events would follow quickly upon one another. Had she given expression to her thoughts, she would have said: "Jesus' hour has now come." By one's hour was meant a period of decisive importance, preordained by God. From Simeon's prophecy, Mary knew that she would be at Jesus' side in His hour when the battle would be raging about Him, and from Gabriel's words she knew that the battle would end in His victory and mark the beginning of His eternal reign. Aware of all this, she felt it her duty to draw close to Jesus and to remain at His side awaiting the time foretold by Simeon, ardently desiring to serve Him in all things.

Mary looked not only upon Jesus, but also upon His disciples, these men whom He had solemnly chosen for His work; in a sense, these men whom He had honored with His confidence became her spiritual sons. This assumption is not founded on exaggerated mysticism, but on the ordinary laws of human life. Would not any mother have done so? A young man brings some schoolmates home with him at vacation time and introduces them to his mother as his close friends. Immediately she begins to have a motherly interest in them. Thus Mary saw in Jesus' earliest disciples the first members of His new kingdom. As she herself had been chosen from poverty and lowliness to be the mother of the Redeemer, she could understand how Jesus had called these simple men of the people to His side.

Jesus meets His Mother after His return from the Jordan

The mother of Jesus was there; Jesus also was invited to the marriage, with his disciples (Jn 2: 1–2).

The accomplishment of a great enterprise and the benefits to ensue will be visualized by a man more vividly at its inception than later, when he is engaged in performing the minor acts that tend to effect his great purpose. Thus, after the days of solitude and recollection in the wilderness and the baptism by John, Jesus had vividly in mind the work He had come to do and the purpose of His mission. He considered not so much the intermediate steps in the work of the redemption as the climax and conclusion of His earthly life, His Passion and death on the cross, by which the world would be redeemed from sin and He would enter into the glory and power of His heavenly Father.

With this in mind, Jesus announced to Peter, upon first meeting him on the road to Cana, that some day he would be called by a new name, that he would be Peter, "the rock." Now, too, Jesus' thoughts were with Mary, who in the beginning, as His Mother, had been incorporated in the work of the redemption and who in the end would occupy a unique position in the work.

When Jesus saw His Mother again in Cana, His heart was filled with a new love for her, a love that was different from the love of a son for his mother, although that earlier filial affection still bound them to each other in the most intimate manner. From that earlier love, as from the heart of a flame, a new love burst forth, the love of the Redeemer for her who was "full of grace" and who had been chosen from among all others to be at His side in the most crucial hour of His life.

Because Mary had been called by the Father to serve in the plan of the redemption and because she had already given her consent, it was not now necessary, as it was with Peter, that she be told for what purposes God had called her. Nor was it necessary to give her a name and an office. She already possessed a name and an office; she was the woman "full of grace," the woman in the plan of the redemption without an equal. It only remained for Jesus to announce to her, who would assist at His sacrificial death, what tasks awaited her in the coming days. That opportunity was given Him at the wedding in Cana.

We are inclined to assume that the meeting of Jesus and Mary in Cana meant the same for both of them; but this was not so. When Mary saw her Son in Cana for the first time after His return from the Jordan, she realized that He came to her clothed with a new role, the Messiah solemnly proclaimed by John. But when Jesus saw His Mother again, He was not only conscious that He was appearing before her for the first time as the Messiah, He saw her now not so much as the earthly Mother to whom He owed His life, but as that woman whom His Father had chosen to be the maternal handmaid in the establishment and continuance of His kingdom on earth. In her humility, Mary had no conception of this new attitude, but after the miracle at Cana it would be clear that He honored His Mother as the maternal cooperator in the redemptive sacrifice.

Mary's request

When the wine failed, the mother of Jesus said to him, "They have no wine." And Jesus said to her, "O woman, what have you to do with me? My hour has not yet come." His mother said to the servants: "Do whatever he tells you" (Jn 2: 3-5).

In the midst of the joyous gathering at Cana, a painful discovery was made: the wine was failing. The ewers were still being filled, but soon there would be no more wine.

Mary had assisted in preparing and serving the meal and was one of the first to learn of the situation; indeed, according to the Gospels, she knew of it before the steward did. This misfortune would be most embarrassing to the young couple, who were rejoicing at the honor Jesus had shown them by His presence. If something was not done, people would talk about how the wine failed at their wedding.

The bridal couple would not be able to excuse themselves on the score of the cost of the wine. Although we have no records of the cost of wine in Palestine at that time, we know that in other Mediterranean countries a quart of wine could be bought for a trifling sum, equivalent to two or three cents in our money. In Galilee wine was probably especially cheap because that was a grape-growing country.

As a last resort, the bridal couple could excuse themselves by saying that the disagreeable situation came about because Jesus' arrival, along with His disciples, had considerably increased the number of guests. Thus the greater part of the blame would fall on Jesus.

At home in Nazareth, Mary had often attended a marriage with her Son, and each time she had asked His advice about what they should give as a wedding present. She had often prepared their gift and presented it on such occasions. Here at Cana she did not doubt that He would avert the threatening unpleasantness. The matter could still be remedied without attracting the attention of the guests. It was, however, no longer proper that Jesus as the Messiah should personally intervene in such a concern; therefore Mary was willing to act for Him and in His name. She had been helping in the preparations for the feast and receiving the gifts and advising about their disposal. In the present quandary, she could be of assistance under Jesus' direction without causing comment. Such indeed was her conception of the future: she thought perhaps that she would continue to remain at His side, ready to serve Him when that time came of which Simeon had spoken. Mary, therefore, went to her Son and said: "They have no wine."

It was not merely a personal request, as if she were asking something for herself. She felt that as soon as she had informed

Him about the situation He would decide to save the poor bridal couple from this disgrace, especially since His presence had increased the number of the guests.

Mary's request included her offer to act as mediatrix, that through her His gift might come to the guests. The request and the offer to act for Him were addressed now, not to the erstwhile carpenter of Nazareth, but to the newly proclaimed Messiah. In His new position she wished to serve Him more perfectly than before and to relieve Him of the duties that were incumbent upon Him as head of the family.

Mary came to Jesus with her request as His Mother, believing that she would continue always to remain with Him and serve Him as His Mother. Under these circumstances, it became necessary for Him to make known to her something of the greatest importance. During the coming time of His public ministry she was not to accompany Him as His solicitous Mother; instead, later, in the critical period of His life when He would be founding the kingdom of God, she would have a place not only as the faithful and solicitous mother but as the divinely appointed cooperator in the work of the redemption and in the kingdom He would establish.

Jesus' reply

And Jesus said to her, "O woman, what have you to do with me? My hour is not yet come" (Jn 2:4).

All that Jesus wished to say to His Mother is contained in His answer to her present request: "Woman, what have you to do with me [i.e., what do we have now in common]? My hour is not yet come." The reply is so succinct that it has received various interpretations.

The first sentence of the answer contains an idiom taken from the vernacular of the people. The sense of such idioms is colored by the immediate circumstances and by the personal relationship of the people engaged in the conversation. All the circumstances surrounding the use of such an idiom must be carefully considered. The question: "What have you to do with me?" was asked in Cana at a time when Jesus and Mary had met in a new relationship, and this fact must be taken into consideration.

Mary had made her request, not for herself, but for the benefit of others. Furthermore, she had offered her own assistance in the difficulty; and she was no longer addressing Jesus as her Son and the head of the house, but as the Messiah. Hence the following were implied in His answer: 1. He declined her personal cooperation; 2. He accepted the situation as pertaining wholly and entirely to Himself, while postponing a decision; 3. He answered not as Mary's Son or the head of the house in Nazareth, but as the Messiah.

To these words by which He declined Mary's assistance, Jesus added: "My hour is not yet come," as though He spoke not for Himself alone. Perhaps the word "woman" belongs to this sentence: "Woman, my hour is not yet come." Jesus used similar expressions on other solemn occasions; for example, when raising the dead to life, He said: "Little girl [or young man], I say to you, arise." Now, as the Messiah, He solemnly addresses Mary with a new title: "Woman." We will explain later how this term is not a general, but a particular and personal, form of address.

From an examination of the Gospels it will be clear that whenever Jesus speaks of His "hour" He has in mind the time of His Passion, death, and Resurrection, those events which He foretold His Apostles in the words: "The Son of man must suffer many things, and be rejected by the elders and chief priests and scribes, and be killed, and on the third day be raised" (Lk 9: 22). In His mind these things were the end and the beginning, the end of His earthly existence and the beginning of His eternal and heavenly existence as the Redeemer. The expression "my hour" used here at Cana referred to that crucial period of His life; but now, used for the first time, it was still obscure and enigmatic.

For Mary, too, these words were vague and mysterious. On other occasions Jesus had given enigmatic answers, from which the hearers understood but one thing clearly: that He possessed greater knowledge about the question than He wished to impart. He gave such answers to His enemies, as when He said to the Pharisees: "Destroy this temple, and in three days I will raise it up" (Jn 2: 19); and also to those who were close to Him, especially when He spoke of what they must suffer for His sake. Thus He said to the sons of Zebedee: "Are you able to drink the cup that I am to drink?" and to Peter: "When you are old, you will stretch out your hands, and another will gird you and carry you where you do not wish to go" (Jn 21: 18). So now, speaking to His mother, He did not wish to make Himself clearer to her.

But Mary possessed knowledge that enabled her to understand these words better than did the others present; at least, she was able to grasp their fundamental significance. She had cherished in her heart the words of the angel telling of the royal throne that Jesus would receive from His Father, and from Simeon's prophecy she knew that the ascent to this throne would be preceded by a bitter conflict in which she and her Son would be united. With this knowledge, she possessed an attitude of mind that prevented her from interpreting these words falsely because of any selfish inclinations.

Out of pure and unselfish motives, Mary wished to remain at Jesus' side, not that she might have the first place in His kingdom, but in order to receive that sword of sorrow according to God's decree. In her judgment of the present question, however, Mary was in error. Like many of her contemporaries, she thought that now, after Jesus had publicly appeared as the Messiah, the development would be rapid, and soon the great conflict would come to an issue. At this time Jesus alone knew that the people would be given a rather long period of grace, during which they could declare themselves for or against the Messiah. Only then, when the period of grace had run its course and the grace had been rejected by the people, would the Redeemer's life reach that painful climax spoken of by Simeon in the Temple.

Inwardly grateful to His Mother for her ready generosity, Jesus pointed out to her that the time when they would suffer together was still distant and therefore her offer of loyal cooperation was premature: "My hour is not yet come."

Mary had expected Jesus to give her some direction as to what she should do; undoubtedly she was surprised at His answer. But He had merely indicated to her that the time had not yet come when He would require her personal assistance; He had not directly answered whether He would or would not come to the aid of the bridal couple. Knowing their predicament and the customs of the country, and understanding her Son's goodness of heart, with sure womanly instinct Mary still hoped for His aid. To prepare the way as much as she could, she went to the waiters and said: "Do whatever he tells you" (Jn 2:5). Mary, as the handmaid of the Lord, submitted perfectly to the will of Jesus; and He, after drawing that line of separation between Himself and His Mother, now fulfilled His Mother's wish because of her persevering maternal trust in Him, which was a symbol and the beginning of her future position as mankind's intercessor with

Him. Similarly, He later rebuked the Canaanite woman, saying that He had been sent only to the children of Israel; but afterward He answered her prayer because she did not cease to trust in His goodness.

The miracle

Now six stone jars were standing there, for the Jewish rites of purification, each holding twenty or thirty gallons. Jesus said to them, "Fill the jars with water." And they filled them up to the brim. He said to them, "Now draw some out, and take it to the steward of the feast." So they took it. When the steward of the feast tasted the water now become wine, and did not know where it came from (though the servants who had drawn the water knew), the steward of the feast called the bridegroom and said to him, "Every man serves the good wine first; and when men have drunk freely, then the poor wine; but you have kept the good wine until now" (Jn 2: 6–10).

In some room of the house or in the courtyard were six large waterpots where the guests washed their hands before sitting at table. Jesus commanded the waiters to fill these waterpots with water. The waterpots contained from seventy to a hundred and twenty quarts, and it took some time to fill them because the water had to be carried from the cistern or the town well. When the waterpots were full, Jesus said to the waiters: "Now draw some out, and take it to the steward of the feast."

To obey this command was a daring venture, unless the waiters thought that Jesus had previously spoken to the chief steward. What would happen if they brought water to the steward, who was expecting a new supply of wine? He would certainly have been displeased at so inconsiderate a pleasantry or would have regarded it as a personal affront. But Mary, who was still active in caring for the comfort of the guests, had prepared the waiters for Jesus' command; and Jesus Himself had made His order emphatic: "Now draw some out, and take it to the steward of the feast." These words give us a picture of Jesus standing by the waterpots and waiting until His orders had been carried out.

Somewhere in the house, in a room close by, stood the large wine jugs to which the waiters had been going to fill their pitchers before carrying these to the chief steward. Now they dipped their pitchers into the water and filled them, and when they brought them to the steward and he dipped his cup into the pitcher, the water was changed into wine. Until then the steward had noticed nothing unusual. But what was this? He tasted, he tasted again to make certain—yes, his first judgment was correct: this wine was much better than the other. It must have been taken from a supply that he had not been told about.

The steward did not know whether he should rejoice or be annoyed, and he expressed his feelings in a saying that was not without a sting of reproach. He called the bridegroom and said to him: "Every man serves the good wine first; and when men have drunk freely, then the poor wine; but you have kept the good wine until now."

But the waiters were standing about ready to explain. They were able to assure the steward that the wine had not come from the household supply, and explained that it came from water they dipped out of the waterpots and carried to him.

The waiters were witnesses and cooperators in this miracle without knowing it. Now everyone gathered about to question them, and they had no reason to hide anything. They told how Mary had come to them and said, "Do whatever he tells you." A question arose now in the minds of some of the guests: When Mary spoke to the waiters, did she know that Jesus would work a miracle? Did she use such general terms because she knew His intention? Perhaps some went to Mary to ask her or, perhaps, amid the excitement, the question was asked openly.

Mary rejoiced that she could give all the honor to Jesus and say that she knew nothing of the miracle. He was now the central figure of the feast. We can easily imagine the excitement that surged around Him. Before the miracle the guests had separated into groups: the older men sat on mats, slow and deliberate in speech and action; the younger men and boys amused themselves in the traditional songs and dances, marking time by clapping their hands; the women and girls sat apart, and chatted with one another. After the miracle, they all came together and formed new groups; some went out into the village to spread the news; and now even more guests came to the house.

The effect of the miracle

This, the first of his signs, Jesus did at Cana in Galilee, and manifested his glory; and his disciples believed in him (Jn 2: 11).

For centuries no miracle had been worked in Israel. The Sacred Scriptures told how the prophet Elijah had multiplied flour and oil for the widow, but that was long ago, in the distant past. John the Baptist had begun to preach, but he worked no miracles like the prophets of old. Now, suddenly, a miracle had been performed.

The miracle came as a surprise to all, for Mary His Mother, for His disciples whom He had just chosen, for His relatives who were present, and for all the guests. But it did not affect them all in the same way.

Of all those who witnessed the miracle, Mary, because of her greater knowledge and understanding, was best able to divine its true significance. For her a new world was dawning. Jesus had said, "My hour is not yet come," and then He had performed the miracle. That "hour" of which He spoke, therefore, was to be preceded by a period of time during which He would reveal Himself by miracles and prepare the people for the revelation of His divine Sonship. She understood now why He had held her aloof from Himself before the miracle. But it was done at her request. In the midst of her joy, this thought startled her—a great distance had been placed between her Son and herself; for her, too, He became inaccessible, He stood alone, united to God in a new way. During the course of the public ministry, more and more light was shed on this experience at Cana. Mary began to realize that her future position at her Son's side was concerned with something above the realm of the natural, with something in a higher plane, especially when she heard the parables about the kingdom of heaven.

For the disciples also the miracle came as a surprise. We may suppose that before they met Jesus they had expected that the Messiah would work miracles, but they had not expected that He would work His first miracle for the benefit of wedding guests in a little village in Galilee. Nevertheless, they were overjoyed, and their eyes were alight with renewed devotion to Him. At the same time, they felt that by the miracle Jesus had withdrawn Himself somewhat from them.

The miracle was also unexpected by His relatives, but they did not receive it with unqualified joy and approval. At first, they took part in the general rejoicing, for Jesus was manifesting Himself as the Messiah in a manner that could be reconciled to their idea of a world-conquering Messiah. Other things, however, that He had done were greatly displeasing to them. Why had He chosen these simple fishermen from the lake country as His disciples and made them such glowing promises, even giving one of them, Simon, a new name? Whatever He might mean by His words, one thing was evident: in His program He was ignoring His relatives and their rights to advancement. According to their way of thinking, His relatives should have been consulted before anyone else, and they should have been chosen as His followers.

The guests, too, were astounded by the miracle. They were all happy about what they had seen, but they were so overcome with astonishment that it took some time for them to recover sufficiently to form a judgment about Jesus. Some sincerely believed that He was the Messiah; some declared for Him with a passing enthusiasm, while others objected because He was merely a carpenter from Nazareth. Thus, within an hour after the miracle had been performed, that division of minds had begun which would continue more intensely during the time of His public ministry.

One question in connection with the miracle at Cana remains unanswered. Was St. John present at the conversation between Mary and Jesus before the miracle? More probably Mary spoke privately with Jesus. The threatened shortage of wine was not yet generally known, and she desired to assist Jesus without attracting the attention of the assembled guests. Of course, the detail of this conversation might have been learned by St. John later from Mary herself.

The symbolic significance of the miracle

To comprehend the miracle at Cana fully, we must not overlook the symbolism that underlies it. Here we are immediately confronted by obstacles, because our minds are not trained to search out the symbolism of events. In this instance, our task is especially difficult because only the words of Jesus addressed to Mary give us the key.

We may, however, cast some light upon the symbolism of this miracle, for it belongs to a definite group of our Lord's miracles that have a special significance and that have certain characteristics in common.

The Gospels relate three miracles that may be distinguished from the others because they are "social miracles," that is, miracles worked for the benefit of a group. These are the multiplication of loaves, the great haul of fish, and the changing of water into wine. In each case our Lord miraculously produces something that is distributed to many individuals in order to supply their need. The bread baskets were empty; He produced bread to feed His hungry listeners. The fishermen's nets were empty; His miracle filled the nets so full that they almost broke. The wine jugs at Cana were empty; He provided the guests with wine.

These three miracles resemble one another in still other ways. They are symbolic of the future society of the kingdom of God. In each a present need is satisfied, and thus they point to the fulfillment of the needs of the soul and to the Messianic gifts that will be bestowed on the community of the faithful. Further, these miracles foreshadowed the position that would be held in the community of the faithful by those persons who under Jesus' direction cooperated in the performance of the miracle.

In the multiplication of the loaves, our Lord allowed the Apostles to make all the preparations that He could delegate to them. Thus this miracle, which provided bread for the physical life of men, was a symbol of a still greater miracle, Jesus' provision of food for the soul. He Himself on the next day pointed to this symbolism, as referring not only to the food of the soul, but also to the position the Apostles would have in the kingdom of God; as they now distributed the bread for the body, so in the future they would be the ministers of the food of the soul.

The miracle of the haul of fishes foreshadowed the Church, which would gather men as the net caught fishes. It also symbolized the position of the Apostles, especially of St. Peter, in the future Church. After the miracle, our Lord said to Peter: "Follow me, and I will make you become fishers of men," thus drawing attention to this symbolic significance of the miracle for Peter. As in this miracle Peter had been the chief of the fishermen, so he would dedicate his life to win souls for Christ as the head of the Church, assisted by these same companions.

At Cana the miracle was indeed intended to forestall the embarrassment of the bridal couple; it was also a symbol of the precious gifts men would receive in the future kingdom of God. And the manner in which Jesus permitted Mary to cooperate in the miracle was a symbol of the place she would have in the kingdom of God. Even though in a different manner, here, too, our Lord pointed out the future significance of the miracle. The difference corresponds to the different relationships Mary and the Apostles would have to the future kingdom. The Apostles, who let down the nets and made the preparations for the feeding of the multitude, were called to their work by Christ; Mary, however, had accepted her calling to the work of the redemption when the angel Gabriel appeared to her, and she answered: "Behold, I am the handmaid of the Lord." Jesus first called Peter at the miraculous catch of fishes; but Mary had no need to be told of her vocation; she had already received it. When He addressed her as "woman," Jesus reminded her of the calling that was already hers, and He made known to her what her future task would be in His kingdom.

In all these instances our Lord's miraculous activity followed upon the preparatory work of His helpers in the same way. He permitted them to make all those preparations that would have been made for supplying the particular need in a normal manner. When these preparations had reached a certain stage, He personally entered into the work, erecting the miracle, as it were, on the basis of the preliminary work of the others. Thus, at the multiplication of the loaves, He directed the Apostles to arrange the people in groups, and to them delegated the distribution of the bread. In the miraculous catch of fishes, He directed the Apostles to let down their nets as if for an ordinary catch of fish. And at Cana, the miracle followed upon Mary's solicitude and sympathy for others, upon her petition addressed to Jesus, and upon her directions to the waiters. By the miracle, this maternal activity became a symbol of that motherly sympathy and solicitude that would be hers for all time in the kingdom of her Son, once it had been established by His death on the cross.

In view of Mary's position in the miracle at Cana, we may rightly ask whether there is any significance in the fact that this was the first of our Lord's miracles. It may have been placed first among the miracles because Mary's close relationship with Jesus was the earliest and most important of all the preparations for the redemption. Perhaps St. John intended to indicate not only this miracle's priority in time, but also its important rank, when he concluded his narrative with the words: "This, the first of his signs, Jesus did at Cana in Galilee."

We may also ask to what extent Mary, the disciples, and the guests grasped the symbolic significance of the miracle. They were undoubtedly in a better position to judge than we are, who only read the account of the miracle. And they had a surer sense and quicker grasp of the symbolism of events, especially the symbolism of the acts of men who were called by God. In the present instance, we should note that a marriage and its outward celebration were more closely associated with each other according to the religious views of the time than they are today. Marriage, the bond of love uniting two people, was an accepted symbol of the relationship of men to God, and the marriage celebration derived some significance quite naturally from the marriage itself and came to be a symbol of man's union with God.

Our Lord's parables comparing the kingdom of God to a marriage and to a marriage feast are striking evidence that this was an accepted viewpoint. He would not have spoken thus unless the people had an understanding of the basis of these comparisons. At Cana those present understood the religious significance of marriage and the marriage celebration. We may say that by the miracle at Cana our Lord paved the way for His parables comparing the kingdom of heaven to a marriage feast.

Mary "the woman"

During the years at Nazareth, Mary had heard the story of Paradise and of Adam's sin, when it was read year after year in the synagogue. She heard the earliest promise of the coming Redeemer: "I will put enmity between you and the woman, and between your seed and her seed; he shall bruise your head, and you shall bruise his heel," in God's words to the serpent.

When the passage had been read, the commentators pointed out that these words referred to the Redeemer. The imagery of this prophecy was one familiar to everyone at that time from his own daily experience. Snakes were greatly feared throughout the land. They crawled along the ground and, when close to a man on foot, made ready to strike. The quickest and surest defense was to crush its head beneath one's foot. Here was an intimation of how the coming Savior would overcome sin. The seed of the woman would triumph over the serpent.

Mary had cherished this prophecy of the Redeemer before she had given her consent to be His Mother. But from the day when she became the Mother of the Redeemer, this passage had a new meaning for her. Now she knew that it was her Child who was the Redeemer spoken of in the prophecy on the first pages of Holy Scripture.

Who was the woman mentioned with the Redeemer and like Him separated from the Tempter by a complete enmity? Did not these words of the sacred text refer to her, the Mother of the Messiah? Was she this woman?

The angel had said: "Hail, full of grace," calling her "full of grace" instead of using her name, Mary. Her cousin Elizabeth, filled with the Holy Spirit, used similar language: "Blessed are you among women, and blessed is the fruit of your womb." As in that first prophecy, Elizabeth mentioned Mother and Child in one breath. Later, Simeon joined the Mother and the Child in his prophecy, and he spoke of that mysterious event in the Redeemer's life when a great conflict would break out, at which the Mother would be present to be wounded by the sword of sorrows.

Mary had been pondering all these things in her soul until that hour came when Jesus for the first time addressed her as "Woman," saying to her: "O woman, what have you to do with me? My hour is not yet come." What effect did this new form of address have on her? What were her thoughts when she first heard it? What did it recall to her mind, she who "kept all these words, pondering them in her heart"?

From the circumstances surrounding this first use of that new form of address, Mary was able to understand that Jesus was making known to her the place she would hold in the scheme of the redemption. From the Scriptures, she knew that often when God called someone for a special office, He conferred on him a significant name. In the days just passed, when Jesus was appearing publicly for the first time as the Messiah, He had given Simon a new name, saying: "So you are Simon the son of John? You shall be called Cephas (which means Peter)." Jesus Himself had assumed a new name. Without previous explanation, He announced to His disciples: "Truly, truly, I say to you, you will see heaven opened, and the angels of God ascending and descending upon the Son of man." In times gone by the prophet Daniel had spoken of the Messiah as the "Son of man." Jesus, however, did not explain the connection between His words and the words of the prophet.

As yet, the disciples did not comprehend the meaning of the phrase, but they felt that Jesus had taken this name because He was the Messiah. Their faith clung to His words as the vine clings to its support. Were not the all-important days at hand when the meaning of this name would be fully revealed? Filled with these thoughts, they came to Cana, and there told how John the Baptist had directed them to Jesus, how Jesus had received them, and how He had given Himself and Peter new names.

More than the others, Mary listened intently and with understanding to these glad tidings, and within her the fire of yearning and expectation flamed anew. But at every word that she heard spoken about her Son, she thought of that great mystery which she alone knew of—the mystery of His divine Sonship. This mystery was a light illuminating all these words and revealing their meaning to her more than to the others. Now, when Jesus appeared as the Messiah, publicly proclaimed by the Baptist, Mary may have expected that soon Jesus would reveal this fundamental mystery to the world.

In these hours of expectancy, Jesus also gave His Mother a new name. As He had told Peter: "You shall be called Cephas," as He had taken a new name for Himself, so now, without any explanation, He addressed Mary as "Woman."

St. Peter Canisius, in his book on the Mother of God, considering the question why Jesus thus addressed His Mother at Cana, quotes the words of one of his contemporaries: "Christ is here referring to that earliest prophecy that the seed of the woman shall crush the head of the serpent. He uses this form of address because it is the most honorable and respectful. Among all others, Mary alone is that great woman who brought forth the seed in whom all the peoples of the earth are blessed." She alone is worthy of those titles of honor, "full of grace," "blessed among women," bestowed on her by the angel and by Elizabeth. With this form of address, our Lord once more spoke to Mary when, hanging on the cross and filled with love for His Mother, He entrusted her to John's care: "Woman, behold, your son." Even in death He wished to honor His Mother and crown her with this title of honor, signifying that she was blessed among women. Far be it from us to think that the Son of God in His agony wished to derogate from His mother's honor when He called her "woman."

To what extent Mary understood this new title conferred on her at Cana by her divine Son, is, of course, not known to us. Nor was it necessary for Mary to understand it completely at that time. Simon, the son of John, did not yet know the meaning of his Messianic title, "the rock," and no one, even until the end, understood that Jesus was rather concealing His divine Sonship than revealing it, when He called Himself the "Son of man."

One thing, however, was clear to Mary from Jesus' words. In His life's work, in the redemption, she was to assist Him at some future time. Now she obeyed Him completely and forsook that intimate domestic manner of living with Him that had been her joy for thirty years. He now belonged to His disciples and to the people; from now on she remained in the background. She would labor for her Son in the background as long as He willed it; but at all times she was ready, whenever His "hour" would come, to be at His side as the handmaid of the Lord.

VI.

The Period of Jesus' Public Ministry

The journeys of Jesus

The twelve were with him, and also some women who had been healed of evil spirits and infirmities: Mary, called Magdalene, from whom seven demons had gone out, and Joanna, the wife of Chuza, Herod's steward, and Susanna, and many others, who provided for them out of their means (Lk 8: 1-3).

These words reveal a side of our Lord's public ministry for which we are not quite prepared. Together with the Apostles, a group of women accompanied the Savior on His journeys in Galilee, some of them belonging to the upper classes. These women, we are told, supplied the needs of Jesus and His disciples. Accordingly, we find two groups in our Lord's following: the group of men led by him and a group of women who served them.

That these women also accompanied Jesus later in Judea, at least occasionally, we may infer from the account of the Crucifixion written by another Evangelist, St. Matthew: "There were also many women there, looking on from afar, who had followed Jesus from Galilee, ministering to him" (Mt 27:55). We should note that the Evangelist does not speak of two or three women, but of "many." Jesus met these women as they were journeying to Jerusalem for the Passover, or perhaps they accompanied Him in Judea as they had done in Galilee.

However, we must not conclude that our Lord and the Apostles depended entirely on the services of these women. In ancient times in the East, women did not have exclusive charge of the household; the men retained a considerable part of the management of the house. The Apostles, therefore, were experienced in caring for themselves.

The group of Jesus' followers was so organized that they were able to dispense with the services of the women. Judas had the permanent office of caring for the little company's money; even until the end he dispensed alms in Jesus' name. When, at the Last

Supper, the Savior said to him: "What you are going to do, do quickly," the Apostles thought that Jesus was referring to some purchases to be made for them or that He was directing Judas to give some alms to the poor.

From the Gospels we know that the women did not always accompany the followers of Jesus. When, for example, He retired into solitude and spent the night with His Apostles in the open air, of course the women were not with them. We may also conclude that the women did not accompany Jesus on the longer and more strenuous journeys into the northern districts about Tyre and Sidon. But when He "went on his way through towns and villages, teaching, and journeying toward Jerusalem" (Lk 13:22), the women in His following probably went ahead, arranged places for lodging, and prepared the meals.

Where was Mary while Jesus went up and down Judea and Galilee? Although we cannot answer the question with certainty, we may suggest some probabilities. Perhaps Mary joined the group of women among His followers whenever they accompanied Him. The Gospel says expressly that she was present at the Crucifixion with the women who followed Him. But she is not mentioned among those women who followed Him in Galilee.

Certainly Mary was not always among those who accompanied our Lord. The Gospel records a visit that she made to Jesus; during the time just preceding the visit, certainly she was not with Him. We may reasonably suppose that at the great feasts of the year she joined Him on the way to Jerusalem or met Him in the Holy City.

Where did she reside during the time when she was not with Jesus? Perhaps at first she resided at Nazareth and later went down to Capernaum to live with some family there, possibly Peter's family or some relatives. After Jesus had been finally rejected by the people of Nazareth, Mary certainly did not remain there. Later, when a similar attitude was manifested in Judea, probably she lived at Bethany with Martha and Mary, the sisters of Lazarus.

From the cross, the Savior entrusted His Mother to St. John, who received her into his house. Shortly before the Passion, Salome, John's mother, had come to our Lord, asking Him to give her sons the first places in His kingdom. For some time, a twofold friendship may have existed between Jesus and the family of Zebedee, arising from the close friendship between Jesus and the brothers John and James, and from a friendship between Mary, the Mother of Jesus, and Salome, the mother of the sons of Zebedee.

In any event, we may confidently say that during all this time Mary remained in the background, in obedience to her Son's will. He had told her in Cana that His "hour," which was also her "hour," had not yet come. Immediately after this declaration, He had performed His first miracle, and Mary understood that the days of the miracles did not coincide with the time of that conflict foretold by the prophet Simeon. But when the people began to hold themselves aloof from Jesus and when the Pharisees began to persecute Him with increasing fury, she realized that the "hour" was approaching.

Until the Passion, Mary's relations with Jesus' disciples were governed by a certain reserve. Jesus was the only one who knew of Mary's miraculous motherhood, and she was still the only one who had been initiated into the mystery of His divine Sonship. He did not yet wish her to give her testimony. Not until He had entered into His glory and until His own revelation had been completed, should she confirm it.

Mary's visit to Jesus

And his mother and his brethren came; and standing outside they sent to him and called him. And a crowd was sitting about him; and they said to him, "Your mother and your brothers are outside, asking for you." And he replied, "Who are my mother and my brethren?" And looking around on those who sat about him, he said, "Here are my mother and my brethren! Whoever does the will of God is my brother, and sister, and mother" (Mk 3: 31–35; see also Mt 12: 46–50; Lk 8: 19–21).

A great crowd had gathered before the door of the house where Jesus was speaking: men, women, boys, and girls, the bright shawls of the women blending with the bleached hoods of the men; on the edge of the crowd, children ran about looking for an opening through which they might press closer to the house.

Meanwhile, Mary was approaching from the street, accompanied by her relatives, perhaps the same who are mentioned elsewhere in the Gospels. They had probably set out together from Nazareth. We are left in ignorance as to the purpose of this visit, unless we associate it with the plots being formed against Jesus. Of these we will speak in the next chapter.

With her relatives, Mary had now come to the house where her Son was speaking; those who stood by the entrance moved aside as they saw the visitors approaching. The relatives may have asked some questions: How long has He been speaking? How long will it be until He finishes? Not being disposed to wait, they let it be known that they were His relatives; they introduced His Mother and said they desired to speak to Him. The word passed from mouth to mouth; inside the house, the listeners were soon turning to see the cause of the disturbance. The impression was given that these relatives had come to speak with Jesus about an urgent personal matter. When the people heard that "His mother and brothers" had come, they immediately yielded to them because, in the popular mind, the relatives were all-important, they were "flesh of His flesh, blood of His blood."

All eyes turned to Jesus, and the listeners were pressing against the walls to make way for Him. What else could He do but go out to them at once? Were they not His relatives?

But He did something unexpected. To those who saw Him, it seemed He had long been waiting for this opportunity; now that it had come, He could at last say something that He had had in mind for a long time and that clamored for expression.

St. Matthew says: "Stretching out his hand toward his disciples, he said. . . ." St. Mark describes the scene as follows: "Looking around on those who sat about him, he said. . . ." We must remember that the Evangelists, like other writers of their time, were sparing in their description of gestures and facial expressions. Undoubtedly, Jesus' action made a deep impression upon His audience. Standing in the midst of the people, He declared solemnly: "Here are my mother and my brothers! Whoever does the will of God is my brother, and sister, and mother."

What astonishment was written on the faces of the listeners! They had already heard the expression "child of God," understanding thereby a man who lived according to the will of God. In the Book of the Jubilees, composed about that time, it was written: "They will keep my commandments, and I will be their father and they shall be my children." Nor was the expression, "do the will of God," newly coined. The listeners had no difficulty in understanding the terms Jesus used.

They must have noticed that He spoke also of sisters, although no one had said that sisters or female relatives wished to speak with Him. By including the word "sister," Jesus made the meaning of His words clearer. Whoever does the will of the Father who is in heaven will be so closely united to Jesus in the kingdom of His grace that the intimacy between brother and brother, between brother and sister, and between son and mother must be gathered into one relationship in order to understand the closeness of that union. This was a fundamental principle of the new kingdom: to do the will of the heavenly Father. The more completely a man dedicated himself to the fulfillment of the Father's will, the closer he approached to Jesus.

In that statement another truth was presupposed: that Jesus was the consubstantial Son of the Father, participating in the divine nature of the Father and also in the divine life of grace in the souls of those men who do the will of His Father. Through this divine life alone could a person become His brother, sister, or mother.

During this visit of His Mother, Jesus was teaching by means of an enacted parable; as though He said: "The kingdom of heaven is like to a relationship that has one head but many members. All those related to the head by blood are subject to him, and with him they form one whole. So also in the heavenly relationship, in the relationship of the children of God, of those who do the will of the heavenly Father: they are all related to one another, they are brothers and sisters and mothers, and their head is the Father in heaven."

Jesus places this heavenly relationship so far above earthly relationships because it has its origin in the nobler part of man, in his soul. Earthly relationships, founded on blood, belong, like the blood, to this world. Jesus did not, however, cast any aspersions on these earthly relationships. Rather, He wished to ennoble them, for as children of God His relatives ascended to a higher plane.

His reply may have surprised Mary, as it surprised the others. But in the fulfillment of God's will she was in entire agreement with Him; and as soon as she knew what Jesus willed, she conformed to His will. But such was not the case with the relatives who had come with her. When they grasped the import of this declaration, they were angered. In their opinion, Jesus' first duty was to do the will of His relatives; furthermore, they were provoked because He did not at once admit His Mother before the assembled crowd. Their ill will did not arise from any unselfish love for Mary; they felt that whatever Jesus had done to His

Mother was also intended for them. But, since He had acted to Mary the same as to the other relatives, they were unable to reproach Him; they could not complain that He had shown favoritism among His relatives. Yet they recalled with what respect and devotion He had lived with Mary in Nazareth for so many years.

The relatives would have been gratified if Mary, His closest relative, had shown displeasure at her Son's words. But they saw that she submitted and bowed beneath the words of Jesus as a maidservant bows beneath the directions of her master.

Angered by Jesus' strange conduct, the relatives vented their ill will on Mary. Periods of reproachful silence followed, and, at times, by their remarks they showed her how dissatisfied they were with her Son.

The conspiracy against Jesus

Then he went home; and the crowd came together again, so that they could not even eat. And when his friends heard it, they went out to seize him, for they said, "He is beside himself" (Mk 3: 19-21).

Today we have difficulty in imagining the rapidity with which news was transmitted in the land of Israel. At that time everybody, almost unconsciously, constituted himself a news reporter. Besides this, people in certain occupations undertook to carry the news for business purposes: camel drivers and mule drivers, who journeyed frequently between the larger centers of population; traders and merchants, who offered the latest news before beginning their business transactions.

In Galilee, various circumstances aided the rapid diffusion of news. That section of Palestine had a network of roads, some leading to Judea, others from the lake of Genesareth to the Mediterranean. At the gate of every city and town and in the streets of the bazaars, news was announced at frequent intervals. Whenever an event of general interest occurred, messengers spread the news with a speed that seems incredible to us. The same thing happens in the East even today. During the First World War, military forces in the East were often chagrined to discover that their supposedly secret marches were already known to the Bedouins. Of course, rumors and false reports were spread with equal rapidity through these news channels.

Amid such conditions we must place our Lord's public ministry. When, for example, He was preaching and working miracles in Capernaum, the news was spread quickly from village to village. The town where He was stopping became for the time the focal point of the country, and from it the news was carried to all parts of the land.

In the open places before the city gates or elsewhere in the city, idlers gathered and discussed the current news. What tales and rumors were told about Jesus in those days! The words of the psalmist (Ps 69: 12) were fulfilled: "I am the talk of those who sit in the gate, and the drunkards make songs about me." Our Lord's deeds were recounted, and each teller colored his tale according to his own attitude toward Jesus. Thus the Savior's cause was injured.

His relatives in Nazareth learned what He was doing, and reports were brought also of the activities of His enemies. The people of Nazareth were simple folk, who continued quietly at their accustomed trades. Now, without their wishing it, they saw themselves becoming involved in a bitter conflict. How could Jesus and His disciples withstand the Pharisees, against whom even the Sadducees, who belonged to the nobility, were powerless? And if He lost in this conflict, His relatives also would suffer the consequences. They would not be pleased to have envious neighbors shout after them: "You also are one of His relatives."

The rumors about Jesus became more and more malicious. Now it was said He was "beside himself." Perhaps not everyone intended the same thing by this expression. The word in the original Greek text has a broad meaning: to be beside oneself because of joy or astonishment or anger or enthusiasm. In the account of the boy Jesus in the Temple at Jerusalem, we read that the doctors of the law were "beside themselves" with astonishment at His questions and answers. Because of its broad application, the expression could be given its worst meaning by a caustic tone of voice. Moreover, we should remember that at this time intimations were being spread that Jesus was in league with the devil.

We may be inclined to believe that such expressions as "was beside himself" and "become mad" should be softened, and that it is unlikely that such monstrous rumors as that Jesus was "mad" were being noised about. But the fact remains that the Gospels record the spreading rumor that Jesus had allied Himself with the devil. Among a people believing in the existence of a real devil, such a charge was far more ominous than a report that He was "beside Himself." The ordinary people did not distinguish clearly between diabolical possession and mental derangement. When, for example, Jesus said: "Why do you seek to kill me?" the people answered: "You have a demon! Who is seeking to kill you?" meaning that He had an obsession with persecution. The two accusations—to be under the influence of the evil spirit and to be beside oneself—in the world of that day were not far apart in meaning.

Under these circumstances, our Lord's relatives were obliged by the customs of the East to take a stand with regard to Him. Either they must approve of what He did and vouch for Him, or they must condemn His activities as improper and strive to bring about His retirement from public life. To say that the things He did were none of their concern would not relieve them from partial responsibility in the matter. The first responsibility rested on the chief relatives, especially now, since Joseph had died. Had Joseph been living, the matter would have been much simpler; they would have gone to his workshop and demanded that he call Jesus back home.

Thus it had come to that action against Jesus which is briefly mentioned by St. Mark, who says that Jesus' friends "went out to seize him" (Mk 3: 21). The statement leads us to ask: Who were to lay hold on Him, and what did they do? The Greek expression may best be translated by "His people"; whether they were relatives or some of His followers remains undecided. Whoever they were, their action was based on the rights people possessed or thought they possessed over their relatives. Whether they themselves believed that Jesus had acted imprudently and had overstepped the bounds of propriety, we cannot say.

What did His people intend to do? They wished "to seize Him," that is, deprive Him of His liberty. Probably they themselves had not yet decided how they would accomplish this, leaving the details to be decided by the circumstances. What was the result of this undertaking? If the attempt was made at the time of the visit of Mary and His relatives, described in the last chapter, we know how Jesus rejected any intervention on the part of His relatives and pointed to the spiritual relationship to which He and all men were more strictly bound than to any earthly relationship. If His relatives came on some other occasion "to seize him," we know only that the attempt ended in failure.

Beneath these meager accounts lies a world of unrecorded sorrow and grief in Mary's life. If the relatives had persuaded her to accompany them when they went to bring Jesus back home and limit His activities, it must have been a journey filled with grief and anguish, a preparation for the way of the cross; and if she had not been drawn into the affair and merely heard later what had occurred, it must have weighed heavily on her mother's heart.

"Blessed is the womb..."

Now he was casting out a demon that was dumb; when the demon had gone out, the dumb man spoke, and the people marveled. But some of them said: "He casts out demons by Beelzebul, the prince of demons"; while others, to test him, sought from him a sign from heaven (Lk 11: 14-16; see also Mt 12: 22-32; Mk 3: 22-30).

The imputation that Jesus was in league with the prince of devils was a calumny so startling and so overwhelming that it seemed to paralyze the reasoning powers of the people. For them the devil was not some mythical hobgoblin, but the enemy of all that was good and the father of lies. Thus the accusation that Jesus made use of the power of the devil in working miracles was the worst calumny that could be hurled at Him. The simple, honest man of the people, who was slow to impute evil to his fellow man, must have thought within himself that such an accusation would not have been made without good reason. Therefore, Jesus opposed these vile slanders with unusual severity, not with long and involved arguments, but with statements that fell like blows upon His enemies, statements that everybody could understand. He said:

"Every kingdom divided against itself is laid waste, and house falls upon house. And if Satan also is divided against himself, how will his kingdom stand? For you say that I cast out demons by Beelzebul. And if I cast out demons by Beelzebul, by whom do your sons cast them out? Therefore they shall be your judges. But if it is by the finger of God that I cast out demons, then the kingdom of God has come upon you. When a strong man, fully armed, guards his own palace, his goods are in peace; but when one stronger than he assails him and overcomes him, he takes away his armor in which he trusted, and divides his spoil. He who is not with me is against me, and he who does not gather with me scatters.

"When the unclean spirit has gone out of a man, he passes through waterless places seeking rest; and finding none he says, 'I will return to my house from which I came.' And when he comes he finds it swept and put in order. Then he goes and brings seven other spirits more evil than himself, and then enter and dwell there; and the last state of that man becomes worse than the first" (Lk 11: 17–26).

Jesus erected His refutation upon ideas that were the common property of all the people. The simplest man among His hearers understood the point of His answer and realized that the Pharisees had suffered a defeat. But not all dared to admit it openly. A woman, however, in her inspired enthusiasm was impelled to exclaim: "Blessed is the womb that bore you, and the breasts that you sucked." Jesus replied: "Blessed rather are those who hear the word of God and keep it" (Lk 11: 27–28).

Such exclamations were natural to these vivacious people, and exclamations including the mother of the one who was praised were especially cherished. Rachel, the mother of Joseph of Egypt, was praised in similar terms: "God Almighty . . . will bless you with blessings of heaven above, blessings of the deep that couches beneath, blessings of the breasts and of the womb" (Gen 49: 25). In the course of time, the form of this blessing was permanently incorporated into the language of the people and, with corresponding changes, was used in imprecations. The expression grew out of the common conviction of the people that there was no greater blessing or happiness possible for a mother than to have given a great man to the world.

Jesus allowed this praise to be accorded to His Mother, for she was indeed worthy of praise. Many years before, she had received the praise of her cousin Elizabeth, and Jesus constantly praised her within Himself for another reason: because she, more than all others, faithfully fulfilled the will of God. In His eyes she was deserving of praise not simply because she was so close to Him by blood, but because the sentiments of her soul were always most intimately united to His.

On other occasions He enunciated this principle, which was the basis of Mary's merited praise. The soul, such was His teaching, belongs to God and is more closely united to Him than a man is united to his family, and the earthly family is not the highest and ultimate goal of man, who possesses an immortal soul. If a man has to choose between his love of God and his love for his family, he must forsake his earthly relationship rather than deny his soul's divine relationship. If some in his family do not decide for God, he must be prepared to separate from them for God's sake. On one occasion our Lord expressed the thought in these words:

Do you think that I have come to give peace on earth? No, I tell you, but rather division; for henceforth in one house there will be five divided, three against two, and two against three; they will be divided, father against son and son against father, mother against daughter and daughter against her mother, mother-in-law against her daughter-in-law and daughter-in-law against her mother-in-law (Lk 12: 51–53).

The same thought underlies the words: "If any one come to me and does not hate his own father and mother and wife and children and brothers and sisters, yes, and even his own life, he cannot be my disciple" (Lk 14: 26).

Whoever separated from his earthly family in order to serve God with greater freedom and perfection would obtain a special place in the heavenly relationship; for as earthly kings gave the first places in their kingdoms to their relatives, so Jesus promised a special reward to His own who would give themselves entirely and wholeheartedly to His service:

Truly I say to you, in the new world, when the Son of man will sit on his glorious throne, you who have followed me will also sit on twelve thrones, judging the twelve tribes of Israel. And every one who has left houses or brothers or sisters or father or mother or children or lands, for my name's sake, will receive a hundredfold and inherit eternal life (Mt 19: 28–29).

Although these words may seem harsh and forbidding, they do not disturb the natural love and affection of the family. Indeed, our Lord often referred tenderly to the love between members of a family. He frequently made use of parables taken from the family life of the ordinary man. He spoke of a father who had retired with his children and was in bed with them and who turned away his friend lest by rising he disturb the slumbers of his children. He told how children ask their father for bread and fish and eggs and are not refused by him. Once, when His disciples forbade little children to be brought to Him, He rebuked them in words they certainly never forgot. More unmistakably than anyone before or after Him, He defended the inviolability of the family bond founded on marital fidelity. All this family love and affection was not to be destroyed, but incorporated into His kingdom. In that Eastern world, this teaching was entirely new, but it was no more than a consequence of that all-important fundamental law of His new kingdom, "to do the will of the Father in heaven," which would be brought to realization by a living union with God.

The rejection at Nazareth

He went away from there and came to his own country; and his disciples followed him. And on the sabbath he began to teach in the synagogue; and many who heard him were astonished, saying, "Where did this man get all this? What is the wisdom given to him? What mighty works are wrought by his hands? Is not this the carpenter, the son of Mary and brother of James and Joses and Judas and Simon, and are not his sisters here with us? " And they took offense at him. And Jesus said to them, "A prophet is not without honor, except in his own country, and among his own kin, and in his own house." And he could do no mighty work there, except that he laid his hands upon a few sick people and healed them. And he marveled because of their unbelief.

And he went about among the villages teaching (Mk 6: 1-6; see also Mt. 13: 54-58; Lk 4: 16-30).

When, during His journeys, Jesus visited His town of Nazareth, He went to the synagogue for the Sabbath services. As He passed along the street, men and women, dressed in their Sabbath garments, came out of the houses that were so familiar to Him. At the door of the synagogue, beggars and cripples gathered every Sabbath to beg alms from those going in. Certainly these beggars heard of the things that Jesus had done in Capernaum and that He had arrived in Nazareth. As He walked by them, some perhaps looked up to Him as if to say: "Here we are if you need anyone upon whom to demonstrate your power." But this attitude was entirely alien to the trust and confidence Jesus required. He passed them by and entered the house of prayer.

The cantor intoned the prayers, or perhaps, if the custom already obtained for the reader of the Prophets to begin the prayers, Jesus led the prayers. The congregation responded briefly, often with the simple "amen," to the long petitions. Now the reader of the Law rose up to read; the doxology was recited; then followed the passage from the Prophets.

Jesus now stood up and came to the reader's desk and was handed the roll. He sought out a passage, and the congregation began to sense that He had something special to say to them. He

179

read the passage in Hebrew, then the interpreter announced the passage in the vernacular, and they heard:

> The Spirit of the Lord is upon me,
> because he has anointed me to preach good news to the
>   poor.
> He has sent me to proclaim release to the captives
> and recovering of sight to the blind,
> to set at liberty those who are oppressed,
> to proclaim the acceptable year of the Lord (Lk 4:18-19).

Jesus rolled the parchment about the rod, returned it to the servant, and sat down. The atmosphere had become tense; Jesus Himself was proposing to decide the question that was uppermost in the minds of the congregation.

Now He was speaking; it was a sentence uttered with a tone of finality: "Today this scripture has been fulfilled in your hearing." Immediately an abyss separated Him from His listeners. According to their way of thinking, this prophecy was not yet fulfilled, and would not be until Jesus had surpassed His other miracles in their presence and for their benefit. Then they would be prepared to acclaim Him. But from His tone, as He spoke these first words, they sensed something else: this was not the Jesus to whom they had once given their orders and directions as the simple carpenter of their village. Jesus made Himself unmistakably clear when He said:

Doubtless you will quote to me this proverb, "Physician, heal yourself; what we have heard you did at Capernaum, do here also in your own country." And he said, "Truly, I say to you, no prophet is acceptable in his own country. But in truth, I tell you, there were many widows in Israel in the days of Elijah, when the heaven was shut up three years and six months, when there came a great famine over all the land; and Elijah was sent to none of them but only to Zarephath, in the land of Sidon, to a woman who was a widow. And there were many lepers in Israel in the time of the prophet Elisha; and none of them was cleansed, but only Naaman the Syrian" (Lk 4: 23-27).

People became uneasy and restless, and in some parts of the synagogue murmuring arose: "Is not this the carpenter, the son of Mary and brother of James and Joseph and Judas and Simon, and are not his sisters here with us? "

The restlessness increased. When Jesus entered the synagogue, He could not number many friends in the congregation;

at most He had before Him men who were willing to acknowledge Him if it was advantageous to their town and to themselves individually. But now, when He resisted them and dared compare them to the unbelieving sons of Israel of ancient times, their hidden resentment broke forth and spread like fire.

The listeners sprang from their benches and crowded around those who were shouting at Him, around those prominent men who occupied the places of honor and who became the leaders of the disturbance, around the doctors of the law who had come to Nazareth to watch Him. The action of the leaders was the signal for the common people; someone shouted: "Cast Him out." Everyone crowded to the exits, benches were overturned, and the air was filled with the sound of seats being dragged over the stone floor. Jesus was cast out by the men and disappeared. He revealed how far above them He was, disappearing from their midst miraculously, so that afterward no one dared to touch Him again.

We do not know whether Mary was present at this scene. Even if she was not present, the disciples may have described to her how He was forcibly expelled from the synagogue. This was the town where the angel of God had solemnly announced to her: "And behold, you will conceive in your womb and bear a son, and you shall call his name Jesus. He will be great, and will be called the Son of the Most High; and the Lord God will give to him the throne of his father David, and he will reign over the house of Jacob for ever; and of his kingdom there will be no end." And now, like one who had blasphemed God, Jesus was cast out from the synagogue of His own city.

Mary knew that she, too, had been outlawed with Jesus in Nazareth. Did they not, when the violence broke out, call Him Mary's Son, almost as if this was the cause of their resentment? She could not now remain long in Nazareth. In these days, the cross was casting its shadow not only on Jesus, but also on Mary. What the people of His own city had begun, the people of Israel as a whole would complete in Jerusalem.

The counsel of Jesus' relatives

Now the Jews' Feast of Tabernacles was at hand. So his brethren said to him, "Leave here and go to Judea, that your disciples may see the works you are doing. For no man works in secret if he seeks to be known openly. If you do these things, show yourself to the world." For even his brethren did not believe in him. Jesus said to them, "My time has not yet come, but your time is always here" (Jn 7: 2-6).

Before the Feast of Tabernacles, circumstances were like those before the Passover following the wedding at Cana. Then Jesus, His mother, and His disciples had come down to Capernaum in order to go up to Jerusalem along the valley of the Jordan. Now He was already in Capernaum with His disciples, while His relatives were coming down from Nazareth to Capernaum. St. John does not say whether Mary was already in Capernaum or whether she had come down with the relatives. But, since it was her custom to go to Jerusalem for the great feasts, we may assume that she was among the followers of her Son.

At this time His relatives offered Him a suggestion. The advice they urged was almost the opposite of what they offered Him on an earlier occasion. Once they had tried to use all the influence they possessed to persuade Him to return home and become a quiet citizen again. Now, filled with paternal advice and solicitude, they urged Him to go to the capital city of the country and show there His power of working miracles and gather His followers about Him.

What was the attitude of His relatives toward Him at this time? In a certain sense their faith had grown; they were willing to admit that He had the power to gather about Himself an enthusiastic populace; and they supposed that such was His intention. But they also thought that He did not know how to choose the proper time and place to carry out His plan.

In general, the people's attitude toward Jesus was not yet antagonistic. They were ready to decide for or against Him; by one clever stroke He could win them all to His side; but if He continued His policy of retirement, He would lose all. A miracle such as the multiplication of loaves would win them all over to His side, and the crowds who came for the Feast of Tabernacles would be transformed into an eager army ready to do battle.

His relatives acted in conformity with their conception of things when they urged Him: "Leave here and go to Judea, that your disciples may see the works you are doing. For no man works in secret if he seeks to be known openly. If you do these things, show yourself to the world." They spoke as benevolent guardians; they wished to help Him overcome His timidity and reserve, and to spur Him on.

Jesus answered His advisers: "My time has not yet come, but your time is always here. The world cannot hate you, but it hates me because I testify of it that its works are evil."

To understand these words, we must keep in mind the task that His relatives had set themselves. They wished to persuade Him to go up with them to Jerusalem on the occasion of the feast and make Jerusalem the scene of His activity. Beyond this, they were hoping that as the Messiah He would establish His headquarters in Jerusalem and return no more to Galilee. Jesus' conception of the events that would follow His entrance into Jerusalem differed from that of His relatives simply because they entertained a false notion of the mission of the Messiah. Like many others, His relatives thought that the Messiah would bestow earthly greatness and glory on them; accordingly, they sought to persuade Jesus to make a powerful manifestation of His Messiahship before the people. He knew that some day He would solemnly enter the Temple of Jerusalem amid the waving of palm branches and shouts of "Hosanna." He knew, too, that this would be the prelude to His death; therefore, the time for His entrance into Jerusalem would come immediately before the time ordained by His Father for His death in Jerusalem. Therefore, He answered the pleadings of His relatives by saying: "My time has not yet come."

Probably this scene took place in Mary's presence. At any rate, she learned of it sooner or later from her relatives. The ominous undertone of Jesus' answer meant more for her than for the others; and now again, when He referred to the tragic end of His life, she vividly recalled the words of Simeon's prophecy.

Did Mary receive any special revelations?

An important question regarding Mary's life is whether our Lord imparted any special revelations to her. By these special revelations is not meant those revelations of His soul which she received during her life with Him at Nazareth; or those inspirations of grace by which her soul was illumined. The question is, rather: Did Jesus impart to her any knowledge beforehand about His public ministry and His death in Jerusalem? Did He, for example, tell her, before He went to John the Baptist on the banks of the Jordan, that He would never again return to His workshop to continue His work as a carpenter? Some writers speak of such revelations, but they do not always distinguish between an inward inspiration and an outward communication. In answering this question, apparently we are not helped by the Gospel narrative. But if we carefully study the background of the passages in which the Blessed Virgin is mentioned, we will incline to the opinion that Jesus did not personally inform His Mother about the plan of the redemption. We do not mean, however, that He did not speak to her in private about those things which He was publicly preaching to others.

During the period of the public ministry, Mary is expressly mentioned only at the marriage at Cana and at the visit of His relatives. At the wedding feast in Cana, He certainly revealed something to her that she did not know before.

When His relatives visited Him in Capernaum, Mary was also present. Hearing that His relatives had come, Jesus answered: "Whoever does the will of God is my brother, and sister, and mother." This reply was intended for Mary as well as for the others, and for her also it was unexpected. These two scenes make it seem very probable that during His public ministry Jesus did not make known His plans or intentions to Mary beforehand.

From what we read of Mary in the Gospels, we may infer that, with regard to asking questions of Jesus, she adopted a reverent reserve. Her faith in Him united her to Him most closely, but it did not destroy her reverence for Him. Precisely by her silence, Mary the woman of great faith differed from the disciples, who often asked Him questions and sometimes even ventured to offer Him advice.

Mary and the mystery of the Holy Trinity

Seldom do Christians appreciate the importance of the mystery of the Holy Trinity; yet within that mystery the ascent of man's soul to God is realized. In our early years, we learned that God the Father created us, God the Son redeemed us, and God the Holy Spirit sanctifies us.

Because we accept the doctrine of the three divine Persons as the foundation of our faith without pondering its fundamental significance, we often base some of our judgments of Mary's life on false premises. We may wrongly suppose that at the Annunciation Mary clearly understood that she was cooperating in a work of the Holy Trinity and that when she gave her consent the three divine Persons were present to her mind. If, however, we wish to understand things as they really were, we must put aside these misleading preconceptions. Not only before, but also after, the Annunciation, Mary did not clearly know the mystery of the Holy Trinity, unless we assume without warrant that she had been granted a special revelation before the mystery was revealed by our Lord. The angel had indeed said to her: "The Holy Spirit will come upon you, and the power of the Most High will overshadow you; therefore the child to be born will be called holy, the Son of God." Mary accepted the full import of these words, but she did not then, as later, possess that deep insight into the divine nature of the Redeemer. The revelation of this mystery was, of course, of far greater significance and moment for Mary than for others, since her very life was drawn into the heart of the mystery. It was her Son Jesus who had come into the world as the Son of God the Father; hence she was closer to the mystery than was any other human being and to her was given a clearer vision of the life of the three divine Persons in the Holy Trinity.

Mary and the mystery of the divine Sonship

Mary stood in a special relationship to the mystery of the divine Sonship. As often as Jesus spoke to her of the great mystery of her own life, the miraculous Incarnation of the Son of God, she saw it as the earthly and temporal reflection of the eternal and divine relationship of Jesus within the Holy Trinity. Gradually, on various occasions, as on the days before the Feast of Tabernacles, the mystery was unfolded before the eyes of her soul. Whether she was present on that occasion or whether she heard Jesus' words from the disciples, they seemed, as it were, intended especially for her.

When the people discussed whether or not Jesus was the Messiah, some exclaimed loudly: "Yet we know where this man comes from; and when the Christ appears, no one will know where he comes from." The Savior heard these words and accepted them as a challenge, and He cried out:

You know me, and you know where I come from? But I have not come of my own accord; he who sent me is true, and him you do not know. I know him, for I come from him, and he sent me (Jn 7: 28–29).

Even if I do bear witness to myself, my testimony is true, for I know whence I have come and whither I am going, but you know not from whence I come or whither I am going. You judge according to the flesh, I judge no one. Yet even if I do judge, my judgment is true, for it is not I alone that judge, but I and he who sent me. In your law it is written that the testimony of two men is true; I bear witness to myself, and the Father who sent me bears witness to me. They said to him therefore, "Where is your Father?" Jesus answered, "You know neither me nor my Father; if you knew me, you would know my Father also. . . .

"You are from below, I am from above. . . .

"I speak of what I have seen with my Father. . . .

"It is my Father who glorifies me, of whom you say that he is your God. But you have not known him; I know him. If I said, I do not know him, I should be a liar like you. . . . Your father Abraham rejoiced that he was to see my day: he saw it and was glad. . . . Truly, truly, I say to you, before Abraham was, I am" (Jn 8: 14ff.).

Of His life before He lived as a man, of His life at the time when Abraham lived on earth and looked for the coming of the Redeemer, Jesus spoke openly; He spoke of His Father in heaven, from whom He had taken His origin. He did not speak as a man who knows nothing of the days when he began his earthly life; rather, He spoke as if His entrance into the world was a free and conscious act, just as when an ordinary man goes from one house into another.

Mary alone knew that Jesus had come from the eternal world of the Father into this passing world. Her heart must have quickened when she heard these words and pondered them in the light of the angel's announcement: "The child to be born will be called holy, the Son of God. . . . The Lord God will give to him the throne of his father David, and he will reign over the house of Jacob for ever; and of his kingdom there will be no end."

As Jesus was unveiling these truths, Mary's relations to His disciples quite naturally underwent a change; she and they came closer together because they were being initiated into the same mysteries. More and more clearly she saw that the Apostles were the chosen ones of her Son, that Peter was the one to whom the keys of that endless kingdom were entrusted. We can hardly visualize Mary's relations to the Apostles in all their details; but we know that, while Jesus was revealing more and more of His divinity and of His kingdom, Mary was being drawn more deeply into the spiritual relationship of His kingdom. Gradually, the Apostles began to see in Mary not only the woman who was His earthly Mother, but also the woman who was united to Him by the most intimate spiritual union. When, on the cross, Jesus said to Mary: "Woman, behold, your son," and to John: "Behold, your mother," it was not the creation of a new relationship, but the culmination of an inner development that had begun much earlier.

The tests of Mary's faith

Christendom has always been one in acclaiming Mary the greatest of all saints. Her sanctity far surpassed that of all other saints, but many erroneously assume that her sanctity was a pure gift of God that knew nothing of the coin of sacrifice with which holiness is purchased. In reality, Mary was not spared even the hardest trials, trials that exceeded in intensity and duration the trials of any other child of the race. In these trials, she distinguished herself from all others in that she never faltered or failed; she carried the burden God had placed upon her with such equanimity that outwardly she appeared to be a woman with nothing unusual about her. Thus we may perhaps think that her sanctity knew no suffering, at least before the Passion of her Son.

This is especially true when we consider the view men commonly take of Mary's faith. She is indeed frequently proposed as the model for the faith of all Christians; but many of us fail to appreciate how she was really an impregnable tower of faith. Many believe that when she miraculously conceived at the Annunciation, she knew that Jesus was the Son of God and did not need to believe as we do. Precisely because she was so close to the mystery of Jesus' divine Sonship, her faith was subjected to the severest trials. She was obliged to witness how all the supernatural glory of the Child whose birth had been foretold by an angel faded away and how He grew up like any ordinary child; she saw how as a boy He began to help His foster father in the workshop and finally became a carpenter Himself.

Because of her miraculous motherhood, she was placed in a unique position. She was no longer like the ordinary women of the Old Testament who prayed fervently for the coming of the Messiah, because she knew He had already come on earth; and she did not yet belong to the New Testament, because Jesus had not yet manifested Himself as the Redeemer. Thus she stood alone in the world. During the entire period of the hidden life, to her and to her alone was entrusted the mission of believing in the redemption of the world by a Savior who was working as a carpenter and who gave Himself so exclusively to His trade that it seemed He had come into the world for nothing else. Daily and hourly the question must have arisen: How can it be that the Son of God leads such a life?

Even greater trials awaited her during the days of His public ministry, when He was preaching and working miracles. Indeed, these very miracles, by which the power of God was revealed to others, were tests of Mary's faith. Jesus multiplied bread for those who were hungry; He provided the coin that Peter might pay the Temple tax. Why had He not multiplied the meager supply of bread in Nazareth and provided the money for the taxes by a miracle? The longer He appeared as the Messiah and the more He revealed His power, so much the more did the hatred of His enemies increase. In all Israel no thief was watched so closely as her Son was watched by the Pharisees. How could God let these things happen to His Son? And lastly came the days of suffering, when Mary's faith was put to the severest test, from which she emerged unshaken and untouched.

Dark hours came when, humanly speaking, it might have been possible for her to commit that sin which underlies every sin, that sin by which man, the creature, calls God to account, as if there were some standpoint outside of God from which man can judge Him, as if there were some law under which both God and the creature stand as equals, a law to which man can appeal against God. With more semblance of reason than others could have done, Mary might have proposed the question: If God sent His Son into the world, why did He not permit Him to appear in such a way that men must acknowledge Him as the Son of God and believe in Him? How could God permit that His Son, who is all-wise, almighty, holy, and eternal, should be so like the rest of weak sinful mankind in the outward circumstances of His life that many of His contemporaries looked down on Him and despised Him? Why did not the Father give Him might and power, which would have suggested the superhuman and the divine? How could God suffer hovel-dwellers, mule drivers, caravan leaders, synagogue officials, doctors of the law, and Pharisees to express their opinions about the Redeemer? How could He permit alien kings like Herod and pagan officials like Pilate to summon the Son of God before their tribunals and sit in judgment upon Him?

Over all these trials Mary triumphed in the most magnificent manner. During all the dark hours of her maternity and especially during those most difficult hours in which she was overwhelmed by the sorrow and anguish of the Passion and death of Jesus, she always maintained that attitude expressed in the words she had spoken at the Incarnation: "Behold, I am the handmaid of the Lord." And at every moment during her trials, even to the last day of her life, the Mother of the Redeemer deserved to hear the words once addressed to her by her cousin in reverent awe: "Blessed is she who believed."

Mary's vision of Jesus' eternal kingdom

He will reign over the house of Jacob for ever; and of his kingdom there will be no end (Lk 1:33).

We have already pointed out that Mary's inner attitude was determined by the angel's prophecy: the Lord God would give her divine Son an eternal kingdom. During the quiet years at Nazareth, while Jesus labored as a carpenter, she pondered these words. But of those things which must come to pass before He would take possession of His kingdom, she knew nothing except what she could glean from Simeon's prophecy and from the Scriptures.

The angel's prophecy: "He will reign over the house of Jacob for ever; and of his kingdom there will be no end," stirred within her to new life when she now heard about the preaching concerning the "kingdom of God" and the "kingdom of heaven." She heard how John the Baptist began his sermon with the warning: "Repent, for the kingdom of heaven is at hand," and how Jesus had taken up the Baptist's cry and said: "The kingdom of God has come near to you" (Lk 10:9).

When Jesus began the Sermon on the Mount by saying: "Blessed are the poor in spirit, for theirs is the kingdom of heaven," He was announcing a new principle to mankind. Mary had long been living according to this principle and had given expression to it in the *Magnificat*. More than others, she understood the Savior's teaching about the kingdom of God, for which He was working among men; although men rebelled against His rule, she knew that ultimately the will of the Father to give an eternal kingdom to His Son would be accomplished.

Perhaps she alone remarked that Jesus, in His labors for the establishment of the kingdom of God, turned only to the children of Israel and not to the Gentiles. Yet Simeon had foretold that Jesus would be not only the "glory to thy people Israel," but also a

189

"light for revelation to the Gentiles." When would the Gentiles be received into Jesus' kingdom? What great changes must take place before those words could be fulfilled?

Thus the thought of the kingdom of God led Mary back to the thought of the conflict of which Simeon had spoken, that conflict in which the kingdom of God would assume the form it was to have for all eternity; and the vision of that kingdom included the period of suffering that, according to Simeon, awaited both her and her Son. In these days immediately preceding the Passion, these thoughts were confirmed by Jesus' prophecies in which He spoke of His suffering and of His glory as two aspects of that one great event, the establishment of His kingdom.

VII.

The Passion and Death of Jesus

Jesus' prophecies about His Passion

When for the last time Jesus went up to Jerusalem for the Passover, His following included some women. Although only the mother of John and James is mentioned, we may assume from the prevailing customs the presence of a group of women, probably corresponding to the group of Apostles and disciples. Later the Evangelist relates: "And there were also [at the Crucifixion] women looking on from afar, among whom were Mary Magdalene, and Mary the mother of James the younger and of Joses, and Salome, who, when he was in Galilee, followed him, and ministered to him; and also many other women who came up with him to Jerusalem" (Mk 15: 40). In deference to custom and the norms of propriety, Mary spent these last days before the Passion in the company of these women.

As Jesus was going up to Jerusalem from the valley of the Jordan, "he took the twelve disciples aside," and told them what awaited Him in Jerusalem: "Behold, we are going up to Jerusalem; and the Son of man will be delivered to the chief priests and scribes, and they will condemn him to death, and deliver him to the Gentiles to be mocked and scourged and crucified, and he will be raised on the third day" (Mt 20: 17-19).

In Bethany, Simon the leper gave a dinner in Jesus' honor. During this meal Mary, Martha's sister, anointed Jesus with precious spikenard. When Judas became indignant at what he called this waste, our Lord answered him with these words of prophecy: "Why do you trouble the woman? For she has done a beautiful thing to me. . . . In pouring this ointment on my body she has done it to prepare me for burial. Truly, I say to you, wherever this gospel is preached in the whole world, what she has done will be told in memory of her" (Mt 26: 10, 12-13).

On the Wednesday before the Passion, the Savior declared the third and last prophecy. He said: "You know that after two days the Passover is coming, and the Son of man will be delivered up to be crucified" (Mt 26: 2). In these words, He prophesied His Passion with terrible clarity; but He also foretold that He would come forth triumphant from the grave after three days and that the joyous tidings of His Resurrection would go into the whole world.

These words affected Mary and the Apostles in different ways. The Apostles became like men who feel they are threatened by some unknown terror, not knowing when or from what quarter it will strike. The most frightening thing was that Jesus Himself, who until now had protected them against all danger and, when it was necessary, saved them by a miracle, announced the coming terror. But, since such an appalling event seemed beyond belief, they did not give full credence to His words and did not unreservedly trust in His leadership. Their protestations of loyalty and love at the Last Supper were really expressions of their uneasiness. Perhaps they regarded the Lord's words not as prophecies but, rather, as expressions of His anguished spirit.

Mary, however, accepted the prophecies with a spirit fortified by faith and prepared for sacrifice, even though they brought the certainty that the hour was near when her heart would be pierced with the sword of sorrow.

Mary's preparation for the Passion and death of Jesus

While these prophecies in which Jesus foretold His death caused an estrangement between the Apostles and their Master, Mary began to prepare to share the coming hours of suffering and death with her Son; indeed, under God's direction, during her whole life she had been preparing herself for this hour.

Soon after the Savior's birth, God had announced to her, through the aged Simeon, that she would have much to suffer on account of her Child: "A sword will pierce through your own soul." On a second occasion, the heavenly Father sent her a message when the boy Jesus in the Temple said to her, "Did you not know that I must be in my Father's house?" This event was like the gathering of clouds in the early morning, presaging the coming fury of the storm.

During the peaceful, secluded years in Nazareth, Simeon's prophecy and the finding of the divine Child in the Temple remained so vivid in Mary's mind that, when Jesus appeared openly as the Messiah, she prepared immediately to stand at His side and await those things which Simeon had foretold. But when

Jesus said to her, "My hour is not yet come," He was intimating to her that she must still wait some time; and He likewise announced to her that the hour was coming when Mother and Son would be united in suffering.

As the hatred of the Pharisees and the hostility of the people increased, Mary knew that the deciding conflict was no longer far distant, and Jesus' repeated prophecies on the way to Jerusalem made her feel certain that the "hour" was near at hand. With growing insight into the sufferings that her Son must undergo and an ever clearer knowledge that the time was now approaching, Mary's love for Him grew apace. A wonderful quality of mother love is that the child's every new trial opens a new fountain of love. At the same time, Mary's love increased her anxiety and anguish, so that her loving care became boundless.

Jesus' words and His attitude brought her comfort and solace; from Him she learned that His suffering and death were the culmination of His life. When opposition reared its head in Galilee, He had begun to speak of His suffering as of some precious secret, as the great task that had been appointed Him. The previous year, at the Feast of Tabernacles, He had spoken of His Passion in these words:

I am the good shepherd. The good shepherd lays down his life for the sheep. . . . I am the good shepherd; I know my own and my own know me, as the Father knows me and I know the Father; and I lay down my life for the sheep. And I have other sheep, that are not of this fold; I must bring them also, and they will heed my voice. So there shall be one flock, one shepherd. For this reason the Father loves me, because I lay down my life, that I may take it again. No one takes it from me, but I lay it down of my own accord. I have power to lay it down, and I have power to take it again; this charge I have received from my Father (Jn 10: 11–18).

Thus the death of Jesus had been willed by the Father, and Jesus knew no rest until He had fulfilled the Father's will and had given His life for men and restored them to life. As the handmaid of the Lord, with unshakable faith, Mary followed Jesus on the road of suffering, even though she was unable to discern its ultimate goal. Like her Son, she was thinking now of the Passion and of the redemption that the Passion would accomplish.

We do not know how much Mary understood of the world-embracing nature of her Son's redemptive work. The Gospels are silent, but the Scriptures tell of men who possessed an amazing grasp of the nature of the redemption. All his life, Simeon had longed for the Redeemer and was contented to depart from this life once he had held the Child in his arms. So too had the prophetess Anna prayed and yearned for the consolation of Israel for sixty years. Simeon already understood that the redemption would not be accomplished by some magnificent stroke of power accompanied by signs captivating men's minds, but by persecution and suffering. How great must have been the yearning in the soul of John the Baptist when, animated only by the thought of the coming Savior, he spent himself in lifelong fasting and prayer! How clearly he must have understood the Redeemer's mission when he constantly preached penance and, pointing to the Savior, said: "Behold, the Lamb of God, who takes away the sin of the world."

Mary's knowledge of sin and its consequences surpassed that of Simeon and Anna and John; therefore she was better able to comprehend the nature of the redemption. Moreover, she had lived with Jesus for thirty years and, during that time, His thoughts and sentiments had become her own in a manner far beyond our imagining. This absorption of her mind in the mind of her Son and this knowledge of the blessings His sacrificial death would bring to mankind endowed her with immeasurable strength when the sufferings of her Son came before her mind in stark reality.

She accepted His prophecies concerning His humiliating suffering and death not only with courage and readiness for sacrifice, but also with an equally firm hope that His words about His glorification and the triumphant spread of His kingdom throughout the world would be fulfilled. "And he will be raised on the third day." The Apostles were so stunned by the heartrending announcements of mockery and derision, of suffering and death, that preceded this prophecy, that they seemed not to hear the prophecy of Jesus' victory over death. Still less did they grasp the significance of the Master's words in Bethany: "Truly, I say to you, wherever this gospel is preached in the whole world, what she has done will be told in memory of her." Jesus spoke of the spread of His kingdom, looking out upon the future and beholding His suffering and death, and the glorification of His name by redeemed mankind. Here the Apostles were unable to follow Him. They, who outwardly, at least, deserted Him in the beginning of His Passion, began in these days to draw away from Him inwardly. Mary alone, in spite of the dreadful prophecies of pain and death and utter destruction, was able to cling fearlessly to Jesus' words about victory, Resurrection, and glory. "And he will be raised on the third day."

Therefore she drew ever nearer to her Son as the great "hour" approached. Now, as during her whole life, she was ready to offer her Son as the lamb of sacrifice for the salvation of mankind.

We must see Mary's greatness not only in this, "that she offered her womb as a dwelling place for the only begotten Son of God that the sacrifice for the salvation of the human race might become possible. It is also a part of Mary's glory that she accepted the office of protecting and nurturing the Lamb of sacrifice and leading it to the altar in due time. Thus there was at no time any interruption in Mary's living and suffering with Jesus, and the words of the psalmist: 'My life is wasted with grief: and my years in sighs,' are true of Mary and her Son" (Pius X, encyclical *Ad illum diem*).

Jesus was filled with anguish at the thought of His approaching Passion; yet He desired it ardently, and Mary participated in that desire. She was prepared for what Jesus' "hour" might bring, and in complete surrender to Him she also longed with all her maternal heart for the salvation of the human race and the glorification of her Son as the Redeemer of the world.

Thus she was now the only one who followed Him without faltering or hesitation, she was the only one who preserved the faith in the coming of the Resurrection during the darkness of the next two days, even though she was wholly overwhelmed by the bitterness and grief of the Passion.

Jesus had now but one thought: to complete the task that had been assigned to Him in the Sacred Scriptures. The biblical prophecies, illumined now by Jesus' own prophecies, were completely unveiled before Mary's mind, and they were her companions even as they were the companions of her Son during the night of suffering and death.

Mary and the Psalms

Better than anyone else, Mary had understood the prophecies about Jesus' sufferings recorded in Scripture. But now, when Jesus openly stated that He would be dragged before the tribunal in Jerusalem, delivered into the hands of the Romans, scourged, mocked, spit upon, and put to death, Mary was given a key that opened up to her the last hidden meaning of the ancient prophecies and psalms. The psalms of the Passion had become so much a part of her being that they seemed always to be present before her mind, they seemed to rise up and say to her: "We await the moment when your Son will make us come true in His life."

The individual prophecies were like messengers sent by God to her, the Mother of the Messiah; according to Simeon's prophecy and Jesus' words at Cana, she would be at His side during His "hour" and would be pierced by a sword of sorrow.

Psalm 110 seemed to be a description of the great conflict:

> Sit at my right hand,
> till I make your enemies your footstool.
>
> The Lord sends forth from Zion your mighty scepter.
> Rule in the midst of your foes!
> Your people will offer themselves freely
> on the day you lead your host
> upon the holy mountains.
> From the womb of the morning
> like dew your youth will come to you.
> The Lord has sworn,
> and will not change his mind,
> "You are a priest for ever
> after the order of Melchizedek."
>
> The Lord is at your right hand;
> he will shatter kings on the day of his wrath.
> He will execute judgment among the nations,
> filling them with corpses;
> he will shatter chiefs
> over the wide earth.
> He will drink from the brook by the way;
> therefore he will lift up his head.

Psalm 22 appeared as a more detailed description of the sufferings foretold by Jesus Himself; the separate details of the Passion, to which He had referred but briefly, appeared in this psalm vividly portrayed in gruesome vividness and accompanied by the bitter lament of grief and anguish.

> But I am a worm, and no man;
> scorned by men, and despised by the people.
> All who see me mock at me,
> they make mouths at me, they wag their heads.
> "He committed his cause to the Lord; let him deliver him,
> let him rescue him, for he delights in him!"

Then, in the midst of this lamentation, reference was made to the mother:

Yet thou art he who took me from the womb;
    thou didst keep me safe upon my mother's breasts.
Upon thee was I cast from my birth,
    and since my mother bore me thou hast been my God.
Be not far from me.

It was as though Mary saw herself mirrored in these verses. When a child was born into the world, he was placed on his father's knee, and the father thus acknowledged the child as his son and publicly accepted the obligation of caring for him. This practice is the basis for the mysterious words of this psalm. The author of the lament declares his relationship to God to be the same intimate relationship that exists between son and father.

Again and again in mysterious language Jesus had spoken of His life with the eternal Father; but no one except Mary understood these references. God was truly the Father of Jesus her Son, in a much higher sense than any son had ever been the son of an earthly father. Were not these words of the psalm an expression of those sentiments which Jesus felt toward His own Father?

Now the picture of the mother disappeared and the lament of the psalmist continued:

I am poured out like water,
    and all my bones are out of joint;
my heart is like wax,
    it is melted within my breast;
my strength is dried up like a potsherd,
    and my tongue cleaves to my jaws;
thou dost lay me in the dust of death.

Yea, dogs are round about me;
    a company of evildoers encircle me;
    they have pierced my hands and feet—
I can count all my bones—
    they stare and gloat over me;
they divide my garments among them,
    and for my raiment they cast lots.

But thou, O Lord, be not far off!
    O thou my help, hasten to my aid!
Deliver my soul from the sword,
    my life from the power of the dog!

Save me from the mouth of the lion,
my afflicted souls from the horns of the wild oxen.

How much suffering and tribulation were contained in these verses! But the same psalm contained some rays of comfort. There were mysterious words of a community of brethren and of a sacrifice that, after all this sorrow and anguish had passed away, would be established among all peoples and would continue for all time.

I will tell of thy name to my brethren;
in the midst of the congregation I will praise thee:
You who fear the Lord, praise him!
all you sons of Jacob, glorify him,
and stand in awe of him, all you sons of Israel!
For he has not despised or abhorred
the affliction of the afflicted;
and he has not hid his face from him,
but has heard, when he cried to him.

From thee comes my praise in the great congregation;
my vows I will pay before those who fear him.
The afflicted shall eat and be satisfied;
those who seek him shall praise the Lord!
May your hearts live for ever!

All the ends of the earth shall remember
and turn to the Lord;
and all the families of the nations
shall worship before him.
For dominion belongs to the Lord,
and he rules over the nations.

Yea, to him shall all the proud of the earth bow down;
before him shall bow all who go down to the dust,
and he who cannot keep himself alive.
Prosperity shall serve him;
men shall tell of the Lord to the coming generation,
and proclaim his deliverance to a people yet unborn,
that he has wrought it.

Once before Jesus had spoken of a spiritual food, which would be Himself. How were all these things related to one another? Mary knew that soon the last veils would fall from these words.

Preparations for the Last Supper

And on the first day of Unleavened Bread, when they sacrificed the passover lamb, his disciples said to him, "Where will you have us go and prepare for you to eat the passover?" And he sent two of his disciples, and said to them, "Go into the city, and a man carrying a jar of water will meet you; follow him, and wherever he enters, say to the householder, 'The Teacher says, Where is my guest room, where I am to eat the passover with my disciples?' And he will show you a large upper room furnished and ready; there prepare for us." And the disciples set out and went to the city, and found it as he had told them; and they prepared the passover (Mk 14: 12-16; see also Lk 22: 7-13; Mt 26: 17-19).

On Thursday, the disciples came to Jesus and asked Him where He wished them to prepare the Passover. Jesus knew what this year's Passover would mean for Him; He Himself would take the place of the paschal lamb and take away the sins for which the paschal lambs could never atone. Before His Passion, however, He provided for a quiet hour of peace. In directing His disciples, He did not specify the location of the house in the city, but veiled it in such a way that Judas the traitor would not know it in advance: "Go into the city, and a man carrying a jar of water will meet you; follow him, and wherever he enters, say to the householder, 'The Teacher says, Where is my guest room, where I am to eat the passover with my disciples?' And he will show you a large upper room furnished and ready; there prepare for us." Jesus says expressly that the master of the house would place a large room at their disposal. From the building customs of the time, we may assume that this upper room was the only room on the upper story and that a staircase led to it from the outside. Jesus and His disciples were, therefore, free to come and go without disturbing the master of the house.

Mary and the other women very likely left Bethany together with Jesus and His disciples and crossed over the Mount of Olives to Jerusalem. In those days one group of pilgrims after another went up from the Jordan valley across the desert of Judea. Here and there among the foot travelers could be seen jogging donkeys and camels with their swaying sedan chairs, and above the pilgrims the clouds of dust shone like a golden mist in the sun.

Besides Jesus, Mary was the only one who steadfastly kept in mind what the next days would bring; she alone accepted His prophecies literally; she knew He was going up to Jerusalem for the last time. As she went along, she saw to the south the hills beyond which lay Bethlehem, she saw the road that led down to Bethlehem from Jerusalem. No mother can forget the place where she gave birth to her only child; and Mary may have thought of that time long ago when she wrapped her Son in swaddling clothes. She looked down on the Temple court, where Simeon had taken the Child into his arms and said to her: "This child is set for the fall and rising of many in Israel. . . . And a sword will pierce through your own soul also, that thoughts out of many hearts may be revealed." The "hour" was close at hand.

As in the past, Mary's greatness consisted in this, that she was the "handmaid" who was not told all the details of what was to come. That she did not know the circumstances of the Passion beforehand was an added suffering, because she was aware that the terrible hour of the Passion was at hand.

Holy Thursday night

And when the hour came, he sat at table, and the apostles with him. And he said to them, "I have earnestly desired to eat this passover with you before I suffer; for I tell you I shall not eat it until it is fulfilled in the kingdom of God." And he took a cup, and when he had given thanks he said, "Take this and divide it among yourselves; for I tell you that from now on I shall not drink of the fruit of the vine until the kingdom of God comes" (Lk 22: 14-18; see also Mt 26: 20-29; Mk 14: 17-25).

Toward evening Jesus with His Apostles entered the room that Peter and John had prepared for the Passover; the paschal lamb had been killed and prepared in the meantime. Jesus observed the rite of the paschal meal with His Apostles, and, during the course of it, He instituted the sacrifice of the New Testament. Then, in the Garden of Gethsemane, He underwent a great agony. Either from Jesus Himself or from the Apostles, Mary had heard the prophecy that Jesus would give His body and blood to His followers as food and drink; but, like the disciples, she did not know in what manner He would fulfill this promise. She had received the words of the promise with the serene unshakable faith that was characteristic of her. She must have felt that, in some new mysterious way, Jesus was separating Himself from her; but with a joyful spirit she consented to what He had promised: to give His flesh to be the food and His blood to be the drink that would nourish life in the souls of the faithful so that on the last day He might raise them up to Himself.

The mysterious promise became clearer when she heard what took place at the Last Supper. Her faith far surpassed the faith of the Apostles, and she was able to understand that the Sacrament of the Altar was Jesus' final gift of love: "This is my body which is given for you. . . . This cup which is poured out for you is the new covenant in my blood."

For Mary these words were full of meaning, in view of the coming Crucifixion; they deepened her understanding of those things which she would witness on Friday. In the Crucifixion Jesus was offering a sacrifice that His disciples would renew in His name after His death.

Hearing these words, Mary was brought into a new and mysterious inner relationship with the Apostles. Aside from their disloyalty, their terror, and their human weakness, Mary saw in them the men to whom her Son had entrusted the office of renewing His act of sacrifice under the appearances of bread and wine when He would no longer be on earth.

Thus she perceived that the maternal right of disposal, which she had exercised over Jesus in the days of His childhood, was being transferred to the Apostles. But she did not feel that she was being supplanted; she saw but one thing, that the work of the redemption was taking clearer form hour by hour. When at last she stood beneath the cross, she knew that this bloody sacrifice would be repeated in an unbloody manner in obedience to her Son's command.

As to the other events that took place during that night, the following question is important: Where did the Apostles flee when the Master was taken prisoner? Did they remain in the protective shadows of the trees on the Mount of Olives, or did they go back to the city and lock themselves in the upper room, as they did on the following Sunday?

If Mary went to the upper room and the Apostles returned there, it was then she learned that Jesus had been taken prisoner. At the latest, she heard of it when Peter sought her out, sobbing after his denial in the courtyard, or when John came and told her about the hearings before Annas and Caiphas. John stood with Mary by the cross. We may suppose he was with her during the darkness and terror of this night.

Man has a strange inclination to erect between himself and the Son of God barriers that do not exist; the inclination is not peculiar to men of modern times. We find it in the early days of the Church, when copyists omitted the record of our Lord's agony in the Garden of Gethsemane because in their opinion it was not fitting for the Son of God. For similar reasons, the narrative of Jesus' temptation by the devil was suppressed as improper. If these two passages were not actually part of the Gospels, no one would dare to invent them, with their accompaniment of detailed description.

If we speak of Mary's temptations, many also will feel that the matter is highly improper. Consciously or unconsciously, some people think there was nothing in Mary's life that can be compared to Jesus' temptations in the wilderness or to His agony in the garden. Yet Mary's life had temptations like those of her Son; but, because she was the Mother of Jesus, these temptations centered on Him and indeed seemed to flow from Him.

Looking at the matter more closely, we see such trials and temptations indicated by the Gospels in the narrative of the loss of the boy Jesus in the Temple, in Jesus' attitude at the wedding in Cana, and in His turning Mary away when she and His relatives came to visit Him; but the hours of the severest temptations were still to come when Jesus left her on Thursday to begin His Passion.

In some books of piety we read that Mary suffered with Jesus on Thursday and Friday because of a special revelation; but her suffering was still greater because during this night she knew only what Jesus had foretold: that on Friday He would be condemned to death and crucified by the Roman soldiers and that He would rise again on the third day. Thus Mary, like her divine Son, suffered an agony on that Thursday night; like Him she was alone in her agony, and no human consolation was possible because no one else believed in the reality of what had stricken her heart with anguish.

We remember how Jesus appeared in the Garden of Gethsemane as a human being, how He was besieged by agony and swayed by fear and terror of what was to come, how He remained faithful to His mission only by praying to His heavenly Father. Recalling all this, we may say that during the hours of that night Mary awaited the morrow with a heart filled with dread and terror because of the sufferings that would be heaped upon her Son. The anguish she had suffered when searching for the twelve-year-old Boy was but a forerunner of the agony that now completely overwhelmed her soul.

The Crucifixion

They led him out to crucify him (Mk 15: 20; see also Mt 27: 31; Jn 19: 16).

On Friday morning, the whole city of Jerusalem with eager interest followed the various steps in Jesus' trial and witnessed the abuse to which He was subjected. The open space before Pilate's house was filled with a sea of faces. From time to time, a wave of excitement surged through the crowds as they shouted against Jesus. Pilate yielded to the clamor and ordered that Jesus be scourged. Then, hoping that the Jews' hatred had been sated, he presented Jesus to them, disfigured almost beyond recognition. At this their hatred blazed into rage, and from a thousand throats, demanding and threatening, the blast of their shouts fell upon the ears of the stricken Man: "Crucify him." Again Pilate yielded. He condemned Jesus to death. Where was Mary while all this was taking place? The Gospels tell us nothing; but we may suppose that she witnessed the proceedings in John's company.

We are certain that she joined her Son on the way to Calvary, because later, as we read in St. John's Gospel, she stood beneath the cross. The fourth station of the cross commemorates that moment when Jesus and Mary met in their sufferings. We can best place this meeting somewhere near the city gate. Any freedom of movement, such as we must suppose, was impossible in the narrow streets filled with pilgrims and onlookers and sometimes lined with detachments of soldiers. At the city gate, a halt was made in the tragic procession. There Simon of Cyrene was compelled to help Jesus carry the cross, and during this time Mary was able to approach the Savior.

Beneath this meeting of Jesus and Mary was concealed something even they did not express in words. In that moment, it was as though they stood before each other with their whole lives present to their minds. Jesus throughout His life had awaited this moment; and, since Simeon's prophecy, Mary had been waiting and preparing for it. Side by side they had expected this hour, their eyes intent upon the decree of the heavenly Father, each knowing that the other was likewise looking for the coming of this time. And now their eyes met, and at once there was a union of their souls. What need could there be for words? Suffering met with suffering, sympathy accepted sympathy, courage joined with courage, and love was united with love.

After this, each moment brought new torments to Mary's soul. Jesus was led up the hill of Calvary; the last preparations were made for the Crucifixion. Someone offered Him a drink of bitter wine, but He merely tasted it and returned it, not wishing to numb his senses.

Then Jesus, her Child, still covered with wounds and blood from the scourging, was deprived of His garments by the executioners. For Mary, this was a suffering that wounded her love to the innermost. Bright red the blood began to flow from the wounds, calling out to her heart. Then, with harrowing rapidity, sorrow followed upon sorrow; the nails were poised above His hands, the hammer fell, and each blow explored new depths in her soul. All during her life she had heard the sound of the hammer as in Jesus' hand it had descended on beams and boards, and, as she listened to the sounds coming from His workshop, she knew that there in obscurity the Redeemer of the world was laboring day after day. Afterward, the hammer blows became pulsations that mysteriously suppressed all the noises of the world into silence.

Now again she heard the sound of the hammer falling, but this time it was not Jesus who directed it to the nail that was to enter the wood; now the arms of the executioners wielded the hammer that drove the nails through His flesh. Blow followed blow, driving the sword of sorrow deeper into Mary's soul.

Jesus' prayer for His enemies

And Jesus said, "Father, forgive them; for they know not what they do" (Lk 23:34).

A mother watching by the side of her dying child experiences extreme suffering when the child no longer speaks to her; she feels that he has gone to some far distant place where she can no longer follow him. How tense she becomes with loving expectation when at last the child speaks again!

Jesus' first word from the cross was a prayer for His enemies: "Father, forgive them; for they know not what they do." Forgive them! His blessed Mother desired what He desired in imitation of His example and for His sake. Forgive them! Filled with compassion, she looked upon the jeering soldiers, on the chief priests who mocked Him, and the people who wagged their heads in derision at Him. Her compassion saw straightway into their souls and was not disturbed by their actions. "They know not what they do." Indeed, compared with her who had been initiated into the mystery of the Son of God, all these who stood about had no understanding of what was now taking place here on Calvary.

Even after many years, a mother can remember the last words of her child before his death. Thus Mary, who cherished in her heart every word of Jesus, always remembered this prayer for forgiveness. Thus she became the mother of all those in need of an advocate with the Father in heaven, for what was true of the mockers about the cross is true of all sinners. In His prayer, Jesus had all sinners in mind, and Mary had compassion on them all; thus the Mother of the compassionate Savior became the Mother of mercy. Now, more than before, she understood that the Savior's Passion was a labor of love for sinners, and she desired only to follow her Son in that love.

Ordinary human beings bearing the stains of sin cannot easily understand Mary's solicitude for sinners. Whoever has been drawn into sinfulness loses thereby his unclouded insight into the nature of sin, and in his mental confusion he strangely imagines that a person who is without sin, as Mary was, can have no true knowledge of the nature of sin.

Next to Jesus, however, Mary had the most profound understanding of the mystery of sin, and, therefore, she suffered with those whom she saw in the wretched state of sin, while the poor beings around about her did not realize how much they were to be pitied. This was especially painful for Mary. Her attitude toward sinful mankind was like that of a mother of maimed and sickly children who do not know how miserable they are. With motherly love, Mary bends down to the sinful children of mankind that she may support and protect them when they come to realize their sorry state.

The inscription

Pilate also wrote a title and put it on the cross; it read, "Jesus of Nazareth, the King of the Jews." Many of the Jews read this title, for the place where Jesus was crucified was near the city; and it was written in Hebrew, in Latin, and in Greek. The chief priests of the Jews then said to Pilate, "Do not write, 'The King of the Jews,' but, 'This man said, I am King of the Jews.'" Pilate answered, "What I have written I have written" (Jn 19: 19–22; see also Mt 27: 37; Mk 15: 26; Lk 23:38).

In the treasury of her remembrances gathered by her maternal heart, every incident of Mary's life continued to live on and every new experience was woven into the fabric of the past or, in the words of St. Luke, Mary "kept all these things in her heart." Every new event in her life became associated with the events of the past, going back to the time in Nazareth when the angel revealed to her that she was to be the Mother of God. Now, beneath the cross, Jesus' whole life was recalled to her mind.

Surrounding His death were circumstances that carried her spirit back to the days at Nazareth. Above all, there was the inscription, which read: "Jesus of Nazareth, the King of the Jews." The inscription was in three languages: Hebrew, the language of religion; Greek, the language of culture; and Latin, the language of the state. Perhaps Mary was able to read the Hebrew writing, but, at any rate, many of those present read it aloud.

"Jesus." She remembered that moment when she had heard the name for the first time, when the angel said to her: "You shall call his name Jesus."

"Nazareth." The word recalled the thirty years in which Jesus worked as a simple carpenter, the years she lived with Him at Nazareth.

"King of the Jews." "The Lord God will give to him the throne of his father David, and he will reign over the house of Jacob for ever; and of his kingdom there will be no end." Such had been the angel's message many years ago. "The throne of his father David." For an entire lifetime Mary had pondered these words in her heart. At first, like the others, she had thought of an earthly throne; but when Jesus began to speak of His suffering, the vision of a throne of gold and ivory, surrounded by soldiers and servants, faded away, and in its place there came the cross, surrounded by the jeering soldiery.

The division of the garments

When the soldiers had crucified Jesus they took his garments and made four parts, one for each soldier; also his tunic. But the tunic was without seam, woven from top to bottom; so they said to one another, "Let us not tear it, but cast lots for it to see whose it shall be." This was to fulfill the scripture

"They parted my garments among them,
and for my clothing they cast lots."
So the soldiers did this (Jn 19: 23–25; Mt 27: 35; Mk 15: 24; Lk 23: 34).

Like Pilate's inscription, an occurrence that took place at the foot of the cross recalled to Mary's mind the days at Nazareth. The soldiers detailed to perform the Crucifixion were unfeeling, brutal men. They appropriated Jesus' garments to divide them among themselves according to established custom.

For a mother, the garments of her dead child become sacred; and, as time goes on, the dearer they seem to be. But no mother desired to keep her child's garments more than Mary did on Calvary. Here on the ground lay His sandals. How often she had handled them at Nazareth! She shuddered to think how the soldier would take them away, wash the blood from them, and either wear them himself or sell them to a comrade.

But the soldiers had no feelings in the matter. They divided His garments, excepting the cloak, because it was one piece of cloth. So they said: "Let us not tear it, but cast lots for it to see whose it shall be."

To lose this garment, which Jesus had probably worn for a long time, was especially painful for Mary. The soldiers cast the dice and counted the spots, and the ownership of the garment was decided. Thus, even before Jesus died, His garments had fallen to new owners without passing through Mary's hands.

The mocking of Jesus

And those who passed by derided him, wagging their heads and saying, "You who would destroy the temple and build it in three days, save yourself. If you are the Son of God, come down from the cross." So also the chief priests, with the scribes and elders, mocked him, saying, "He saved others; he cannot save himself. He is the King of Israel; let him come down now from the cross, and we will believe in him. He trusts in God; let God deliver him now, if he desires him; for he said, 'I am the Son of God' " (Mt 27:39-43; see also Mk 15:29-32; Lk 23:35-37).

The chief priests and scribes, the soldiers and executioners, and the populace that had gathered on Calvary were not satisfied to see Jesus hanging on the cross. To His bodily suffering they added mental torment; they mocked and ridiculed Him by recalling the days of His public ministry, when the people had followed Him everywhere, regarding Him as a prophet, when some had even believed that He was the promised Messiah. The populace shouted to Him on the cross: "You who would destroy the temple and build it in three days, save yourself. If you are the Son of God, come down from the cross."

The chief priests held themselves aloof from the common herd, but in spirit they were one with the crowd. They mocked Him saying: "He saved others; he cannot save himself. He is the King of Israel; let him come down now from the cross, and we will believe in him. He trusts in God; let God deliver him now, if he desires him; for he said, 'I am the Son of God.' " Mary needed a vast reserve of strength in order that her heart might endure all this and that she might conform to the inexhaustible patience of her Son. The words: "For he said: 'I am the Son of God,' " pierced her inmost soul as they led her back in spirit to that hour when the angel had said to her: "He will be called the Son of God."

Now, one of the thieves who had been crucified with Jesus began to blaspheme. His heart overflowing with bitter hatred, he said to the Savior: "Are you not the Christ? Save yourself and us!" This mockery was an even greater humiliation for Jesus than the reviling of those who stood below, for now this criminal with whom they had associated Him renounced Him and scorned Him. He made the words of the scribes and priests his own, hoping thereby perhaps to be freed from the cross. Even in his dying moments, a man reviles and scorns the Son of God!

Was Jesus' mission then to be all for nothing? No, it was not to be so. The other thief, hearing these blasphemies, came to Jesus' defense: "Do you not fear God, seeing you are under the same sentence of condemnation? And we indeed justly, for we are receiving the due reward of our deeds; but this man has done nothing wrong." And he said, "Jesus, remember me when you come into your kingdom."

How lovingly Mary looked up to the thief who was defending her Son! Turning to her Son, she seconded the petition of the contrite thief, and Jesus, opening His lips, said to him: "Truly, I say to you, today you will be with me in Paradise."

It was indeed a great consolation for the thief to hear that his soul was saved, and for Mary too these words were a consolation; but they also contained the announcement of Jesus' death. He said: "Today you will be with me in Paradise." His death, therefore, was close at hand.

Her heart recoiled from the thought of His death and united itself to Him and His unspeakable torments for the last few moments of His life. However much she suffered now, seeing Him thus on the cross, it would be a greater suffering when He would be no more. But before He died, He was to be torn from her in His desolation in a manner that was even worse than physical death.

Mary's dereliction

And when the sixth hour had come, there was darkness over the whole land until the ninth hour. And at the ninth hour Jesus cried with a loud voice, "Elo-i, Elo-i, lama sabach-thani? " which means, "My God, my God, why hast thou forsaken me? " And some of the bystanders hearing it said, "Behold, he is calling Elijah" (Mk 15: 33–35; see also Mt 27: 46–46).

Jesus was now more alone than He had ever been during His whole life. Mary, indeed, was intimately united with Him in His sufferings. But at every moment she realized that He was not living with her as closely as she was living with Him; He was living according to the will of His Father. Therefore, she too must withdraw within the will of the Father, and in His will she must persevere beneath the cross. She was so close to her Son and yet so far from Him; it seemed that now she could only approach Him through the Father in heaven, now she could no more unite her heart to His, and her sorrow to His sorrow.

After Jesus had given John to her and entrusted her to John, a mysterious thing began to happen to Him. The hour had come when the Son of God was mysteriously forsaken by His heavenly Father.

No person, not even Mary, had any knowledge of what was happening to Jesus. He Himself made it known; and not least of all, that Mary might follow Him into this new trial. With a loud voice He cried out: "My God, my God, why hast thou forsaken me?"

This cry of anguish wrung from His soul by His inexpressible suffering was perhaps Mary's severest trial. Following her Son and bowing to His will, she had submitted in all things to the will of the Father in heaven, as though her whole soul had been absorbed into the will of God. But now, suddenly, the will of the Father seemed to dissolve into nothing, no longer able to give a meaning and a purpose to this suffering.

Following her Son, Mary's soul had sped to God on wings whose every stroke seemed to leave an entire world behind. Before her now, however, her Son seemed to stand still, as though the Father's voice had never said: "This is my beloved Son, with whom I am well pleased." For Mary too, the Creator now seemed far distant.

The dereliction of Jesus, the Son of God made man, was an incomparable thing, and Mary's dereliction was that of the purest and holiest of God's creatures at a time when she was least prepared for such desolation. Humanly speaking, a monstrous temptation loomed before Mary's mind, the temptation to be no more concerned about the Father because He had abandoned His Son, no longer to turn to Him because He no longer showed Himself to His Son.

In this most difficult hour, Mary remained faithful. Every faculty and sense of her being seemed to be consumed and annihilated in this crushing desolation. But one thing remained: to repeat the words spoken so long ago to the angel: "Behold, I am the handmaid of the Lord."

Mary at the foot of the cross

Standing by the cross of Jesus [was] his mother (Jn 19:25).

Now, when Jesus was in His death agony, Mary stood close by at the foot of the cross; the other women, so the Gospels record, "stood afar off beholding these things." Because she was His Mother, she was permitted to come closer; perhaps John had obtained this permission from the soldiers, as on the night before he had obtained permission from the portress for Peter to enter the courtyard of Caiphas' palace.

During these hours in which Jesus hung on the cross, surrounded by the mocking soldiers, the jeering populace, and the triumphant Pharisees, Mary at the foot of the cross realized that now Simeon's prophecy had come to fulfillment: "This child is set for a sign that is spoken against, and a sword will pierce through your own soul also." Now that, too, which Jesus had referred to at Cana, had come to realization: His "hour" had come, and hers too.

All during her life, Mary had longed for the days of salvation; now the time of waiting had passed, now with Jesus she had reached the hour of accomplishment. With that exultation which great souls can feel in moments of even the deepest sorrow, Mary now rejoiced; with the psalmist she could pray: "My heart is ready, O God, my heart is ready," as she went down with Jesus into the valley of humiliation and death.

We have unusual difficulty in understanding how great a sacrifice Mary was now making. We may perhaps somewhat appreciate the magnitude of her sacrifice if we make a comparison with the sacrifice of the mother of the Maccabees during the execution of her youngest son. Six sons had already been done to death; the youngest alone remained. She could have saved him by persuading him to obey the command of the king to eat the meat and openly transgress the Law. Instead she said to him:

My son, have pity on me. I carried you nine months in my womb, and nursed you for three years, and have reared you and brought you up to this point in your life, and have taken care of you. I beseech you, my child, look at the heaven and the earth and see everything that is in them, and recognize that God did not make them out of things that existed. Thus also mankind comes into being. Do not fear this butcher, but prove worthy of your brothers. Accept death, so that in God's mercy I may get you back again with your brothers (2 Mac 7: 27–29).

The mother of the Maccabees not merely consented to the martyrdom of her son, she also urged him to persevere and remain faithful, realizing that neither she nor her son ought to prefer anything, even life, to obedience to the commandments of God. Like the mother of the Maccabees, Mary consented to the death of her Son; but in a more exalted manner, because He was also the Son of God.

God had sent His Son into the world to redeem it; the angel Gabriel had announced to her that her Son would be the Redeemer of the world; and she had answered: "Behold, I am the handmaid of the Lord." Now, when Jesus was about to accomplish the redemption by His Passion and death, she persevered in that act of obedience and surrender to the will of God, repeating within herself those words spoken long ago: "Behold, I am the handmaid of the Lord."

As Jesus, in the Garden of Gethsemane, seeing before Him His coming suffering, recoiled before it but was unable to refuse the chalice of suffering because it was offered by the hand of His Father, so Mary His Mother, during the Crucifixion, saw, beyond the hands of the executioners, the hand of the heavenly Father, who had decreed that the Son of God who had been born of her should thus take away the sins of the world. She did not rebel against what was done by the Father's hand.

Had Mary been permitted to speak but one word to Jesus in this hour of suffering, she would have addressed Him with the words: "May the will of the Father be done." Whereas the mother of the Maccabees exhorted her son to remain steadfast, in the redemption it was the Son who preceded, and the mother who followed in complete surrender to her Son's will.

Hence, throughout the time of the Passion, Mary was obliged to remain completely passive. We would be misunderstanding the severity and magnitude of her sorrow if we supposed that she maintained an attitude of composure simply for the sake of prudence or in order not to enrage the soldiers. Now, more than before, she was the handmaid of the Lord, freely consenting to what the Father had decreed for His Son for the sake of mankind. Such was her attitude toward her Son and the redemption during the harrowing hours of the Passion.

Mary's assistance in the redemption

Mary assisted in the sacrifice of her Son on the cross. We cannot easily understand how much she contributed to our Savior and His work by this assistance, and how much this assistance meant for Him during His Passion. Her assistance included everything that a human being could have offered to Jesus during His sacrifice.

A man can persevere in pain and suffering only to the extent to which he sees some value and purpose in his suffering. The more he values the good for which he suffers, the more he will be able to bear; the more certain he is of obtaining the good by his sufferings, the more clearly, above all his pain and anguish, the thought will arise that it is not in vain. In the depths of his soul, a spark of joy unquenched by pain will let him know that his suffering is a conflict that will end in triumph.

No man ever lived whose suffering had such an all-embracing purpose and value as the suffering of Jesus on the cross, nor did any man have such a complete understanding of the purpose and value of his suffering. While Jesus' pains flared like flames about Him, and His body was being consumed as in a holocaust, there was in the depth of His soul a mute inexpressible joy because these sufferings were restoring the glory of the Father. It mattered not whether those who stood about the cross, or all men throughout the world, entered into the sacrifice or not.

While He suffered thus, only one help was possible for him, which would not soften or diminish His pains. This help or assistance consisted in the knowledge that He was not alone in His suffering, that there were others who would appreciate the value and purpose of His suffering, who would see that His death was really a victory bought not too dearly, and who would celebrate it with thanksgiving. To have but one human being with Him in these hours of deadly pain was for Jesus a real benefit and true assistance that could not be outweighed by anything else.

Every thoughtful reader of the Gospel narrative of the agony on the Mount of Olives will realize that Jesus was able to receive such human consolation, and that as a man he stood in need of it. He pleaded with the Apostles for the comfort of their presence; more than once He fled from the terror and darkness into their company, even though He knew they would be asleep. Then the angel came to comfort Him. And now it was Mary who supported Him with all the strength of her soul.

In the plan of redemption, Mary's assistance was more significant than that of the angel at Gethsemane. It was assistance offered the Redeemer by a human being, by one of His own kind. Besides this, His desire for understanding and support increased from hour to hour as His interior and exterior desolation increased. Deprived of His freedom, He was unable to give expression to this desire, and thus the union of Mary's will, persevering with His own until death, was all the more important for Him.

While He was being overwhelmed by a raging stream of abuse and derision, He knew that the purest woman of the race, the only one unstained by sin, was standing at the foot of the cross. As often as the cruel language of mockery fell upon His ears, thoughts of adoration and surrender to the will of the Father rose up to Him from Mary's heart. While He was mocked and derided, Mary adored Him as the Redeemer of the world. "Even if no one else understands, you understand," was the thought that went from Jesus to Mary; and the answer: "Yes, even though all these deride and mock, I remain faithful," came uninterruptedly from Mary's heart. This consent and support of Mary's soul was the only possible assistance that a human being could have offered the Redeemer in the labor of the redemption.

Mary not only suffered with Jesus, but with Him she looked beyond to the blessings that would come to the human race from these sufferings. In the soul of Jesus, beneath the waves of pain and suffering that surged over it, was an ineffable joy because the glory of the Father was being restored on earth and the kingdom of grace was being established for mankind. So, too, in Mary's soul, in the midst of all her anguish, there was a similar joy because Jesus the Son of God and her Son was taking away the sins of the world by His Passion and death and was making it possible for men to become the children of the heavenly Father.

All Mary's glorious titles, elevating her above all other saints, are based upon this assistance during the Crucifixion, upon this union with the Redeemer in His sacrifice. She is called the assistant at the sacrifice offered by Jesus for the redemption of the human race. This thought is emphasized in Pius X's encyclical *Ad illum diem*. He says: "Mary's thoughts were not completely absorbed by the sight of the terrible tragedy; at the same time she rejoiced because her only Son was offered in sacrifice for the salvation of mankind."

How great a consolation it would have been for Jesus if He had seen Peter standing at the foot of the cross or if in John's soul there had been more than personal loyalty—a profound and living faith in the inestimable value of these sufferings! But Mary alone understood and thus she alone bore in her heart the knowledge that what had taken place was of infinite value for the race; she alone treasured this knowledge in her heart during those dark hours until the Resurrection, when His faithful disciples, the ordained messengers of the faith, were sitting devoid of understanding and appreciation in the upper room, because they knew not what else to do. Mary's faith was all that remained of Jesus' kingdom of God in the hours after His death; her faith was the bridge that joined His Passion and death to the nascent Church of Easter morning.

Mary's new maternity

But standing by the cross of Jesus were his mother, and his mother's sister, Mary the wife of Clopas, and Mary Magdalene. When Jesus saw his mother, and the disciple whom he loved standing near, he said to his mother, "Woman, behold, your son! " Then he said to the disciple, "Behold, your mother! " And from that hour the disciple took her to his own home (Jn 19: 25–27).

The grace of God in all its wealth and depth and power was brought among men in the Incarnation of Jesus, but it remained hidden from men and even from Satan. Gradually, however, men began to feel that in Jesus a new power had come into the world, a power that they must acknowledge in submission or that they must oppose with bitterness. Then those who, in the words of Simeon's prophecy, arose to contradict broke the vessel of grace in order to destroy it; but they only shattered its shell and freed the treasure of grace that it might be poured out upon the whole world.

Thus the Savior's death was at the same time a birth, not as two events following each other closely, for His death simultaneously effected a new creation. His death was like a light that by its flame dispels and annihilates the darkness. Just as there is never a moment when the darkness has disappeared and the light has not yet come, so at the death of Jesus there was never a moment between the coming of the kingdom of grace and the departure of Jesus from this world. The Savior's sacrificial death and His establishment of the kingdom of grace are inseparable from each other and from Himself, the incarnate Son of God and the permanent head of the Church.

Just as there was no interval between the death of Jesus and this second creation of grace, so there was no separation of the two aspects of His death for Mary, who was assisting with full knowledge and full consent. As the Mother, she lost her Son and thus died inwardly with Him. She died with Him because of the Father's will, which had decreed that so the salvation of the world should be accomplished; therefore she was to participate and assist as the mother at the new creation, which was founded in the death of Jesus.

Each man's position in the eternal kingdom of God will be determined by his position in the kingdom of God here on earth. To the Apostles Jesus promised that, because of their labors in the kingdom of God on earth, they should sit upon twelve thrones in the world to come; as they were the first to declare themselves for His kingdom here, so they should have a comparable place in the eternal kingdom.

But Mary, under much greater difficulties, had done much more for the kingdom of God than the Apostles had, and for that reason she deserved a throne above the thrones of the Apostles. More than this, there was a profound difference between Mary and the Apostles. They declared themselves for His new kingdom after He ascended into heaven and sent the Holy Spirit down upon them; but at the crucial time of the conflict, when the kingdom was being founded, they had deserted their Master or, like John, had not possessed that faith which would have enabled them to enter into His sacrificial death.

This is the great and essential difference that elevates Mary above all men, even above the greatest saints. Before and during the death of her Son, therefore before and during the founding of the Church through His death, Mary willed to suffer with Jesus that the kingdom of God might come upon earth. She not only sacrificed and suffered in the kingdom of God after it had been established, she willingly suffered and joined in Jesus' sacrifice at the birth of the Church. Therefore, her relationship to the Church should be that of a mother who in sorrow gives life to her children.

The new creation of grace was still hidden from the eyes of men. Mary, the mother of the Redeemer, alone in this hour beneath the cross believed firmly that the work of the redemption would not fail but would be accomplished. She who knew in what miraculous manner Jesus had come into the world, who until now had been obliged to observe His works from a distance, was given a place in His work by His last words. St. John says: "When Jesus saw his mother, and the disciple whom he loved standing near, he said to his mother, 'Woman, behold, your son!' Then he said to the disciple, 'Behold, your mother!' And from that hour the disciple took her to his own home." In these words Mary's relationship to the faithful was established for all time.

These words of Jesus must have immediately recalled to Mary the words He spoke at the wedding in Cana. There too He addressed her as "woman." This address linked the last words of her dying Son with the words He spoke at the beginning of His public ministry: "Woman, my hour is not yet come." Now that hour had come. In that hour when, humanly speaking, everything for which He had labored was laid waste, when all that He had gathered was dispersed, He united Mary to the only disciple who had persevered and made them the first beginning of His future Church. He entrusted Mary to John as to her son, and asked John to look upon her as his mother.

Because Mary's sacrifice for the establishment of the Church was made at the very moment of its being founded, her position in the Church was now established for all time. In his hour when Jesus, by His sacrifice on the cross, communicated and distributed to all men the grace of God, which would make them children of the Father and His own brothers, Mary assisted as the deacon of the sacrifice.[1] Accordingly, in the kingdom of God she was to be the mediatrix, standing close to Jesus the Son of God, from whom the channels of grace would flow out upon the children of men.

This word of Jesus: "Woman, behold, your son," was also the last word Mary heard from His lips. The other important words addressed to her, the words of Simeon in the Temple, the words of Jesus at Cana, referred to the future, indeed to this hour itself, when Jesus spoke the word that no longer referred to the future but referred to her relation to the disciples and to His Church. Now Mary became the mother of St. John, the mother of the Apostles, the mother of the nascent Church; because the early Church is identical with the Church of all times, she also became the mother of all the faithful.

This word by which Jesus gave His Mother to St. John was received by the Church in all times and places. It was not only the faithful of the early Church who assembled about Mary in prayer; in ages to come the relationship to the Mother of the Redeemer remained something living and life-giving. The faithful felt themselves attracted in a special manner to appeal to her in their necessities and trials, to call the Mother of Jesus their own mother, since she had not only given life to the Redeemer but, in the great hour of the redemption, had been most intimately united to Him in suffering and sacrifice.

The death of Jesus

After this Jesus, knowing that all was now finished, said (to fulfill the scripture), "I thirst." A bowl full of vinegar stood there; so they put a sponge full of the vinegar on hyssop and held it to his mouth. When Jesus had received the vinegar, he said, "It is finished" (Jn 19: 28-30). Then Jesus, crying with a loud voice, said, "Father, into thy hands I commit my spirit!" And having said this he breathed his last (Lk 23: 46).

After His cry of dereliction, another lament came from the lips of Jesus. In the torments of a raging fever, He cried: "I thirst."

The first service of love which a mother renders her child is to give him drink; and whenever a mother is at the bedside of her dying child, this is also the last service. Often when Jesus was a

---

[1] The Church refrains from the use of such expressions as "the priestly virgin" or "the virgin priest" because Mary's position at the sacrifice of the cross corresponds to the position of the deacon in the solemn celebration of the Sacrifice of the Mass.

boy He had said these same words, "I thirst," to His blessed Mother. Then she had offered Him the vessel with cool water and watched Him as He drank. Now she was standing near Him, as close as in those days, but now He no longer belonged to her. He had been delivered up to the executioners. If only they had allowed her to get a vessel with cold water and once more quench His thirst.

Her pain at hearing these words of her Son was increased when she heard the cruel mocking words of the soldiers. The cry, "I thirst," came soon after the words, "My God, my God, why hast thou forsaken me?" The soldiers were not Jews, but they had some acquaintance with Jewish religious notions, and they thought the word "Elo-i" ("My God") referred to Elijah, the great prophet of the people and the helper in every need, and they made this the occasion for further abuse. One of the soldiers arose and dipped a sponge in sour wine, which they had brought with them in a vessel, and lifted it to Jesus' mouth on a reed. The acid wine burned His inflamed lips. The soldiers said: "Wait, let us see whether Elijah will come to take him down." Mary looked up to Him and saw how His face was distorted, while the callous laughter of the soldiers rang in her ears.

Now all things that had been prophesied about the Passion and death of the Redeemer had been fulfilled. With the knowledge that the joy of victory would prevail over all this suffering, Jesus cried out: "It is finished." These words were the first comfort that came to Mary's soul; but they announced a new sorrow. Jesus bowed His head like one who lays himself to rest, and spoke once more to His Father: "Father, into thy hands I commit my spirit."

Once more that word so confident of love, "Father," came from Jesus' lips. That desolation of spirit in which He had cried out to God His Father had now passed. "Father, into thy hands I commit my spirit." Here is the first gleaming of the light of the Resurrection; the Father will not retain His spirit but will return it to Him that it may once more be united to this body from which it now takes its departure. Pain and sorrow were passed for Jesus, but for Mary they took a new form: Jesus was dead.

The lamentations for the dead

The lamentations for the dead are an ancient custom of the East. As death approaches, relatives and neighbors gather about the sick person. If, in Eastern hospitals conducted according to European methods, the relatives are not permitted in the sick room, they will wait for hours, or even for days, outside the door. When the person dies, they begin the lamentations, which, although observing certain ancient forms, are prompted by genuine grief. Those who are unable to be present at the funeral chant the lamentations later while visiting the grave.

Besides those who were moved to genuine grief by the bereavement in a family circle, certain women, professional mourners, were hired to chant the lamentations.

To us this practice is strange and, if we witness such a scene in the East, our dislike of the custom becomes greater. Nevertheless, these lamentations, in the atmosphere of Eastern life, are not so unreasonable as they appear to us. They do not indeed bring any solace to the dead; but the living are comforted and consoled when they hear the dead being praised.

These preliminary remarks I thought necessary to prepare the way for a discussion of certain events that occurred at the time of our Lord's death. Although we are principally concerned with Mary, in our consideration we will include the other women who were present at His death. These women, true daughters of the East, could not permit Jesus' death to be deprived of the customary lamentations. Their neglect of the usual expression of grief would have been a failure to manifest their love of Him.

If we wish to reconstruct the scene according to the customs of the time and place, we must assume that at Jesus' death the women intoned the lamentations in accents and phrases that they had heard on similar occasions. The Gospel merely says that the women "stood at a distance and saw these things." But frequently the Gospel narrative omits obvious details. Who could have been present at such a death and not break forth in lamentations? The weeping women on the way of the cross had already begun a sort of lamentation.

How did Mary conduct herself at Jesus' death? In the later Middle Ages, features were woven into her life that corresponded to the emotional reactions of the time. She is accordingly pictured as being so overcome that she sank beneath her great burden of grief. Later, the opposite view was taken; the fact was stressed that Mary "stood" beneath the cross. Perhaps the word "stood" was too much insisted on, and she was at times

219

represented not as the living, suffering Mother, but as an unfeeling statue.

The Gospel mentions that Jesus wept at the grave of His friend Lazarus. If He did not think it unbecoming His divine dignity to weep publicly for His deceased friend, we may reasonably suppose that His blessed Mother gave outward expression to her grief at His death. It is only human to give decent and dignified expression of our sorrow, as it is unnatural and unreasonable to give way to frenzied lamentations or to suppress our grief within ourselves. Probably Mary joined in the customary lamentations of the dead, avoiding, of course, anything unbecoming or excessive.

St. Ephraem, the Syrian poet who died about 350 and was therefore close to the Passion in time and place, wrote a poem that he called "The Lamentation of Mary." It is composed very much according to the style of Eastern lamentations for the dead, with alternating questions and exclamations. The following lines are excerpts from the poem:

My dearest, most beloved Son, how is it that thou must suffer the torments of the cross?

My Son and my God, how canst thou endure all these things, the nails and the lance, the blows upon the cheek, the mockery and derision, the crown of thorns, the purple mantle, the sponge with vinegar and the reed, the gall and the vinegar?

How is it that Thou hangest naked upon the cross, Thou, my Son, who didst cover the heavens with the clouds?

Thou sufferest thirst, and art Thou not the Creator who didst make the sea and the fountains of water? Thou art the most innocent and Thou diest between two criminals.

What hast Thou done of evil? In what, my Son, hast Thou offended the Jews? Why have these unjust, ungrateful people fastened Thee to this cross? Didst Thou not heal their lame and sick, and raise their dead to life?

Where are now Thy friends, Thou my dearest Son, my great God?

I am consumed with sorrow when I behold Thee hanging on this tree of torments, fastened with nails and covered with wounds.

Where is now Thy beauty and Thy comeliness? The sun has hidden his glory and refuses to give his light. The light of the moon has disappeared and she is hidden in darkness. Great rocks are shattered and graves are opened, and the veil of the Temple is rent in twain.

O Simeon, thou holy seer, now I feel the sword which thou didst foretell piercing my heart.

My Son and my God, I behold Thy terrible suffering and this unjust death
to which they have condemned Thee, and I cannot come to Thy
assistance.
O mourn with me, all ye disciples of the Lord, you who see my great
sorrow and the grievous wound in my heart.

But the poet does more than describe Mary's suffering. He also
considers her the woman who consented to Jesus' Passion and
who saw beyond the Passion and His death. The lamentation
ends with these lines:

My Son, I venerate Thy sufferings, I praise and adore Thy mercy and Thy
magnanimity.
The humiliation which Thou hast taken upon Thyself has become the
glory of all, Thy death has become the life of the world.

Preparations for the burial

Since it was the day of Preparation, in order to prevent the bodies from
remaining on the cross on the sabbath (for that sabbath was a high day),
the Jews asked Pilate that their legs might be broken, and that they might
be taken away. So the soldiers came and broke the legs of the first, and of
the other who had been crucified with him; but when they came to Jesus
and saw that he was already dead, they did not break his legs. But one of
the soldiers pierced his side with a spear, and at once there came out
blood and water. He who saw it has borne witness—his testimony is true,
and he knows that he tells the truth—that you also may believe. For
these things took place that the scripture might be fulfilled, "Not a bone
of him shall be broken." And again another scripture says, "They shall
look on him whom they have pierced" (Jn 19:31-37).

By Jesus' death Mary was placed in an entirely different world.
During all the vicissitudes of the past, one thing had remained
always the same: her life and suffering had been like the shadow
of His life and suffering. But now His life was ended, and she lived
on. When a mother stands by the dead body of her child, a change
takes place in her soul. Until he breathes his last, she is intent
upon his sufferings, fearful lest she fail to support him by her
presence in his last moment. But when death has come, love's
attention turns back to the past and lovingly gathers all the sweet
memories of the dead. The child's body is, as it were, a book in
which are written the incidents of the life that is now closed.
Thus the burial of the body is the climax of the mother's sorrow.

With regard to those who stood by the cross, Mary's position was also altered. In the ordinary course of things, the body would be taken down from the cross and then buried or, since Jesus had been condemned as a rebel who wished to make Himself king, the body might be burned as part of the sentence according to which the last vestiges of a rebel were to be destroyed. Even though Pilate was convinced of our Lord's innocence, many of the Jews were of a different opinion. Once Pilate issued the death sentence, he could not readily act in a way that would reflect on his first judgment.

Mary was stricken with a new fright when she saw a detachment of soldiers come from the city and approach the cross. A group of Jews had gone to Pilate and, quoting a provision of their law, asked that the legs of the crucified be broken and their bodies removed. The soldiers came and broke the legs of the two thieves, then the bodies were taken down for burial.

Mary had seen how the "good thief" had died, after the Savior promised Paradise to him. She also had seen how the other thief, who blasphemed Jesus, remained obdurate to the end. These two men, it seemed to her, were symbols of Simeon's prophecy: "Behold this child is set for the fall and rising of many in Israel."

Meanwhile, Mary's heart was torn by apprehension. What would the soldiers do with the body of her Son? Would it be taken down also, loaded on a cart, and buried in some ditch? Every mother cherishes the feeling that she has a right to the body of her child; because of that feeling, she may rise up in defense of the body if malicious hands dare to touch it.

But events took another course. When the soldiers saw that Jesus was already dead, one of them thrust his lance into the side of the dead body. Mary saw the spearhead enter and be withdrawn, leaving an opening from which flowed blood and water. No mother could have witnessed such a happening without feeling a pain enter her own heart. That thrust of the lance also entered Mary's heart.

The burial

And when evening had come, since it was the day of Preparation, that is, the day before the sabbath, Joseph of Arimathea, a respected member of the council, who was also himself looking for the kingdom of God, took courage and went to Pilate, and asked for the body of Jesus. And Pilate wondered if he were already dead; and summoning the centurion, he asked him whether he was already dead. And when he learned from the centurion that he was dead, he granted the body to Joseph. And he bought a linen shroud, and taking him down, wrapped him in the linen shroud, and laid him in a tomb which had been hewn out of the rock; and he rolled a stone against the door of the tomb. Mary Magdalene and Mary the mother of Joses saw where he was laid (Mk 15: 42–47; see also Mt 27: 57–61; Lk 23: 50–56; Jn 19: 38–42).

Because Jesus had been executed as a criminal, Pilate could have disposed of His body. Besides Pilate, Mary was the only one who needed to be consulted about the arrangements for the burial. It was probably soon after our Lord's death that Joseph of Arimathea and Nicodemus made known to Mary that they wished to bury Him in a sepulcher near at hand.

This was the first consolation Mary received from others after the Passion of her divine Son. She still hovered between hope and fear, for Pilate must first give his consent to the burial, and even then the possibility remained that the enemies of Jesus would put obstacles in the way.

Nicodemus hurried into the city and went to the bazaar to purchase spices. Joseph of Arimathea went to Pilate and asked for permission to bury the body of Jesus. Pilate wondered when this noble counsellor appeared before him, announcing the death of Jesus and asking for His body. Only a short while before, other important men, the chief priests, had come and obtained an order that the legs of the crucified men should be broken; now this nobleman announces that Jesus has died. Pilate called the centurion and, upon hearing his report, gave Joseph permission to take the body of Jesus.

Soon after the soldier had opened Jesus' side, Joseph and Nicodemus came to Calvary to prepare the body for burial. With them came servants and disciples carrying spices and linen cloths. Mary was consoled at the sight of these preparations for burial: they were the first visible pledge that Jesus' words about the Resurrection on the third day would be fulfilled.

The men began to take the body down from the cross. The darkened blood was washed away, and the wounds stood forth clearly. Then Jesus once again, as when He was a child, was laid in Mary's arms. In those years of His childhood, often she had looked on Him with faith and adoration, and said: "This is He who will redeem the world." Now she looked on Him again, and with all the faith of her soul she said: "This is the Redeemer of the world."

The body was placed in linen cloths and bound with linen bands. That had been the service she rendered Him in the crib in Bethlehem; now others were doing it for the last time. Afterward, she was reminded of the little body wrapped in swaddling clothes in the manger. Mary saw how reverently these men lifted the body of her Son; she saw how they grieved because of her sorrow; and her heart went out to them in gratitude.

They carried the body into the burial chamber. The tomb, located in a garden that had a wall of rock at one end, was hewn in this. Just within the entrance of the tomb was an antechamber where the body was prepared for burial. From this room a low entrance led into the burial chamber itself.

Only those actually engaged in the burial could enter this chamber because of the restricted space. When the men had gone, Mary went into the inner chamber. The men believed that they had said their last farewell to Jesus, but Mary knew that on the third day He would rise again. Even now she had a presentiment that, after the Resurrection, He would no longer be her Son as He had been before His Passion, and that He would never again live together with her in the old intimacy. Therefore, she, too, in a certain sense, bade Him a last farewell.

When she had left the tomb, the men rolled a stone before the opening. The Sabbath was about to begin; any moment now they might hear the trumpets announcing that all work must cease.

The little group returned to the city. The streets had been swept and cleared; people were wearing their Sabbath garments. They seemed already to have forgotten the day's events, while the women and the disciples were so stricken with grief that they had no thought for the present.

For Mary everything was now changed. She knew that mankind had been redeemed by the Savior's death and that a new light had arisen for the world. As once she had borne within her the faith in the Messiah, so now she was the depositary of the faith that the world had been redeemed by Jesus. To the others, even to the Apostles, it seemed not only that His work had been ended, but that it had failed. From Good Friday until Easter morning, the mystical body of Christ reposed in Mary alone.

VIII.

Mary in the Early Church

The Resurrection

The women who had come with him from Galilee followed, and saw the tomb, and how his body was laid; then they returned, and prepared spices and ointments.

On the sabbath they rested according to the commandment (Lk 23: 55-56).

And when the sabbath was past, Mary Magdalene, and Mary the mother of James, and Salome, bought spices, so that they might go and anoint him (Mk 16: 1; see also Mt 28: 1-4; Jn 20: 1).

According to the customs of the time, Mary probably spent the time from Friday until Sunday in the company of the women who stood with her at the foot of the cross. It is also likely that these women did not separate, but returned together to the house where they had found lodging as pilgrims to the paschal feast.

The question arises whether the women occupied the same house as the disciples. The Gospels throw little light on the question, since the movements of the women and of the disciples on Sunday morning are so interwoven that we cannot determine the order of their occurrence. This may be because the women and the disciples lodged in different houses and each group acted independently of the other. Perhaps the women were not all lodged in the same house. Only when the great event of the Resurrection became known to them did they again communicate with one another. Mary Magdalene hurried to the Apostles. The Gospel seems to imply that she did not go to the tomb from the house where the Apostles lodged, but that she knew where Peter and John could be found. There the women and the Apostles came together. After this, they all seemed to act separately again: Peter and John went to the tomb alone; Mary Magdalene also went alone, and after Jesus had appeared to her she went, in obedience to His command, to inform the disciples that the Lord had risen.

Outwardly, Mary the Mother of Jesus had some association with the other women because she lodged in the same house with them or close by. But inwardly, she was separated from them. She grieved, indeed, over Jesus much more than they, but not in their hopeless way, for she believed in His Resurrection on the third day. Meanwhile, these women had but one thought: to go out to the tomb on the morning following the Sabbath to complete the anointing of the body and make it ready for final burial. Mary is not mentioned as taking part in these preparations. The women sympathized with her in her sorrow, but for themselves they felt that all hope must now be abandoned.

In this loneliness from Friday until Easter, Mary became a stranger to all about her. The women were unable to speak a word of consolation without adding to her sorrow, for, like the disciples on the road to Emmaus, they would have had to say that her Son was indeed a great prophet, "mighty in work and word," but not, as they had hoped, the promised Messiah.

The day after Good Friday was a Sabbath, a holy day of obligation, and Mary certainly did not omit the prescribed visit to the Temple. As is recorded of the Apostles in the following weeks, she also went up to the Temple to pray. Only a week had passed since Jesus had made His solemn entrance into Jerusalem; the palm branches still lay, trodden under foot and covered with dust, by the roadside. A week ago, the populace waved these palm branches as they acclaimed the Messiah King. With indescribable sentiments of prayer, Mary lifted her soul to God on this Sabbath. All hope for the Resurrection had been concentrated in her heart. How the Resurrection would take place, what Jesus would do thereafter—all this was still unknown to her.

An ancient and commonly accepted belief in the Church is that after the Resurrection Jesus appeared first to Mary alone because, as His Mother, she had suffered with Him the torments of the Crucifixion and because His appearing to her possessed a significance different from His appearances to the women and the disciples. Faith had to be reestablished in the hearts of the women and the disciples. Mary was to receive the reward for her perseverance in faith.

The scene was one of unspeakable calm and intimacy. Mary, the Mother of Jesus, was sitting alone in her chamber; outside, the world, after the Sabbath rest, aroused itself to a new workday. Mary thought of only one thing: He will rise. For her the element of surprise, which so astounded the disciples, did not exist. As she had known and felt the pangs of the Passion long before it took place, so now she was fully prepared by her faith for the Resurrection.

We do not, of course, know under what circumstances our Lord's appearance to His Mother took place. He appeared to Mary Magdalene in such form that she did not recognize Him and mistook Him for the gardener of the place. He appeared to the two disciples on the way to Emmaus as a stranger. He appeared to the assembled Apostles behind locked doors, and to the five hundred followers in Galilee as if at a reunion of friends. Doubtless He appeared to His Mother Mary in such a way that she understood He was now in the state of transfiguration and glory and that He would not continue His former mode of existence on earth. His relationship to Mary had already changed, since He had entrusted her to John and made John her son.

From Easter to the Ascension

After the Resurrection, Jesus appeared to His disciples in Jerusalem and Judea, and these appearances strengthened the women and the disciples and gathered together the dispersed flock. The faith of the disciples had been shattered. They had persistently hoped for an earthly kingdom. But now, from the ruins of their shattered faith, illumined by recent happenings, a new faith was rising. Jesus was not only He who would save Israel, He was the Son of God. Formerly they called Him "Master"; now they began to call Him "the Lord."

The disciples found themselves in a precarious position. The enemies of Jesus did not believe in the Resurrection and were compelled to advance another reason for the disappearance of the body from the tomb. Only one such explanation suggested itself: the disciples had stolen the body. The penalty for such a desecration was death. Some years ago an inscription was discovered in Nazareth containing an imperial edict fixing the death penalty for those who violated the graves of the dead. If the disciples had heard the current rumors that they had stolen the body of Jesus, they must have expected to be arrested at any time. Not without reason, therefore, they hid themselves behind barred doors in the upper room. Not only the Apostles, we are told, but also "those who were with them" (Lk 24: 33), a group of

Jesus' followers, including probably also the women and Mary, had assembled in the upper room.

In obedience to the Lord's command, the Apostles and Mary left Jerusalem and went to Galilee. This return to Galilee was a great humiliation for Mary and the disciples. What reports had been carried back to Nazareth about Jesus by the pilgrims returning from the Passover! The chief news was that Jesus of Nazareth, Mary's Son, had been taken prisoner in Jerusalem, condemned to death, and crucified. Then the usual flood of invidious comment followed, including not only Jesus, but also Mary and the disciples. What would this Mary do now? Had she not always been an unusual person? And what would these fishermen do now, they who had let themselves be taken from their occupation by Jesus? Nothing remained for them but to go back to their nets.

Returning to Galilee, Mary and the disciples entered into an atmosphere where such questions and comments flew back and forth, and it seemed that the Apostles were actually following the suggestions of the people of Nazareth: they went out from Capernaum to catch fish. But wherever they guided their boats, they were reminded of the times when Jesus was with them. Then, one morning, after a laborious and fruitless night, He appeared to them; He stood on the shore and directed them to cast out their nets once more. They did as He told them and caught such a great number of fish that their nets broke. John was the first to recognize the Master in this stranger, and probably also the first to tell Mary of the appearance, since she probably lived with him now at Capernaum.

The days from Easter to Pentecost were days of mingled joy and sorrow for Mary. Every step of the journey from Jerusalem to Galilee was a step into the past, into that life with Jesus. She entered the house at Nazareth, where she had lived with Him for so many years. Here was the fireplace at which she had stood so often and thought of Him whether He was near or far; here the mats on which He had sat, the vessels from which He had eaten, the tools with which He had worked, the hammer He had used to drive nails into the wood. Everything she saw reminded her that she was now alone. And what had she become in the eyes of the people about her? In the first hour of her return to Nazareth the news had gone from house to house: Mary, the mother of Jesus the crucified, has come home.

The Ascension

And while staying with them he charged them not to depart from Jerusalem, but to wait for the promise of the Father, which, he said, "you heard from me, for John baptized with water, but before many days you shall be baptized with the Holy Spirit."

So when they had come together, they asked him, "Lord, will you at this time restore the kingdom to Israel?" He said to them, "It is not for you to know times or seasons which the Father has fixed by his own authority. But you shall receive power when the Holy Spirit has come upon you; and you shall be my witnesses in Jerusalem and in all Judea and Samaria and to the end of the earth." And when he had said this, as they were looking on, he was lifted up, and a cloud took him out of their sight. And while they were gazing into heaven as he went, behold, two men stood by them in white robes, and said, "Men of Galilee, why do you stand looking into heaven? This Jesus, who was taken up from you into heaven, will come in the same way as you saw him go into heaven."

Then they returned to Jerusalem from the mount called Olivet, which is near Jerusalem, a sabbath day's journey away; and when they had entered, they went up to the upper room, where they were staying, Peter and John and James and Andrew, Philip and Thomas, Bartholomew and Matthew, James the son of Alphaeus and Simon the Zealot and Judas the son of James. All these with one accord devoted themselves to prayer, together with the women and Mary the mother of Jesus, and with his brethren (Acts 1: 4-14).

And they returned to Jerusalem with great joy, and were continually in the temple blessing God (Lk 24: 52-53; see also Mk 16: 19).

Forty days after the Resurrection, the disciples met in Jerusalem in obedience to Jesus' command. The period of rest had come to an end; soon they were to go out into the world as the heralds of the new kingdom. Mary accompanied the disciples to the Holy City.

Everywhere she saw reminders of the Passion, of Jesus' condemnation, the way of the cross, and His death on Calvary. The bazaars were open, merchants cried their wares in the streets, but for Mary they were only figures that recalled the days of the Passion, when Jesus had offered the great sacrifice for the redemption of the world.

The disciples lodged again in the house where Jesus had bade them farewell before His Passion. Now He was to bid them a final farewell; He would appear to them once more. He spoke to them of what they must do in the future: "These are my words which I spoke to you, while I was still with you, that everything written about me in the law of Moses and the prophets and the psalms must be fulfilled. . . . Thus it is written, that the Christ should suffer and on the third day rise from the dead, and that repentance and forgiveness of sins should be preached in his name to all nations, beginning from Jerusalem. You are witnesses of these things. And behold, I send the promise of my Father upon you; but stay in the city, until you are clothed with power from on high" (Lk 24:44-49).

Then they all left the upper room and went to the Mount of Olives. They went down into the Cedron valley, crossed the brook, and ascended the steep slope on the other side. Jesus saw again that place where on the night of terrors He had prayed and agonized. Now all that was past. As they went up, they had a better view of the city; below they saw the Temple place encircled by its colonnades, and beyond that the towers of Herod's palace, and farther north the hill of Calvary. Jesus blessed the disciples and His Mother and then lifted Himself up and disappeared from them in a cloud.

Frequently nothing is said of Mary's life after this event. True, the Gospels report no further details of her life, but the words of Jesus on the cross, "Woman, behold, thy son—Behold, thy mother," contained a commission both for Mary and for John, and this commission gave their lives a purpose.

After the Ascension, the disciples returned to Jerusalem "with great joy." There was a contrast between this farewell and the farewell before His Passion. Then they had known nothing of a presence of Jesus that did not presuppose His visible nearness; now they understood that He was present with them even though they could not see Him.

But as they returned to Jerusalem, Mary's joy was greater than that of the Apostles; it was the joy of the Mother of the Redeemer, rejoicing that now her Son's work might bud forth like a grain of wheat and grow until it covered the whole world. Turning toward the south, she saw the district where Bethlehem lay; there in a stable, in the dark of night, in a miraculous manner, her Son had begun His earthly life; now the earth was the footstool from which He had ascended into heaven.

Few things unite men so intimately as to have been together in bidding farewell to one they all love. The picture of the one who has gone is deeply impressed upon them all and binds them to one another. Children are never closer to each other and to their mother than on the day when they return together from the grave in which they have laid their father to rest.

Thus, too, it was with Mary and the disciples. They were closely united, and in this little community Mary began to have a more exalted position, because Jesus had now become for them "the Lord."

After the Ascension, the disciples no longer expected further appearances. Jesus had frequently and expressly foretold that He would leave them and that He would send another Comforter. Now, too, the breach between the relatives of Jesus was closed; for the first time these relatives who had "not believed in him" are mentioned among His followers.

This change was probably brought about by the sojourn of Mary and the disciples in Galilee after the Resurrection. There they had mingled with His relatives, who also had been given an opportunity of seeing Him. Perhaps that appearance which Jesus had prearranged for His faithful followers was of special significance for His relatives. Then they who had known Him from the days of His youth and therefore refused to believe that He was the Son of God saw Him coming from another world, the same Man indeed whom they had seen laboring as a carpenter; and then they believed.

Mary rejoiced because now they were united not only as blood relatives, but also as spiritual relatives. Indeed, the old physical relationship had been dissolved when Jesus entrusted her care to John; when John took Mary "unto his own," the action was so unprecedented that it must have occasioned a break with her relatives. After this, according to their view of things, they could no longer count themselves among her relatives, but they entered now into the community of the faithful, not as members of her family, but as members of the same spiritual kingdom.

The Ascension was the ending of Jesus' earthly life with His disciples; it also marked the conclusion of His earthly life with Mary. From now on, all her energies were dedicated to the work of the Apostles.

He had died for the salvation of mankind. His last wish and commission to her had been that after His death she should not withdraw into that circle of relatives at Nazareth but should enter the spiritual community He had founded. Could Mary have been unconcerned about the work her Son had entrusted to the

Apostles? Did she not, more than all others, comprehend the significance of that work?

Thus all her love was absorbed in the work Jesus had begun. When the disciples began to pray in preparation for the coming of the Holy Spirit, Mary joined them. The Scriptures give but a meager description of this early community of the Church. We know that they numbered somewhat more than a hundred persons and that they assembled in an upper room, probably the room in which Jesus had celebrated the Last Supper. They did not, of course, all live there; the upper room was merely the place where they gathered for prayer.

Mary and the coming of the Holy Spirit

In the Old Testament, the Spirit of God had already been mentioned and was understood to be God operating in the souls of men. In those days, men had as yet no knowledge of the existence of a third divine Person. Even when the angel announced to Mary: "The Holy Spirit will come upon you, and the power of the Most High will overshadow you," she did not understand the nature of the Holy Spirit and His relationship to the Father and the Son in the same manner as she did after Jesus began to preach His doctrine.

To illustrate by parables the Person of the Holy Spirit and His operation was not so easy as to explain the Father and the Son. The existence and operation of the Holy Spirit would be revealed as an article of faith only after faith in the Father and the Son had been firmly established.

Jesus in His public teaching spoke of God as His Father and made known that He was the consubstantial Son of the living God from all eternity, co-equal to the Father. Only a short time before His death He began to speak of the existence of a "Comforter" besides Himself and the Father. For the Apostles, the matter remained clouded in mystery; when Jesus spoke of the third Person as the "Comforter," the term was not so descriptive as "Father" and "Son."

When Mary miraculously conceived the Son of God, she was endowed with a special mysterious knowledge that enabled her to understand, better and more readily than the Apostles, the revelations Jesus made about the Father in heaven and about Himself, the consubstantial Son of the Father. So when He began to speak about the Holy Spirit, Mary was reminded of the angel's words at the Annunciation: "The Holy Spirit will come upon you, and the power of the Most High will overshadow you." The Holy Spirit whom Jesus was now promising was the same as had come upon her when she became the Mother of Jesus. Her longing for the Holy Spirit, whose light illumined all things, can be compared only with that desire she once had for the coming of the Redeemer before the angel brought the message from heaven. During these days of preparation, the disciples prayed with her, placing their petitions in her prayers, kindling their longing at the flame of her desire; because of her presence in their midst, they felt themselves united in a special manner to Jesus, who had ascended into heaven.

Pentecost

When the day of Pentecost had come, they were all together in one place. And suddenly a sound came from heaven like the rush of a mighty wind, and it filled all the house where they were sitting. And there appeared to them tongues as of fire, distributed and resting on each one of them. And they were all filled with the Holy Spirit and began to speak in other tongues, as the Spirit gave them utterance.

Now there were dwelling in Jerusalem Jews, devout men from every nation under heaven. And at this sound the multitude came together, and they were bewildered, because each one heard them speaking in his own language. And they were amazed and wondered, saying, "Are not all these who are speaking Galileans? And how is it that we hear, each of us in his own native language? Parthians and Medes and Elamites and residents of Mesopotamia, Judea and Cappadocia, Pontus and Asia, Phrygia and Pamphylia, Egypt and the parts of Libya belonging to Cyrene, and visitors from Rome, both Jews and proselytes, Cretans and Arabians, we hear them telling in our own tongues the mighty works of God." And all were amazed and perplexed, saying to one another, "What does this mean?" But others mocking said, "They are filled with new wine" (Acts 2:1-13).

The descent of the Holy Spirit brought the Apostles to the full stature of their vocation. Through His illumination they saw the life of Jesus in its proper place in the history of the Jewish people; they understood its relationship with the Sacred Scriptures and its significance as the foundation of the kingdom of God. What they had until then perceived only in separate detail, they were able to view as a whole.

233

Peter, whom Jesus had chosen as the chief of the Apostles, was the first to go forth and proclaim publicly what the Holy Spirit had revealed to their souls. Fearlessly he addressed the people, saying:

Men of Israel, hear these words: Jesus of Nazareth, a man attested to you by God with mighty works and wonders and signs which God did through him in your midst, as you yourselves know—this Jesus, delivered up according to the definite plan and foreknowledge of God, you cruci- fied and killed by the hands of lawless men. But God raised him up, having loosed the pangs of death, because it was not possible for him to be held by it. For David says concerning him,
"I saw the Lord always before me,
    for he is at my right hand that I may not be shaken. . . ."
Brethren, I may say to you confidently of the patriarch David that he both died and was buried, and his tomb is with us to this day. Being therefore a prophet, and knowing that God had sworn with an oath to him that he would set one of his descendants upon his throne, he foresaw and spoke of the resurrection of the Christ, that he was not abandoned to Hades, nor did his flesh see corruption. This Jesus God raised up, and of that we all are witnesses. Being therefore exalted at the right hand of God, and having received from the Father the promise of the Holy Spirit, he has poured out this which you see and hear. For David did not ascend into the heavens; but he himself says,
"The Lord said to my Lord, Sit at my right hand,
    till I make thy enemies a stool for thy feet."
Let all the house of Israel therefore know assuredly that God has made him both Lord and Christ, this Jesus whom you crucified (Acts 2: 22–36).

These passages from Peter's sermon show that he now saw in Jesus the fulfillment of all the prophecies concerning the Mes- siah. As to the nature of the redemption, he now possessed an understanding that was essentially different from his earlier con- ception of the kingdom of God.

The Holy Spirit had come upon Peter and illumined the souls of all who were present. Mary, the Mother of Jesus, was also filled by the Holy Spirit, working wonderful effects in her soul. Once before, when she had become the mother of Jesus, He had come upon her in a special manner; now He filled her with His graces for a new calling. He strengthened and equipped her for the last part of her life, when she would no longer be united with Jesus but with His work. Like the Apostles, she received new illumina- tions about the significance of Jesus' life and also an illumination of her relationship to Him and His work. These were given in view of her past life, but much more for the future, when she was to hold the position of the Mother of Jesus in the community of those who believed in Him.

The changes produced by the Holy Spirit in the souls of Mary and of the Apostles brought about a closer union between them. Each day they came closer to each other by reason of their living faith and their burning zeal for the work of the redemption. Now, too, the time had come when the veil might be lifted from Mary's life, when she might come forth as a witness and give testimony to those things in Jesus' earthly life which she alone knew.

Mary's testimony to the divine Sonship of Jesus

Only when the hidden glory of Jesus' life, the glory of the only-begotten Son of the Father, had been revealed, could the fundamental mystery of Mary's life, the mystery of her divine maternity, be made known. Any earlier unveiling of this mystery would have made known Jesus' divinity by a revelation that did not proceed from Him and would have been an anticipation of His own revelation. He did not, however, reveal Himself as the Son of God so much by word as by action, especially by His Resurrection. Therefore, Mary could reveal her faithfully guarded secret only after the revelation of Jesus had been completed by His Resurrection and by the coming of the Holy Spirit.

To whom did she first speak of those happenings in her life, which she had kept secret and which, if revealed, would have made known the miracle of the Incarnation? We cannot be greatly in error if we assume that she entrusted all these secrets to John, that disciple whom Jesus had given her as her son. It was John, the beloved disciple of Jesus, who first learned in what manner Mary became the Mother of the Son of God.

John's soul was so perfectly conformed to the spirit of Jesus and Mary that he was prepared to receive the account of that mystery which, after the Savior's death, was known to Mary alone. It was a solemn moment when Mary recounted to John, "her son," how the angel appeared to her and brought her the message from heaven. The revelation made such a deep impression upon John that everything he knew about Jesus centered on that mystery, so that it became indeed the central thought of the Gospel that he wrote a generation later.

The mystery later became the common possession of the faithful. Mary, who during Jesus' lifetime had remained in the background, became now the maternal witness of the divine Sonship of Jesus.

In the Litany of Loreto, Mary is called the Morning Star. The morning star heralds the coming day, and when day has come the light of the star is extinguished. Mary, filled with grace, heralded the birth of Jesus, but when He Himself appeared, Mary receded, as the stars retire before the brilliance of the sun. When the sun has gone down, the morning star appears again, though now it is called the evening star. So when Jesus' earthly life had ended, Mary appeared again, reflecting the light of His earthly sojourn.

The Evangelists recount numerous events in the Savior's life that must have been communicated to them by Mary.

St. Matthew relates the miraculous conception of Jesus, the visit of the Magi, and the slaughter of the innocents by Herod.

St. Luke, in the beginning of his Gospel, declares that he "followed all things closely for some time past" that he might "write an orderly account." After this introduction, he describes the following events in the life of Jesus: the announcement of John the Baptist's birth, the angel's message to Mary, Mary's visit to her cousin Elizabeth, the birth of John, the birth of Jesus, the visit of the shepherds, the presentation in the Temple, and the finding of the boy Jesus in the Temple. For this knowledge he had to depend on witnesses, especially on Mary, and in his Gospel he remarks on two occasions that Mary "kept all these things in her heart." These words can have but one meaning: that St. Luke based his narrative on Mary's testimony.

Remembering that our Lord had entrusted His Mother to John and that she lived with him after the death of her divine Son, we expect John's Gospel to tell us more than the others regarding those events in Jesus' life in which Mary was concerned. But that Gospel speaks of Mary only twice: at the wedding in Cana and beneath the cross. For the account of the Crucifixion, John was not obliged to rely on Mary's testimony because he himself was present there; and he needed Mary's testimony for the events at Cana only if he had not been present at her conversation with Jesus.

In studying the contents of the Gospels, we must consider what persons exercised any influence in the composition of the Gospel. We know, for example, that the Evangelist Matthew was especially attached to the ancient faith of Israel, and that, therefore, he selected those occurrences in our Lord's life which were fulfillments of Old Testament prophecies. Thus the expression: "This was done that the word of the Scripture might be fulfilled," appears again and again in his Gospel.

St. Mark in his Gospel shows that he was influenced by St. Peter's teaching. In his narrative he makes use of the lively and realistic expressions that are characteristic of Peter even in the other Gospels. Mark was Peter's companion and interpreter. The Gospel of St. Luke shows a similar relationship to the preaching and ideas of St. Paul. As St. Paul declared himself teacher of the Jews and Gentiles, so Luke speaks of our Lord as the Savior of the world, who has appeared for all men. St. Luke was the companion of St. Paul on his missionary journeys.

As St. Matthew had in mind the spiritual concepts of the Jews, as St. Mark and St. Luke reflect the minds of St. Peter and St. Paul, the Gospel of St. John reflects that world of ideas in which Mary and John lived after the Ascension.

The great mystery of Mary's life was the Incarnation of the eternal Son of God. Her thoughts were not so much of her physical motherhood, for then she would be making herself the center of her own thoughts, but of the divine Sonship of Jesus, of which the earthly sonship was only a reflection.

This faith in the divinity of our Lord also dominates the Gospel of St. John. In carefully selected passages, St. John illustrates this chief central thought, which he also solemnly proclaims in the introduction to his Gospel: Jesus, the only begotten Son of God, has come into the world and manifested Himself to the whole world in grace and truth. Every part of the Gospel describes how Jesus manifested Himself, and the Gospel itself concludes with the solemn statement that John is the witness of these revelations.

Another mystery was contained in this mystery of the Incarnation: the mystery of Mary's life in God, which was begun and completed in seclusion. This life in God was the source from which she drew all her knowledge of the divine.

This thought appears as the second central thought of St. John's Gospel, and it is announced after the principal theme in the introduction. All men who have received grace feel themselves drawn to Jesus, and by the grace in their souls they are able to recognize Christ's divinity; all who "are born of God" and have the divine life within them believe in Christ and in His divinity. They strive to come forth from the darkness to Him, the true light. Our Lord Himself said: "He who does what is true comes to the light, that it may be clearly seen that his deeds have been wrought in God" (Jn 3:21). These two thoughts manifest the attitude of John's soul and the extent to which he was imbued with Mary's spirit in the writing of his Gospel.

Throughout, he expresses himself with reserve; he does not even once mention his own name. All that he received from Mary was embodied in his Gospel and became his own word. He speaks as Mary's "Son," and his Gospel is the revelation of the spirit of Mary his "Mother," who bore in her soul the knowledge of Jesus' origin as man and the faith in His heavenly glory, and finally bequeathed it to the early Church as a precious inheritance.

Mary and the Psalms

In the last years of her life, Mary, like other Christians, continued to recite the prayers and psalms of the Old Testament. But now the meaning of the psalms had changed. Before they had been like a mountain that lay before her and must be ascended; now, when she stood on the heights, she looked back on them as on the road over which she had traveled.

Now the twenty-second psalm, which begins: "My God, my God, why hast thou forsaken me?" sounded like an account of the Crucifixion. Jesus had spoken these words while He hung on the cross, and then the sword of sorrow had pierced her soul. His sufferings and desolation were described in detail in this psalm:

> Why art thou so far from helping me, from the words of
>   my groaning?
> O my God, I cry by day, but thou dost not answer;
> and by night, but find no rest.
>
> Yet thou art holy,
>   enthroned on the praises of Israel.
> In thee our fathers trusted;
>   they trusted, and thou didst deliver them.
> To thee they cried, and were saved;
>   in thee they trusted, and were not disappointed.

But I am a worm, and no man;
    scorned by men, and despised by the people.
All who see me mock at me,
    they make mouths at me, they wag their heads;
"He committed his cause to the Lord; let him deliver him;
    let him rescue him, for he delights in him!"

Thus they had mocked Him as He suffered on the cross. Then came those words that reminded her of the time when the Redeemer had been born and the time when she stood beneath the cross:

Yet thou art he who took me from the womb;
    thou didst keep me safe upon my mother's breasts.
Upon thee was I cast from my birth,
    and since my mother bore me thou hast been my God.
Be not far from me.

She heard again how her dying Son cried: "I thirst," when she read the words:

I am poured out like water,
    and all my bones are out of joint;
my heart is like wax,
    it is melted within my breast;
my strength is dried up like a potsherd,
    and my tongue cleaves to my jaws;
thou dost lay me in the dust of death.

The cross bearing her Son surrounded by the executioners appeared before her again:

Yea, dogs are round about me;
    a company of evildoers encircle me;
    they have pierced my hands and feet—
I can count all my bones—
    they stare and gloat over me;
they divide my garments among them,
    and for my raiment they cast lots.

But thou, O Lord, be not far off!
    O thou my help, hasten to my aid!
Deliver my soul from the sword,
    my life from the power of the dog!
Save me from the mouth of the lion,
    my afflicted soul from the horns of the wild oxen.

Then followed the chant of joyous thanksgiving:

I will tell of thy name to my brethren;
  in the midst of the congregation I will praise thee:
You who fear the Lord, praise him!
  all you sons of Jacob, glorify him,
  and stand in awe of him, all you sons of Israel!
For he has not despised or abhorred
  the affliction of the afflicted;
and he has not hid his face from him,
  but has heard, when he cried to him.

From thee comes my praise in the great congregation;
  my vows I will pay before those who fear him.
The afflicted shall eat and be satisfied;
  those who seek him shall praise the Lord!
  May your hearts live for ever!

Now Mary knew of the sacrifice that the poor would eat of and be filled. Jesus had instituted it before His Passion when He said: "This is my body which is given for you. Do this in remembrance of me. . . . This cup which is poured out for you is the new covenant in my blood" (Lk 22: 19, 20). Mary thought of the future, when praise and thanksgiving would never cease, but would continue from generation to generation:

All the ends of the earth shall remember
  and turn to the Lord;
And all the families of the nations
  Shall worship before him.
For dominion belongs to the Lord,
And he rules over the nations.

Yea, to him shall all the proud of the earth bow down;
  before him shall bow all who go down to the dust,
  and he who cannot keep himself alive.
Posterity shall serve him;
  men shall tell of the Lord to the coming generation,
and proclaim his deliverance to a people yet unborn,
  that he has wrought it.

Psalm 110 was like a song of triumph:

The Lord says to my lord:
"Sit at my right hand,
till I make your enemies your footstool."

The Lord sends forth from Zion your mighty scepter.
  Rule in the midst of your foes!

Your people will offer themselves freely
  on the day you lead your host
  upon the holy mountains.
From the womb of the morning
  like dew your youth will come to you.
The Lord has sworn,
  and will not change his mind,
"You are a priest for ever
  after the order of Melchizedek."

The Lord is at your right hand;
  he will shatter kings on the day of his wrath.
He will execute judgment among the nations,
  filling them with corpses;
he will shatter chiefs
  over the wide earth.
He will drink from the brook by the way;
  therefore he will lift up his head.

Standing before the chief priests who condemned Him, Jesus had solemnly announced in the words of this psalm: "But from now on the Son of man shall be seated at the right hand of the power of God" (Luke 22:69); and these words had been fulfilled in the Ascension. Now, too, Mary understood those other words: "You are a priest for ever after the order of Melchizedek." She recalled the Last Supper, when Jesus, like Melchizedek, had taken bread and wine in His holy hands and instituted that new sacrifice which would continue for all time.

After describing Jesus' solemn entry into Jerusalem, St. John says that it was a fulfillment of the prophecy of Zechariah: "Rejoice greatly, O daughter of Zion! . . . Lo, your king comes to you, . . . humble and riding on an ass, on a colt the foal of an ass" (Zech 9:9); and then he says that the disciples had not understood at the time. But when Jesus was glorified, "they remembered that this had been written of him and had been done to him" (Jn 12:16). Thus we are told expressly that, after the Ascension, in the minds of the disciples the passages of Sacred Scripture began to stand forth clearly in their relationship to the life of Jesus. The same thing was true of Mary in a much higher sense.

How her soul must have been illumined when, reading a passage in the sacred books, she realized that this also had been prophesied about Jesus. The prophecy was now fulfilled; indeed, everything that had been foretold of Jesus had taken place. The tragic things had come true with greater tragedy, the glorious things with greater glory than anyone had thought.

But her soul did not find perfect rest in this knowledge of the victory of Jesus the Son of God; she longed to behold Him in His glory at the right hand of His Father, to whom He had ascended.

Mary's Assumption

The light of Mary's life cast its rays upon an ever widening circle. At first, she had been the Mother of the Redeemer living only for her Son and separated from others; later, as the Mother of the Redeemer she had persevered beneath the cross and, after His death, had preserved the faith in His redemption and in His Church; and lastly she was the Mother of the Redeemer gathering the newly formed Church about her.

As the circle gradually widened about her, she remained ever the woman and the mother. In no way did she interfere in the direction of the affairs of the early Church in Jerusalem. With a generous heart, she gave the Church her holy life, her faith in the kingdom of Jesus, her prayers, and, to the disciples, the support of her presence in the labors and sufferings they assumed for her Son's sake. Inasmuch as she was not only the earthly Mother of Jesus but also the woman who from the beginning had known that mystery of mysteries, the Incarnation of the Son of God, she brought great comfort to the disciples and in some small way compensated for the loss of Jesus' presence.

After Pentecost, the Scriptures furnish no information about Mary's life. From then on her life was entirely devoted to the work of her Son, to the Church to which He had given her; and we may consider her as having an intimate concern in all those things which are recorded of the labors of the disciples.

The city of Jerusalem, outside whose walls Jesus had been crucified, continued for some time to be the headquarters of all the faithful. St. Luke describes their life as follows:

And they devoted themselves to the apostles' teaching and fellowship, to the breaking of bread and the prayers.

And fear came upon every soul; and many wonders and signs were done through the apostles. And all who believed were together and had all things in common; and they sold their possessions and goods and distributed them to all, as any had need. And day by day, attending the temple together and breaking bread in their homes, they partook of food with glad and generous hearts, praising God and having favor with all the people. And the Lord added to their number day by day those who were being saved (Acts 2: 42-47).

The upper room where Jesus celebrated the Last Supper was now too small for the number of the faithful; but they remained united by the spirit animating them. They continued to assemble for the breaking of bread and for prayers, and Mary was present at these gatherings, taking her place, according to custom, with the women, although she was the spiritual center of the group.

Just as when Jesus had appeared among the people as a miracle worker, so now, when the Apostles did signs and wonders, the people realized that the power of God was in their midst. The simplicity and kindness of the faithful won the hearts of the people, who saw so much dissension and hatred on all sides.

However, in Jerusalem, the principal men, who had crucified Jesus a few weeks before, were determined to root out faith in Him. John, Mary's protector, and Peter were arrested and arraigned before the great council. Like Jesus, their Master, they stood before Annas and Caiphas and were ordered to promise that they would cease preaching and teaching in the name of Jesus. They answered: "Whether it is right in the sight of God to listen to you rather than to God, you must judge; for we cannot but speak of what we have seen and heard" (Acts 4: 19-20). Then the council threatened them with punishment if they continued to preach in the name of Jesus, and dismissed them.

When Peter and John returned to the faithful and told what had happened, the assembled brethren cried out joyfully:

Sovereign Lord, who didst make the heaven and the earth and the sea and everything in them, who, by the mouth of our father David, thy servant, didst say by the Holy Spirit,
    "Why did the Gentiles rage,
    And the peoples imagine vain things?
    The kings of the earth set themselves in array,
    and the rulers were gathered together,
    against the Lord and against his Anointed"—
for truly in this city there were gathered together against thy holy servant Jesus, whom thou didst anoint, both Herod and Pontius Pilate, with

the Gentiles and the peoples of Israel, to do whatever thy hand and thy plan had predestined to take place. And now, Lord, look upon their threats, and grant to thy servants to speak thy word with all boldness, while thou stretchest out thy hand to heal, and signs and wonders are performed through the name of thy holy servant Jesus (Acts 4: 24–30).

After this outburst of prayer, the miracle of Pentecost was renewed, "the place in which they were gathered together was shaken; and they were all filled with the Holy Spirit" (Acts 4:31). Mary was among those faithful believers who looked forward to persecution, confident of victory.

As the number of the faithful increased, the Apostles chose seven men to distribute alms to the poor. Among these was Stephen, who was the first to be martyred for Jesus' sake. After his death, the persecution raged on, and the faithful left Jerusalem. Only the Apostles remained, and Mary probably remained with them. A certain Pharisee from Asia Minor, called Saul, was especially active against the Church, "breathing threats and murder against the disciples of the Lord" (Acts 9: 1).

But the persecution made new converts to the faith. The believers who had fled the city announced the new faith in Samaria, where very many were converted. Although Jesus had entrusted His mother to John, John did not consider it a task that should limit his work as an Apostle; with Peter he went to Samaria to administer the sacrament of confirmation.

The end of Mary's life on earth is entirely a matter of surmise. If we consider the great sufferings she underwent at the time of her Son's death, we may naturally assume that she did not long survive Him. These sufferings took their toll of Mary as they would have done of any other human being, and, as she felt more deeply than others the pangs of spiritual anguish and bodily suffering, they must have been especially ravaging in their effects. She had suffered much in the silence of her soul during the years when Jesus was on earth, and she suffered much when she witnessed the persecution of her Son's faithful followers.

In these days, too, she was filled with a vehement longing for Jesus. Once during His lifetime He had said to the disciples: "The days are coming when you will desire to see one of the days of the Son of man, and you will not see it" (Lk 17: 22). The Lord was announcing to His disciples that the time would come in which they would long in vain for the days when they had lived together with Him and that they would vainly desire to see the Son of God even for one day. Such a time had come for Mary after the Ascension; indeed, she desired to see Him more ardently than did the disciples.

Some are of the opinion that, after the Ascension, by reason of her motherhood, Mary often desired and obtained the appearance of her Son. More probably, however, Jesus never again appeared to her after His Ascension.

Even in these days, Mary's love for Jesus grew uninterruptedly because it was fed by her desire to be united to Him. Once she had desired more than anyone else that the Redeemer might come down upon earth; now she desired with all the ardor of her soul to join Him in heaven. Once her longing had moved the Son of God to descend to earth; now her longing moved Him to make ready to lift her up to heaven. As once He had united Himself to His Mother as the Son of man and dwelt within her, so now His Mother would not be compelled to await the resurrection of the body on the last day but would be assumed, body and soul, into heaven. The Mother and the Son would be united in glory in their humanity as they had been united in suffering. This was the complete fulfillment of the longing that burned in Mary's soul, and, according to the sacred tradition of the Church, Mary's glorified body was taken up into heaven at the end.

Mary's birth had brought the first rays of the light of the redemption to the world. After her assumption into heaven, the afterglow of the brilliant light of Jesus' earthly life was finally extinguished. Those who had followed Him while He was on earth and had been witnesses of His Resurrection and Ascension were completely separated from Him when His Mother departed from this world.

The hearts of the Apostles were filled with joy because, after a life of devotion to the Son of God in the form of man, Mary would now be permitted to behold Him in the glory He had received from His Father. But sorrow was mingled with their joy because they were not able to leave the world and witness the reunion of Jesus with His Mother in the kingdom of the Father.

Mary in heaven

Great was Mary's joy and exultation when, brilliant as the sun with the glory of grace, she was assumed to Jesus in heaven and beheld Him not only with the eyes of her soul, but also with the eyes of her glorified body.

There was no part of her body that had not served Jesus with perfect devotion. Her chaste womb had born the Son of God; her hands had laid Him in the manger, had given Him food and drink, had led Him when He took His first steps in childhood, had labored unceasingly for Him. Those hands had ground the meal and baked the bread, they had spun and woven His clothes for Him, until He was a man ready for the sacrifice; then in the hour of suffering she had folded those hands in complete surrender to God's will beneath the overwhelming burden of sorrow.

Her feet had taken so many steps for His sake: to the well for water to quench His thirst, up the stony hillside to gather wood for the fire; innumerable steps in the home, such as mothers take for their children without counting them, steps on pilgrimages to the Temple in Jerusalem, hurried and anxious steps when she sought Him in the Temple, still more anxious and painful steps when she ascended the mount of Calvary.

Her eyes looked upon Him, the same eyes that had joyfully gazed upon Him in the manger, the eyes that had watched Him grow and had followed Him as He went about the house in Nazareth. Now her eyes would behold Him for all eternity.

Her ears had heard His voice, the voice of the Son of God, when He spoke to her at His labors in the workshop, when He preached and taught the people, when in a commanding tone He had worked miracles and driven out devils, and at last when He had prayed for His enemies on the cross and cried out in desolation. Now she heard His voice again, the voice of the glorified Son of God.

Her heart had longed for the Messiah from the time she had been able to understand anything about the promise of His coming. When the angel came with his message, this heart of hers had become the heart of a Mother for Jesus. Fearlessly she heard the words of the aged Simeon: "Thy own heart a sword shall pierce," and from that moment her heart had been beating for her Son and for those whom He had come to save. Her heart was beating for Him when He rested in the tomb and when He had ascended into heaven; it was beating for Him and for His Church while His disciples waited for the Comforter. And when the Comforter had come, her heart was filled with the joys and sorrows of the newborn Church.

Now, in heaven, her love was poured out into the love of Jesus' heart, a sea of love into an infinite ocean of love; thus her love was absorbed into His love for men, for whom He had suffered so much on earth and for whom she too, for His sake, had borne so much.

In one great vision she now comprehended Jesus' position as the Redeemer of the world. Illumined by the light of her Son's divine knowledge, she saw the individual and his place in the economy of salvation; she understood the relationship of Jesus to each human being and the relationship of each individual to Jesus Himself. She understood also the position of the Apostles in Jesus' kingdom. With the same maternal benevolence she turned to the lowliest human being who was moved by a desire to learn something of Jesus' teaching. She poured out her maternal love upon every creature who was able to know and love Jesus her Son.

It was also the culmination of joy for Jesus when He beheld His Mother again. It was a perfect reunion, not merely a union of soul with soul, but the reunion of two bodies in the glorified state. In a sense, Mary's Assumption into heaven was a complement of Jesus' Ascension into heaven.

Many things Jesus had not been able to tell Mary on earth. As the Son of the heavenly Father, He had come on earth to carry out His Father's commission without giving an account of His mission to anyone. Strangely enough, perhaps because she was so close to Him, He had kept many things from her; He had been silent in Nazareth, silent when He remained in the Temple as a twelve-year-old boy, silent during the failures of His public ministry, silent during His desolation on the cross.

Now at last He could make everything known to her and reward her for her faithful silence. Now He could allow her to look down from heaven and behold the mystery of His kingdom, the mystical life of His Church. Now, in her maternal love for Him and for all those whom He had redeemed, she should stand close to His throne, because during His sacrificial death on earth she had been close to His cross. Because she had suffered with Him then as much as a human being could participate in the sacrifice of the Son of God, so now when the fruits of the sacrifice were to be distributed she would be given as much power to dispose of these graces as was possible for a human being to have. Now, in her Assumption, that new maternity with which Jesus had endowed her beneath the cross attained a glorious fulfillment.

The woman of the Book of Revelation

And a great portent appeared in heaven, a woman clothed with the sun, with the moon under her feet, and on her head a crown of twelve stars; she was with child and she cried out in her pangs of birth, in anguish for delivery. And another portent appeared in heaven; behold, a great red dragon, with seven heads and ten horns, and seven diadems upon his heads. His tail swept down a third of the stars of heaven, and cast them to the earth. And the dragon stood before the woman who was about to bear a child, that he might devour her child when she brought it forth; she brought forth a male child, one who is to rule all the nations with a rod of iron, but her child was caught up to God and to his throne, and the woman fled into the wilderness, where she has a place prepared by God, in which to be nourished for one thousand two hundred and sixty days.

Now war arose in heaven, Michael and his angels fighting against the dragon; and the dragon and his angels fought, but they were defeated and there was no longer any place for them in heaven. And the great dragon was thrown down, that ancient serpent, who is called the Devil and Satan, the deceiver of the whole world—he was thrown down to the earth, and his angels were thrown down with him. And I heard a loud voice in heaven, saying, "Now the salvation and the power and the kingdom of our God and the authority of his Christ have come, for the accuser of our brethren has been thrown down, who accuses them day and night before our God. And they have conquered him by the blood of the Lamb and by the word of their testimony, for they loved not their lives even unto death. Rejoice then, O heaven and you that dwell therein! But woe to you, O earth and sea, for the devil has come down to you in great wrath, because he knows that his time is short! " (Rev 12: 1-12).

St. John is here describing a vision. A woman full of glory is threatened by a dragon, not because of herself but because of the child that is to issue forth from her womb. But the dragon cannot devour the child; the child lives and finally comes to the throne of God.

Who is this woman? On the first pages of Sacred Scripture we are told how the serpent that had seduced our first parents was cursed by God in these prophetic words: "Because you have done this, cursed are you above all cattle, and above all wild animals; upon your belly you shall go, and dust you shall eat all the days of your life. I will put enmity between you and the woman, and between your seed and her seed; he shall bruise your head, and you shall bruise his heel" (Gen 3: 14-15).

Here the "woman" and her seed, and the serpent and his seed, are mentioned in prophecy; and here, too, as later in St. John's

Revelation, mention is made of the conflict that will arise between the woman and her seed, and the serpent and his seed.

Even before the birth of our Lord, at the time when the books of the Old Testament were being translated into Greek, the opinion was already prevalent that the seed of the woman referred to one individual. This may be inferred from the dialogue between Justin Martyr and the Jew Trypho. St. Justin and Trypho are agreed that the passage about the one who is to kill the dragon refers to the Messiah. The dialogue is concerned with the question whether the prophecy was actually fulfilled in Jesus or not. St. Justin is refuting the arguments proposed by Trypho against the Christian belief that Jesus Christ is the seed of the woman by whom God destroyed the serpent and delivered all those who repented of their sins and believed in Him.

From Revelation it is also clear that St. John understood the words about the child who was threatened by the serpent as referring to the Redeemer who had ascended into heaven. It is by "the blood of the Lamb" that men are able to overcome the great dragon, "that ancient serpent, who is called the Devil and Satan." But the blood of the Lamb is the blood of Jesus Christ, which was shed on the cross for the remission of the sins of the world.

Who then is this woman "clothed with the sun, with the moon under her feet, and on her head a crown of twelve stars" who brings forth her child amid the threats of the great dragon?

It may be that the "woman" refers to the people of God, that part of mankind which remained faithful to God: the faithful before Abraham, the faithful of Israel, and, lastly, the faithful of the Church of Christ.

But perhaps more clearly we can see in this "woman" Mary, the mother of Jesus, who was so intimately connected with the Incarnation and birth of Jesus. Mary was chosen from among all others, she was "blessed among women," she was "full of grace." As in the vision the serpent threatened the mother and tried to devour her child after birth, so the child Jesus after His birth was exposed to great danger because of Herod. As the mother of the serpent-killer in the vision fled into the desert, so Mary fled with her Child through the desert into Egypt.

It remains a moot question whether the "woman" of the vision refers primarily to Mary or to the people of God, but the more we insist that the "seed of the woman" in the prophecy of Genesis refers to Jesus, the more plausible it appears that the "woman" of Revelation refers to Mary.

St. John composed his writings in advanced age, after preaching for an entire lifetime about the life and teachings of Jesus, and thus the great events of his own early days were constantly present to his mind.

It would be interesting to determine which events in St. John's writings about Jesus were more important in his mind. Among these more significant occurrences is the simultaneous appearance of the "Lamb of God" and the "woman." St. John's first meeting with the Savior took place under this sign. "Behold the Lamb of God, who takes away the sin of the world." With these words the Baptist had directed the future Apostle John to Christ, and, a few days later, at the wedding feast in Cana, Christ Himself addressed His mother as "woman" and spoke to her of that "hour" which would be of decisive importance for them both. This passage of the Gospel, therefore, begins with the calling of the Apostles, when the Baptist speaks of Jesus as the "Lamb of God," and concludes with Jesus Himself addressing His Mother as "woman."

On a second occasion, beneath the cross, St. John is again associated with the "Lamb of God" and with the "woman." Here Jesus is the "Lamb [of God] who was slain" (Rev 5: 12), and here, too, Jesus addresses His Mother as "woman."

For the third time, "the Lamb of God" and the "woman" appear together to St. John in the vision of Revelation.

St. John wrote the Book of the Revelation before he wrote his Gospel, and perhaps the vision of the Revelation had some influence on his presentation of the "woman" with her Child in the Gospel. With the thought of the "woman" and the Child in mind, John may have selected those two instances in the life of Jesus when Jesus addressed His mother as "woman": the wedding at Cana and the incident at the foot of the cross. From a comparison of the two passages, it seems probable that St. John recognized Mary in the "woman" of the vision of Revelation. Thus the first picture that the Scripture presents of the redemption, the picture of the "woman" and her Child, corresponds to the picture presented in the last book of the sacred text.

The testimony of that disciple whom Christ loved while He was on earth and who remained as a witness after the other Apostles had suffered martyrdom was eagerly accepted and treasured by the faithful of the early Church. We know this from discoveries made in recent times. As early as a generation after St. John had written his Gospel, copies of it existed in Egypt.

The praise of Mary the Mother of God, which he inaugurated, was never silenced on earth. From then on, in Africa, in Asia, and in Europe, Mary was glorified as the Woman who had freely consented to become the Mother of Jesus, the Son of God.

St. John's disciples immediately accepted and in their turn taught to the faithful what he had handed down to them. Ignatius of Antioch (d. 117), a disciple of St. John, accorded Mary those beautiful titles which would form the basis for the veneration of the Mother of God for all time. In his letters, when he speaks of Jesus, the incarnate Son of God, he refers to Mary, the daughter of David. He says that Jesus was conceived of the blood of David and of the Holy Spirit; he calls Jesus the Son of Mary, born of the Virgin.

The veneration of the Mother of God was handed down as follows. St. Justin (120–185), who came from Asia to Europe, wrote, about A.D. 159: "We know that Jesus took His origin from the Father and was born of a virgin. In the same manner in which disobedience came into the world through the serpent, so also would salvation come. As an inviolate virgin, Eve had consented to the word of the serpent and thus disobedience and death were born. With joyous faith, Mary the Virgin received the message of the angel that the Spirit of God would descend upon her and that the power of the Most High would overshadow her and that the Holy which would be born of her would be the Son of God, and she had answered: 'Be it done to me according to thy word.'"

Irenaeus, a disciple of St. Polycarp and, through him, a disciple of St. John, associated with the Christians of Asia Minor and Europe, also compares Mary to the first mother of the race: "At the time when Adam was her spouse but when she was still a virgin, Eve sinned against obedience and thus became the source of death for the human race. Mary, remaining a virgin while she was espoused to a man, by her obedience became the source of salvation both for herself and for the human race. Thus the problem created by Eve's disobedience was solved by Mary's obedience."

In Africa, Tertullian raised his voice in praise of Mary's maternity:

251

God redeemed His image and likeness [mankind] in the same manner in which the devil had taken it captive. The word which was the origin of death had found a place in Eve when she was still a virgin, and accordingly the Word of God that was to create new life must also find a place in a virgin. Only in this way could mankind, which had been brought to destruction by a woman, also be brought back to the way of salvation by a woman. Eve had believed the serpent, Mary believed the angel Gabriel; the error Eve had committed by her belief was repaired by Mary's faith.

Like St. John, these three witnesses, Justin, Irenaeus, and Tertullian, behold in Mary the woman who corresponds to Eve, and they recognize that Mary's greatness consists in this, that she knowingly and willingly consented to become the Mother of the Redeemer.

In the religious life and thought of all peoples, Mary has become the greatest of all women; in the words of the simple faithful she is the "Mother of God," "our Lady," "our Mother," and "our Queen." Almost a thousand years ago, Herman the Lame, a monk of Reichenau, celebrated her as "our Lady," and since that time her praise has been heard in every part of the world, and with this praise we too conclude this book:

> Hail, holy queen,
> mother of mercy, our life, our sweetness, and our hope;
> to thee do we cry, poor banished children of Eve,
> to thee do we send up our sighs,
> mourning and weeping in this valley of tears.
> Turn then, most gracious advocate,
> thine eyes of mercy toward us,
> and after this, our exile,
> show unto us the blessed fruit of thy womb, Jesus.
> O clement, O loving, O sweet Virgin Mary.

INDEX OF PROPER NAMES

See table of contents for major topics.